W0232867

CONGRESS RADIO

ADVANCE PRAISE FOR THE BOOK

The underground Congress Radio played a small but significant part in India's struggle for independence, and Usha Mehta was at its centre. Sadly the story of her involvement, activities, arrest, trial and conviction has so far not been told. This finely structured and affectionately written book, based on probing questions, detailed knowledge of Mumbai and deep understanding of Usha Mehta more than fills the gap. Having myself known Ushaben closely for over forty years, I can say with confidence that the book presents an image of her that is as true to reality as any image can be.

—Bhikhu Parekh, House of Lords, UK

This book on the Congress Radio of 1942 is a thrilling and moving account of how a daring underground operation was conceived and carried out, and of how it was busted by the colonial police. It is meticulously researched, drawing on a wide range of primary sources. At the centre of the story is the remarkable figure of Usha Mehta, a slight, slender, twenty-two-year-old freedom fighter of exemplary courage and resolution. The book deserves a wide readership, within and beyond the academy.

—Ramachandra Guha,
author of *Gandhi: The Years That Changed the World, 1914-1948*

CONGRESS RADIO

USHA MEHTA *and the*
UNDERGROUND RADIO
STATION *of 1942*

USHA THAKKAR

PENGUIN
VIKING
An imprint of Penguin Random House

VIKING

USA | Canada | UK | Ireland | Australia
New Zealand | India | South Africa | China | Singapore

Viking is part of the Penguin Random House group of companies
whose addresses can be found at global.penguinrandomhouse.com

Published by Penguin Random House India Pvt. Ltd
4th Floor, Capital Tower 1, MG Road,
Gurugram 122 002, Haryana, India

Penguin
Random House
India

First published in Viking by Penguin Random House India 2021

Copyright © Usha Thakkar

All rights reserved

10 9 8 7 6 5 4 3

The views and opinions expressed in this book are the author's own and the facts
are as reported by him/her which have been verified to the extent possible, and the
publishers are not in any way liable for the same.

ISBN 9780670095667

For sale in the Indian Subcontinent only

Typeset in Sabon by Manipal Technologies Limited, Manipal
Printed at Replika Press Pvt. Ltd, India

This book is sold subject to the condition that it shall not, by way of trade
or otherwise, be lent, resold, hired out, or otherwise circulated without the
publisher's prior consent in any form of binding or cover other than that in
which it is published and without a similar condition including this condition
being imposed on the subsequent purchaser.

www.penguin.co.in

MIX
Paper from
responsible sources
FSC® C016779

This is a legitimate digitally printed version of the book and therefore might not
have certain extra finishing on the cover.

To Usha Mehta and all her colleagues in the Congress Radio who endeavoured to spread the message of freedom

Contents

Foreword

The story of the underground Congress Radio is a fascinating but yet to be explored segment of history that demands attention because of the integral role it played in India's freedom struggle. It is the story of a zealous group of young patriots who operated the Congress Radio, passionately propagating the message of freedom and disseminating information about the struggle against the coercive rule of the British government. The account of their enterprise is both compelling and inspiring, for not only did they make history within a brief span of time, but they also transmitted reliable news to the people, generating confidence among them and unnerving the British. Equally impressive was the power of the Radio to kindle the flame of freedom in the hearts of its listeners and inspire them during those bleak and difficult times. At the same time, it communicated to the youth the immense value of ideals and dreams and how significant voluntary and arduous efforts were to make these seemingly impossible dreams a reality.

The contribution of the courageous and empathetic Professor Usha Mehta (Ushaben), the only woman in the group, is particularly important. Born on 25 March 1920 at Saras village in the Surat district of Gujarat, she grew up to be a bright student in Bombay (now Mumbai) and carved a niche for herself as a freedom fighter in India's history. Despite being awarded the prestigious Padma Vibhushan by the government of India and known as a scholar of eminence, she never lost touch with people at the grassroots level. She had imbibed Gandhian values early in her life: her friends and well-wishers were charmed by her simplicity, humility and warm-heartedness. Her contribution to the operation of the underground Congress Radio in 1942 was exceptional.

'The times of 1942 were exhilarating; those days were so wonderful! How do I describe them?' Ushaben said, her tiny frame erect, her hair neatly tied in a bun and her large shining eyes overwhelmed by memories of those electrifying days. Recapturing the quintessence of those times she murmured her favourite lines from William Wordsworth:

Bliss was it in that dawn to be alive
But to be young was very heaven.

* * *

I would often ask Ushaben about her participation in the operation of the underground Congress Radio. On many afternoons we would have cups of hot milky chai (Mumbai's mounting temperature and humidity never interfered with our routine of having tea in the afternoon) and biscuits. Years of imprisonment had blunted her appetite, and she survived mainly on two or three cups of tea and/or coffee and a few eatables limited to some biscuits, Cheeslings or *khakhra* (Gujarati cracker). A string of questions would come gushing to my mind: How did the Congress Radio come into existence? Who operated it? Where? How? Who helped? What did it broadcast? How long did it last? How were the operators arrested? How was the case conducted? What was the incriminating evidence against them? What was the judgment? In hindsight, the idea of operating an underground radio in the troubled India of 1942 is indeed adventurous and exciting. But how was it made possible? Who were the doers and where? Many pieces of this jigsaw puzzle needed to be put together—the actual operation which lasted for almost two and a half months, the management of regular programmes, the content of the written reports and the records, and the places for operation, etc. Often, during our discussions, Ushaben in her characteristic manner would say, 'Oh, yes, those were the days! People braved through!' Or 'Oh, you were not fortunate like us. You did not live in our times to take part in the freedom struggle.' I would nod my head saying, 'Yes, but we are at least fortunate to have a person like you amidst us,' and would continue to urge her to talk about the days of 1942. And she would talk, becoming nostalgic about those days filled with the romance of nationalism and fired by the spirit of patriotism.

One day, she casually showed me a bunch of carefully preserved files, consisting of papers, neatly wrapped in old newspapers, and asked, 'Would you like to see these?' I eagerly took the bundle in my hands and slowly opened it. The reading and re-reading of those precious papers at my own easy pace transposed me to the times when the atmosphere reverberated with Gandhi's mantra of 'Do or Die', and when the nation's freedom was of utmost

importance for many, such as this group running the
Congress Radio. The amber hidden in those pages that
had faded with the passage of time had not lost its fire.
Unfortunately, Ushaben passed away soon thereafter and
I was left with those precious documents and even more
precious memories. Juxtaposing the contents of those
pages with the ones I had collected from the archives and
Ushaben's narrations have helped me to put the pieces
of this narrative together. Slowly the story, exciting and
real, vibrant and intense, unfolded, giving glimpses of the
defiant mood of the freedom fighters and the bold resolve
of the team that was involved in the operation of the
Congress Radio.

Glimpses of the roles played by persons like Ushaben
in 1942 makes us realize that the Quit India movement is
a chapter in our history brimming with sacrifice and the
suffering of people determined to achieve independence.
The chronicle of the movement is stirring and gripping—
much had taken place, much has been written about it, and
a few things still remain partly hidden, elusive but alluring.

As the story unfolded, I realized that though situated
in Bombay, the Congress Radio reverberated far beyond
the city's shores; it inspired freedom lovers in various parts
of the country. A re-exploration of the working of the
Congress Radio is both educating and energizing; it is like
a fresh breeze blowing the ideals of freedom and selfless
work into our uneasy and despondent times.

1

Simmering Times in Bombay

The year 1942 was a tumultuous one, with the passion for freedom reverberating through the nation. But even before 1942, the city of Bombay had begun to simmer with political unrest and movements. The youth of the city, particularly the students, were motivated by the nationalist fervour of the times and had started getting active much before they became immersed in the massive wave of the Quit India movement.

Various meetings of students were organized in the city, posters and information by word of mouth being the most effective means of communication. A poster in 1940 for a meeting is very interesting.[1] This poster by the Bombay Students' Union gave a call for a students' meeting on 3 December 1940 at Chowpatty 'to express the solidarity of the student world with the National Liberation Movement'. It informed that special tricolour flags were prepared for the occasion, bearing the stirring words of Jawaharlal Nehru: 'Freedom is in peril. Defend it with all your might.' It urged every student to buy a flag and pin it on prominently as a mark of protest. The spirited slogan given here was: 'Every Student behind the Students' Union! Every Union for the Freedom Movement! *Inqilab Zindabad!*'

Recapturing those times Ushaben said, 'We were drawn to the (Quit India) movement. I had wanted to join the individual satyagraha when Gandhiji announced it. I had even written to him about my desire to do so, but he conveyed that I should complete my studies and serve my parents; he would call me when needed. However, in 1942 there was no question of asking him. We took a plunge into the movement and we were playing our roles the way we understood them.'[2] Being a bright student well-versed in politics and philosophy, she could easily find the connection between what was happening in Bombay with the beginnings of the underground Congress Radio.

Political Ferment in Bombay Before the Quit India Call

The city was the stage for political activities and meetings. Since the resolution of 'Complete Independence' passed at the All India Congress Committee (AICC) session at Lahore in December 1929, 26 January was celebrated as Independence Day all over the country. Bombay did not lag behind, and in 1942, 26 January was enthusiastically observed as Independence Day. In the morning of that day, Bhulabhai J. Desai unfurled the Congress flag at the Congress House. Volunteers of the Bombay National Guards, Bombay Seva Dal, Sevika Dal and Balika Dal were also present. A number of students had chosen to absent themselves from the schools and colleges and some went round the city on cycles shouting slogans. Similar flag salutations were held in the different wards of the city: the municipal garden opposite the King George High School, held under the auspices of the North Bombay Students' Union and where Raja Kulkarni unfurled the flag; Esplanade Maidan under the auspices of the Fort Students' Union and presided over by K.L. Shah; and Chowpatty attended by the students of Wilson College.[3]

On the same day Chowpatty witnessed another mammoth meeting, attended by about 20,000 persons, and presided over by Bhulabhai J. Desai. He made a short speech stressing the importance of the 'Independence Day' and read out the pledge in Hindi, which proclaimed that

> We believe that it is an inalienable right of the Indian people, as of any other people, to have freedom and enjoy the fruits of their toil and have the necessities of life, so that they may have full opportunities of growth. We believe also that if any government deprives a people of these rights and oppresses them, the people have a further right to alter it or to abolish it. . . . We pledge ourselves anew to the independence of India, and solemnly resolve to carry out non-violently the struggle for freedom till Purna Swaraj is attained.[4]

The mill areas too were getting caught up in the same excitement. Some members of the Bombay Girni Kamgar Union joined the volunteers of the North Bombay Students' Union as they took a cycle procession through the mill area exhorting the people to observe Independence Day.[5]

* * *

In 1942 there was a distinct outburst of widespread anger against the British rule, which had been ignited by the inspiring and often fiery speeches of the leaders. As the leaders realized, this mobilization of people was essential for the movement for independence, and needed to be politically channelized before the August AICC session in Bombay. The Congress machinery swung into action, and meetings were organized in different parts of the city by the Bombay Provincial Congress Committee (BPCC) to popularize the resolution based on the demand of 'Quit India' taken by the Working Committee on 14 July at Wardha. (The official records of the British government call such meetings 'propaganda meetings'.) Thus, the period between the Wardha session and the AICC meeting in Bombay was one of preparation both by the Congress and those opposed to the projected movement.[6]

People outside the A.I.C.C. meeting in August 1942

The Congress was aware of this fact, and channelized its energy in boosting the enthusiasm of the people. Towards this end, a series of important meetings were held throughout the city presided over by eminent leaders. Leaders like Yusuf Meherally, Ashok Mehta, Purshottam Trikamdas, B.G. Kher, Shankarrao Deo, Achyut Patwardhan, Nagindas T. Master and S.K. Patil were largely successful in motivating people and mobilizing the students to participate in the movement. The first of these was held at Chowpatty on 26 July, presided over by Nagindas T. Master.[7]

On 27 July, Shankarrao Deo addressed a meeting of students at the People's Jinnah Hall.[8] On the same day an urgent meeting of the BPCC, presided over by Jinnabhai P. Joshi, was held at the Congress House. The Committee called upon the people of Bombay to be prepared for 'trials and sacrifices, hitherto unknown in the history of our great struggle for national freedom'. A resolution was passed at the meeting expressing unfaltering obedience to the Working Committee and the AICC.[9]

Another important public meeting, attended by about 1,000 persons, was held under the auspices of the BPCC, in the compound of the Pallonji Sojpal building at Dadar on 28 July. In it, Shankarrao Deo evoked the memory of the struggle of 1857, and appealed to the citizens of Bombay to participate in the coming rebellion. He stated that if we were free, we would be able to defend our country against foreign aggression. S.K. Patil, the president of the meeting, proudly proclaimed that Bombay was the place where all previous movements of the Congress were not only launched but also carried out successfully.[10]

On the following day, 29 July, the BPCC held another meeting at Lal Baug Maidan. Ashok Mehta, the president, said that many problems had affected the people since the outbreak of the war: increase in the prices of foodstuffs and the difficulties workers faced to maintain themselves on scanty wages. Such problems could only be solved if there was a national government in the country. He hoped that the workers and the people would support the movement launched by the Congress for complete independence of the country. However, Shankarrao Deo warned his audience that the coming struggle would be different from the previous ones and the people should be prepared to face bullets and death if necessary.[11]

Ushaben remembered a huge public meeting, attended by about 50,000 persons, when Vallabhbhai Patel made a powerful speech on 'the task before the country'. This colossal meeting was organized by the BPCC and held at Chowpatty on 2 August. Vallabhbhai Patel, speaking in Gujarati, commented on the prevailing political situation and the adamant attitude of the British government. He also mentioned the war situation over the past six months, noting the failure of the British government to hold Malaya, Singapore and Burma. In his opinion, the international scene had changed a lot over those past six months and India should not be an idle spectator to it. The resolution passed in Wardha on 14 July had asked the British to quit India so that Indians could meet foreign aggression. Moreover, the government supporters were wrong in declaring that the Muslims, Harijans and the students were against the movement. He was of the view that the ban on the Communist Party had been removed after the Wardha resolution probably because the British government intended to use the communists against the Congress. However, he was sure that the communist friends had sufficient patriotism not to fall for such tactics.

He added that this was the last movement to be launched by Gandhi and undertaken at an advanced age, knowing fully its implications. During the movement, schools, colleges and factories would have to be closed and merchants would have to close their business. There would be a complete standstill. He earnestly appealed to the people of Bombay to support the movement as wholeheartedly as Bombay had always done in the past. When asked by some as to what would happen if all the leaders were arrested, he made a compelling observation that the movement might create such a force among the masses that it would be impossible for the government to hold leaders under restraint for a long time. Understandably, the government authorities noted: 'The general tone of the speech was provocative.'[12]

Lumley, then governor of Bombay, reported to the Viceroy, Linlithgow, that after Patel's first enormous meeting in Bombay, which was attended possibly by a lakh of people, the atmosphere completely changed and became revolutionary in outlook.[13]

* * *

The atmosphere was politically charged as Bombay prepared itself to respond to the call of the leaders. To this end, the BPCC efficiently and effectively organized a series of public meetings over the following days.[14]

The communists too had their own views about the movement, and held a public meeting at Lalbagh Maidan on 3 August. S.S. Mirajkar said that the Communist Party fully supported the demands made by the Wardha resolution about the formation of a national government in India, but they disagreed with the proposal to launch a countrywide movement without first bringing about unity between the Congress and the Muslim League. China could only counter Japanese aggression for over four years because of their united strength and courage. Under the prevailing circumstances, however, if the Congress launched a movement as contemplated, it would be inviting Japanese aggression.[15]

* * *

On the eve of the AICC session, people started gathering to warmly welcome the leaders coming from different parts of the country for the occasion. The session was to be held on 7 and 8 August, and as the dates approached, Bombay witnessed the arrival of several important leaders. When Gandhi, accompanied by Kasturba, Mahadeo Desai and Pyarelal, arrived on 3 August, he was affectionately greeted by almost a thousand people at Dadar station, including many leaders. Gandhi stayed at Birla House, Mount Pleasant Road.[16]

The next to arrive on 4 August was Maulana Abul Kalam Azad, the Congress president. He was welcomed warmly at Victoria Terminus by a huge crowd and leaders like Nagindas T. Master, Jaishri Raiji, S.K. Patil, Yusuf Meherally, Shantabai Vengaskar and Kisan Dhumatkar. Sarojini Naidu, S. Satyamurti and Dr Pattabhi Sitaramayya also arrived by the Madras Mail.[17]

The leaders had come to Bombay to voice the aspirations and perspectives of the people of their regions and deliberations started soon after their arrival. The Congress Working Committee presided over by Maulana Abul Kalam Azad met at Birla House from about 3 p.m. to 6 p.m. on 4 August. Gandhi's presence boosted the morale of the participants.[18] Deliberations continued on the next day, 5 August, for three hours in the morning and three

hours in the evening at Birla House.[19] The Committee at
Birla House spent about three hours in the morning and
an hour in the evening on 6 August giving final touches
to the plan of action.[20] The tempo of the movement under
Gandhi's leadership was rapidly building up.

The heady excitement of those times did not weaken—
meetings continued to be held and the people were as
enthusiastic and the organizers as energetic. The BPCC held
a public meeting at Nare Park, Parel, on 5 August. Almost
12,000 persons including about 1,000 women attended
the meeting. Jawaharlal Nehru emphasized that only a free
India could face any foreign aggression. Urging the people
to follow Gandhi's instructions, he advised them not to
lose courage but to form their own working committees
and carry on the struggle even if the Congress was declared
illegal and all communications were stopped.[21] Meetings
were also organized in different parts of the city. More than
3,000 persons, mostly labourers, gathered at the maidan
opposite Phoenix Mill, Fergusson Road, on 6 August.[22]

The dream of independence had captured the students'
imagination. Copies of a cyclostyled circular issued by the
Students' Action Committee were surreptitiously distributed
among them on 5 August, stating that Bombay's communist
students were holding a meeting to present their point of
view. It proclaimed proudly that, 'The students of Bombay
are pledged to the Independence and integrity of their beloved
country.' Evoking Nehru and Lenin it further asserted that,

The students have been asking for an all-out-struggle
for Freedom all those months and years. Now has come
the time, when such a struggle has become urgent, if
the Nation is to survive. It is our good fortune that the
Congress had decided to launch such a struggle. Let us
lead it to SUCCESS.[23]

It was because of these meetings and tireless efforts of the organizers and the speakers that the fire of patriotism was fanned in the hearts of the people of Bombay, strengthening the movement.

The AICC Session in August 1942

The two-day historic session of the AICC was held on 7 and 8 August in a specially erected pandal on the Gowalia Tank Maidan (now August Kranti Maidan). Attending the session were some 10,000 persons, including about 250 AICC members from different provinces. About 3,000 volunteers of the Bombay National Guards, Bombay Seva Dal and the People's Volunteer Brigade, including 500 Desh Sevikas were present to keep order. Besides the audience within the pandal, there were about 5,000 persons who heard the proceedings outside with the help of loudspeakers that had been specially installed. Almost all the notable leaders of India were present at this session.[24]

Special arrangements were made for the accommodation, tea and conveyance of the delegates as well as for the management at the pandal. The AICC members, invited guests and the guests of the BPCC had been lodged at places like Sardar Graha, Arya Nivas, Welcome Hotel, Great Eastern Hotel, Windsor Hotel, Madhavashram, Aryapatikashram and National Hindu Lodge. There were five entrances to the pandal for the AICC members and distinguished guests, holders of tickets of Rs 100, Rs 25 and Rs 10, the press and the Congress workers. Photo permits were issued with instructions not to use movie cameras. Out of nearly 350 press passes issued, 50 were for foreign correspondents from different countries.[25]

Maulana Abul Kalam, who presided over the session, opened the proceedings in Urdu. He talked about the war situation and the importance of India's freedom. Jawaharlal Nehru moved the main resolution and spoke in Hindi. Vallabhbhai Patel, who supported the resolution with a speech in Hindi, appealed to the people to follow Gandhi faithfully. He announced that if Gandhi and other leaders were to be arrested, there would be no need for guidance. Every man and woman born in India had to be his or her own leader and carry on the struggle with non-violence.[26]

Gandhi said with conviction, 'At a time when I am about to launch the biggest fight in my life there can be no hatred for the British in my heart.'[27] Emphasizing the importance of non-violence, he stated:

When I raised the slogan 'Quit India' the people in India who were then feeling despondent felt I had placed before them a new thing. If you want real freedom you will have to come together and such coming together will create true democracy—democracy the like of which has not been so far witnessed nor have there been any attempts made for such type of true democracy.[28]

This concept of participatory democracy made an indelible imprint on young Ushaben's mind, one that she would remember vividly, years later.

On 8 August, Acharya Narendra Deo and others spoke in support of the resolution. Nehru replied to the criticisms made by the communists and said that what was really needed was the popular support of the Asiatic and African people and the change in the entire atmosphere of the world. He wanted the defeat of Hitler and fascism, so that a new world order could be built. This was the aim of the Congress throughout the movement. At the suggestion of the Congress president, all the amendments except those of Dr Ashraf, Sajjad Zahir and Sardesai were withdrawn. When the amendments made by the three communists were put up, they were thrown out by a huge majority, with only twelve voting for them. The main resolution in its original form, without any change, was then put to vote and carried with an overwhelming majority, thirteen voting against.[29]

On 8 August, Gandhi emphasized the importance of Hindu–Muslim unity. According to him,

> The bond of the slave is snapped the moment he considers himself to be a free being. [. . .]
>
> Here is a mantra, a short one, that I give you. You may imprint it in your hearts and let every breath of yours give expression to it. The mantra is: 'Do or Die'.[30]
>
> [. . .] I trust the whole of India to launch upon a non-violent struggle on the widest scale. I trust the innate goodness of human nature which perceives the truth and prevails during the crisis as if by instinct. But even if I am deceived in this, I shall not swerve.[31]

He also said that he would write to the Viceroy and wished to publish the correspondence with the Viceroy's consent.[32] He told the people that 'Every one of you should, from this moment onwards, consider yourself a free man or woman, and act as if you are free and are no longer under the heel of this imperialism.'[33] He wanted the message to travel at the international level. Through the representatives of the foreign press assembled there, he wished to say to the world that the United Nations had now the opportunity to declare India free and prove their bonafides.[34]

Sadiq Ali remembered years later that 'Gandhiji poured out his heart at the AICC meeting at Gowalia Tank in Bombay. I think it was the longest speech he had made at any AICC meeting.'[35]

An announcement had been made that a flag salutation would take place the next morning, Sunday, 9 August, at the Gowalia Tank Maidan, followed by an address by Nehru to students in the Congress pandal. Also that Gandhi would address a public meeting at Shivaji Park, Dadar, the same evening, to be presided over by Nagindas T. Master. The session ended at 10 p.m. on 8 August. Nagindas T. Master, president of the BPCC, proposed a vote of thanks to all who contributed to make the event a success. Nehru, in his turn, thanked the BPCC for all the arrangements they had made.[36]

Khwaja Ahmad Abbas, who was also present at this momentous session, said,

> At 10.30 p.m. the historic session of the All-India Congress Committee came to an end amidst scenes of unprecedented excitement and twenty thousand people streamed out of Gowalia Tank Maidan, Bombay, their hearts aflame with the patriotic sentiments they had heard expressed through the cool but resolute voice of Gandhiji, the fiery eloquence of Maulana Azad, the impassioned speech of Nehru. [But,] Shortly after midnight the office telephone was found 'dead'. The line was not working. The corner public telephone was 'dead' too. So were the telephones in all the other offices in the neighbourhood.[37]

A day or so before the session began, there had been rumours about warrants being issued and the arrests of

AICC members. Although no such calamities disturbed the proceedings, the whispers proved to be true.

Early next morning Gandhi and all the important Congress leaders were arrested in a swift swoop by the government. The list of the arrested leaders of Bombay on the morning of 9 August under the Defence of India Rules, 1939, included B.G. Kher (Khar), D.N. Wandrekar (Khar), M.K. Deshpande (Bandra), G.D. Bhatt (Vile Parle), I.M. Oza (Vile Parle), R.B. Mehta (Ghatkopar) and V.N. Purao (Chembur).[38]

***

The arrest of the Congress leaders on 9 August led to an outbreak of incidents of throwing stones and soda-water bottles at trams, buses and cars and also at the police. Some buses were burnt and the tyres of several buses punctured. The post office at Panjrapole was broken into and papers burnt. Grain shops at Khetwadi, Madhav Baugh and near the Panjrapole post office were looted.[39] The incidents of unruly behaviour continued on the next day as well.[40] The reports of the British officers record the uneasy atmosphere in the city and the restlessness among the students.[41]

In fact, the agitations and the protests that followed the AICC session in August 1942 in Bombay exasperated Viceroy Lord Linlithgow to such an extent that he wrote to Prime Minister Churchill on 31 August 1942 that 'I am engaged here in meeting by far the most serious rebellion since that of 1857, the gravity and extent of which we have so far concealed from the world for reasons of military security.'[42]

The Adventurous Idea

The AICC session on 7 and 8 August 1942 was unparalleled in the history of the nation. The leaders' patience had reached its limit and the mood of the people was at boiling point. The Mahatma's call for 'Do or Die' had fired the minds of the people, and the thousands sitting in the pandal at Gowalia Tank firmly resolved to sacrifice everything including life for the nation's independence. If the government was geared up for atrocities and oppression, the people were ready for the inevitable suffering and sacrifice.

Ushaben and her friends were present on both the days and were 'electrified', absorbing the speeches and infused with the spirit of 'Do or Die'. She would often share with us how this political meeting had filled the hearts of young persons like her and her friends with excitement. They felt energized and decided to contribute their bit to the freedom struggle. It was during this time that they decided to take up the adventurous initiative of reaching people through the medium of the radio. The trigger for the inception of the Congress Radio had thus been pressed.

In Ushaben's words:

'The die was cast. The patriotic urge moved the people to challenge the authority of the government in all conceivable ways. Sometime before the Quit India struggle started, some of my colleagues and I were thinking of what to do in case the movement was launched, because it was our hearts' desire to contribute our humble might to the freedom movement. Demonstrations and public meetings did not appeal to us much from the very beginning. During the Dandi Satyagraha, some of my friends and I had done the work of distributing the illegal Congress bulletins by going from house to house. Now we began discussing how best we could contribute to the Quit India struggle. Babubhai Khakar, a businessman and a co-student in the *rashtra bhasha* (national language) class, joined us in the discussion. Based on my study of the history of revolutions in other countries of the world, I suggested that if we could establish a radio station of our own, it would help us very much in keeping the people informed about the latest developments in the movement. A perusal of the history of the campaigns had convinced us that a transmitter of our own was perhaps the need of the hour. When the press is gagged and news banned, a transmitter helps a good deal in acquainting the public with the events that occur. We had realized the tremendous propaganda value of a transmitter, and the idea that with a powerful transmitter we could reach foreign countries thrilled us. So, Babubhai, I and other colleagues decided to work for a Freedom Radio.

'We began discussing ways and means for raising the necessary finances. Most of us were students and young individuals who had not yet settled in life. We discussed for many long hours but could not find a solution. Our only income then was the pocket money we used to receive from our parents and that was hardly adequate for financing our project. Just when we were on the point of dispersing in a dejected mood, my old aunt who was a widow and one who had participated in earlier freedom struggles and who was listening to our discussion from the adjoining room came out along with Manu, a close relative, with a box in her hands, and boosted up our morale by saying, "Children, do not worry. Here is my *stree dhan*, the box containing my jewellery gifted to me at the time of my marriage, which I have preserved all these years with

great care. You sell it and use the money for your work."
When we hesitated, she said, "I am not sorry to part with
my jewellery. What better use could I make of it than by
putting it as an offering at the feet of Mother India?" All of
us were so deeply moved that we did not even say "Thank
you" to her; we only bowed down to her, returned the box
saying that we would take it when it became absolutely
necessary for us to do so and asked for her blessings.'[43]

The Launch of the Project

Once the decision of launching the radio station was taken,
Babubhai (Vithaldas alias Babubhai Madhavji Khakar) got
busy garnering the resources required for the underground
enterprise. According to the history sheet prepared by the
Bombay police, he was the chief organizer of the Congress
Radio enterprise and was said to be directly responsible to
Ram Manohar Lohia for the success of the scheme. He also
received the necessary funds from the latter.[44]

The most formidable challenge was getting the
technical expertise until Nariman Adarbad Printer
(Printer) appeared on the scene as the answer.[45] For
Printer it was financial gain that was the motivating force,
and he was willing to take whatever risks to attain it. His
track record was not above board, but the members of the
group for the project of the underground radio believed
that under the circumstances he was perhaps the best
available person. It was reported that this accused had no
sympathies for the Congress as such. He was, however,
an 'unscrupulous individual and will not hesitate to
engage in unlawful activities for the sake of profit if he
thinks he can get away with it.'[46] Before the outbreak of
the war, Printer held an amateur transmitting licence in

connection with his activities with the Bombay Technical Institute. This licence was cancelled when war broke out in 1939 and he dismantled the transmitter. He had, however, kept some parts of the transmitting apparatus with himself. In his search for a lucrative business, he invented a mechanism called 'Kerogas' for running motorcars on kerosene in August 1941, obtained a patent for it and advertised for its sale. Babubhai and Ravindra A. Mehta (R.A. Mehta) approached him and obtained the sole selling agency for India, Burma and Ceylon. Their office was on the third floor of Noble Chambers at Sir Pherozshah Mehta Road. The sole agency continued till the beginning of 1942, when the government of India prohibited the sale of Kerogas due to the scarcity of kerosene. Consequently, the selling agency came to an end, and according to Printer, he had transacted business worth Rs 20,000 during that period.[47]

Police using tear gas during the A.I.C.C. meeting in August 1942

Printer next invented Hydrogas, borrowing Rs 3,000 from Babubhai and R.A. Mehta to conduct his experiments since they were to be his partners. That invention, however, failed, but Printer was not deterred. He then asked them to join him in his business of manufacturing calcium carbide and procured another advance. But in July 1942 or so, they expressed their inability to join him in the business as they were uncertain not only about the political future of India but were also afraid of losing their investment.[48]

Babubhai thereafter started Nigos Corporation with a partner in Noble Chambers, but when the partnership dissolved, he started B. Madhavji & Co. in the same space. That was around the end of July 1942. Printer had been in touch with Babubhai, and according to him, that company did not transact any business though the office was used as a meeting place for Babubhai, R.A. Mehta, Ushaben and others. Printer used to go there twice or thrice a week 'to seek financial help' and used to have frequent conversations with them. Sometimes he used to accompany Babubhai to a Hindi class held near the Congress House. Vithalbhai Kanthadbhai Jhaveri (Vithalbhai) also used to be there.[49] He also knew Ramchandra Mohanlal Killewala (Killewala), who used to teach Hindi to the military and naval officers.[50]

It's a matter of speculation as to what must have transpired between Printer and Babubhai and who approached whom. Driven by financial concerns, Printer could have approached Babubhai. Later, the judge observed that it was immaterial who started the idea; probably Printer wanted to make some money by using the parts lying with him.[51]

In due course, Babubhai made the proposal for starting the radio and Printer agreed; he was in need of money and Babubhai and his team needed technical help. Printer thereafter asked his assistant Rustom Cowasji Mirza (Mirza) to clean the parts in his possession and to check whether any were missing. Mirza reported that some minor parts were missing,[52] and these were purchased by Babubhai and Printer from places like India Radio Services and J.W. Mehta & Co. Printer then assembled the transmitter and it was ready for trial.[53]

Printer fitted an aerial in one of the classrooms in his own house,[54] and invited Babubhai, Vithalbhai, R.A. Mehta and some others for the demonstration one evening.[55] He had also asked some friends to receive the messages which were to be transmitted on wavelength 41.78. Unfortunately, the experiment proved to be unsuccessful and the station could not be heard anywhere. But this did not discourage Printer, who made attempts to rectify the mistake. That night and on subsequent nights, when R.A. Mehta tuned his radio receiver to 41.78 metres, he heard the radio broadcast at 7.45 p.m. This happened around the end of August.[56] Soon after, Printer wanted the station to be shifted elsewhere as soon as possible, as he did not want to keep it in his house.[57]

The required special equipment and parts were bought around this time. Later, during the proceedings of the case against the persons involved with the Congress Radio, questions were raised in court as to who bought them, for how much and for whom.[58] One of the most important evidences were two bills-cum-receipts from Chicago Radio Company, because they mentioned how the apparatus and articles/parts were bought, pointing to the possible involvement of Babubhai and others in the transactions. On 14th August 1942, Printer had purchased the amplifier, one pick-up and one volume controller from Chicago Radio Company (for Rs 599-8-0).[59] Babubhai had accompanied him. According to Printer, the bill was made in Printer's name because the salesman Vishvanath D. Deshpande knew him; however, the original bill was given to Babubhai as he had made the payment.[60]

A week or so later, Printer found that the microphone was not working satisfactorily, so on 24 August 1942 he asked Babubhai to get a new one. As it was late in the evening, he told Babubhai that the only place to get one was Chicago Radio Company. Babubhai asked him to go in his car with Killewala.[61] According to Killewala, on that day Babubhai said that he was busy and did not want the Hindi lesson. Instead, he asked him to go with Printer who wanted to buy something. Since Printer did not have any money, Killewala agreed to pay even though he too did not have much money. They made a stop on the way so that Killewala could pick up money from his sister who stayed in Kandewadi, Girgaum. When they reached Chicago Radio Company, Printer gave Killewala a note giving the details of the article he wanted. Killewala went inside and brought the microphone.[62] Printer remained in the car as he did not want to expose himself too often.[63] However, the judge stated that Killewala's story could not be believed since it was difficult to believe that Killewala would pay Printer Rs 250 without taking any documents from him, especially when he himself had had to borrow the funds from his sister. Moreover, if Killewala had bought the microphone for Printer, he would have either given his own name or Printer's name as the purchaser. Besides, on the cash memo it showed that the purchase had been made in the name of Messrs Babubhai & Co., Laxmi Building, Fort, Bombay, but no such company was found in existence, and it was also significant that Babubhai was also the name of the accused Babubhai. According to the judge, Killewala could not even remember the exact amount he paid for the microphone (the cash memo showed that the amount was Rs 250, but Killewala said that he paid only Rs 200). If he had really borrowed the amount from his sister and if, as he claimed, it was returned to him by Printer, two or three days later, he would not have forgotten the amount. This indicated that money did not go out of Killewala's pocket, but that Babubhai must have given it, as alleged by Printer.[64]

To conclude, it is to the credit of Babubhai, Ushaben and their friends that despite all the obstacles and difficulties, the project of the Congress Radio was launched soon after they had decided to start it. By 1942 the radio had become an important means of communication. As pointed out by G.C. Awasthy,

> When the Second World War broke out, broadcasting was in its teens. In the absence of peaceful conditions, one thought, it might want still more time to grow and develop. But, surprisingly enough, the tragedy of war itself demonstrated beyond any shadow of doubt the immense possibilities of broadcasting as an important medium of mass contact. For speed in communication, for imparting to millions scattered over the globe a sense of participation, for keeping alive a glimmer of hope in the hearts of underground patriots, radio proved to be the only effective means.[65]

The people in India wanted to know more about the actual happenings and were suspicious about the news presented by the British government. Thus, the radio was an important means of communication. In the first-ever listener research, conducted by All India Radio (AIR) in May 1940 in five major Indian cities, covering 13,507 listeners, it was found that more Indians were using the radio for news, and that too, for news hostile to Britain.[66]

2

A Trailblazing Adventure

In August 1942, the prevailing mood was such that the people were ready for the launch of the Congress Radio. The decision had been a conscious and determined one, driven by the young team's vision of freedom and their commitment to disseminate information and news about the movement and the troubled times they lived in. They knew that what they considered as an act of patriotism would be in the eyes of the British rulers a criminal offence. They were fully aware of the impending threat of being nabbed by the British government but were willing to take the risk. They were venturing on an unknown path which, even though exciting, was not free from troubles. The task required skilful operation coupled with swift changes in the locations as operating from a single place would invite attention and possible arrest. When their project was launched, the only technical support they received was from Nariman Printer (and his associate, Mirza). Ultimately, this was to prove to be a huge hurdle in the operation of the radio.

Locations for the Congress Radio

When Printer wanted to shift the radio station from his house and relocate it elsewhere, he along with Babubhai, Ushaben and R.A. Mehta started looking for other places they could rent in the city. Babubhai had shown him two or three places, including one in Malad and a bungalow in the suburbs. Finally, on 26 August, they hired the top floor of the building in Chowpatty called Sea View, which Printer considered to be suitable.[1] Ahmed Umarkhan, who lived on the second floor in the same building, said in his evidence that his son was the owner of Sea View, and that he and his son used to let out the premises. He told the court that he rented the flat on the top floor for Rs 165 to Keshavlal Chhaganlal (a fictitious name used by the team) who wanted the place for his uncle who was arriving from Jamnagar.[2]

Later, Daraskhan Ambaskhan, the Pathan watchman at Sea View, said in his evidence that one Bania (identified as Babubhai), one Parsi (identified as Printer) and a lady who was squint-eyed (identified as Ushaben) had come to the premises and had wanted a room on the top floor; he had shown the place to them. He had seen them bringing some chairs, two beddings and a radio set. An aerial was put up by a boy (not Mirza) and was connected with the flat on the top floor. Babubhai, Printer and Ushaben would come there sometimes at noon or 1 p.m. or at night and would remain there for an hour or so. Nobody lived there permanently.[3] The Congress Radio team was thrilled with this place. Here Printer and Mirza fitted an aerial with the help of R.A. Mehta. That transmitter was to be used for 'Congress propaganda'.[4]

Printer and Mirza worked the transmitter at Sea View. Later, when the others started learning how to handle the equipment, Babubhai and R.A. Mehta began to work on it, and sometimes Ushaben. Babubhai would bring the programmes for the broadcast, which were mostly typed; once or twice they were handwritten, as pointed out by Printer. The typewritten material was typed in the 'Kerogas' office at Noble Chambers (Babubhai's office), by different persons, including Ushaben. In the beginning Babubhai, Ushaben and Printer used to speak into the microphone. Later R.A. Mehta was assigned this work.[5] The broadcasting was commenced on 41.78 metres wavelength from 27 August 1942.[6]

When the Bombay Congress bulletin of 3 September 1942 announced that the Congress Broadcasting Station would be broadcasting at 8.45 p.m., there was much excitement among the people. The police records confirm that the Congress Radio came on the air as stated in the Bombay Congress Bulletin. Thereafter, the wavelength of the broadcast was changed to 42.34 metres (from the location of Laxmi Bhuvan). The location of the station was, however, given as 'somewhere in India'. The broadcasts were a nightly feature (shortly before the set was seized, morning programmes were also put on the air) and they continued till the station was identified and seized while actually in operation on 12 November 1942.[7]

It is interesting to note that the Military Intelligence Officer, Bombay, intimated that the station was situated somewhere along a line at 353 degrees from Bombay which passed 50 miles west of Ahmedabad, through the Western Rajputana desert, West Punjab and 50 miles west of Multan, near Dera Ismail Khan and thence through Tribal Territory to and through a point 50 miles west of Kabul. The matter of effecting the exact location of this station had been left in the hands of the military intelligence officer. It was also noted that this broadcast was in addition to the

Bombay Congress Bulletin.

No. 58   Wednesday, 14-10-42

WE APPRECIATE, BUT

It is our misfortune that having accepted the distorted and one-sided stories doled out by the British censor as facts, Prof. Tan Yan-Shan, the Chinese Savant, attached to Vishwa Bharati has taken the liberty to condemn the Indian people for acts for which they are not responsible. It is a matter of superfluity to recall to the man of the type of the learned Professor the unparalled resistance that his own thick and thin are offering in occupied and unoccupied China against the cold barbarism of Yellow Imperialists. Will he be surprised that such practices of hideous barbarism enacted by the White imperialists on Indian women and children are resisted tooth and nail by our people ?

Much as we appreciate his sympathy and earnestness in the cause of India, we must beseech him not to indulge in statements which cannot stand impartial scrutiny. India made the cause of China her own and the learned professor does certainly remember that it was the Indian people, through their accredited organ the Indian National Congress, who sent a Medical Mission to serve the wounded Chinese in the battlefield when Britain closed the Burma Road, the life-line of supplies to china.

ADHERE TO TRUTH

"It is clear........that the resentment over the Congress revolt and the desire to suppress them have taken precedence over the need to get the country as a whole........." Says Mr. T. R. Venkatarama Sastri, an ex-President of the National Liberal Federation of India, commenting on the India debate in the British House of Commons. It is indeed sad that there are still Indians who talk in terms of "Congress revolt", knowing full well that the truth is that it was the Congress that sought on bended knees and with all the earnestness it could command a settlement but that it was the British Government which spurned the approach, imprisoned the Congress leaders and launched unprovoked agression on the people. We do hope that such friends like Shri Sastri will at least adhere to the truth.

CLEVER WOMEN OF BANGALORE

When the mounted police were let loose in the streets of Bangalore during the recent disturbances the women of the City organised parties to throw well-boiled Sago rice on the streets. The streets became so slippery that practically all the horses of the police slipped and fell down. Immediately after this the women threw buckets after buckets of chilly powder on the fallen 'heroes.' The mounted police came to realise that all their brute force was impotent against the ingenuity of women and decided not to send further reinforcements to these areas.

JAPANESE SABOTEURS IN OKHA:

On 1-10-42 five persons, apparently Madrasis, landed from a rubber boat on the coast of Okha Madhi. It is not known why they landed but after landing they went to the town of Okha Madhi for making some purchases. There Patel suspected them and took them into custody and later took them in a cart to Dwarka. There they were handed over to suba Saheb. These five men had five hundred rupees each on their person. They are not regularly imprisoned but are under constant police vigilence. Police is constantly with them. Their evidence was taken by Suba Saheb, and he has telegraphed to the addresses these men had given. It is to be seen what steps are being taken after the replies are received. One man said that they were Congressmen and that many persons like them have landed on the entire coast of India. More will be known later. It is likely that they may have landed from some submarine. They were only with the clothes they wore, which were clean and dhobi washed. Each wears a wrist watch.

RESPECTS TO SJT. MAHADEV DESAI

Tomorrow will witness the completion of two months of Sjt. Mahadev Desai's incredible death. It is but befitting that we offer our grateful respects to a man who has left behind him for the posterity such an immortal history of private and public conduct. There will, therefore, be a congregational prayer at Gowalia Tank tomorrow (Thursday) at 5-30 p.m. when people will pay their tribute to his immense services to the nation and offer peaceful prayers to the immortal spirit which ever remains a guiding star for those who have taken upon their shoulders the arduous task for achieving the object which he set himself to and which cost the nation his precious life. As it is a day of prayer, indulgence in any kind of demonstration or slogans must be avoided.

DO OR DIE.   Congress Radio

                                  8-45 P.M. Metres 42.34

Bombay Congress Bulletin, No. 58. 14, October 1942

one emanating from Azad Hind, Berlin, on the 19-metre wavelength.[8]

The Bombay Congress bulletin with its message 'Do or Die' often urged its readers to listen to the Congress Radio at 8.45 p.m.[9] In the beginning there was only one programme at 8.45 p.m. for fifteen to twenty minutes. Later, morning programmes were also introduced. The record of 'Hindustan Hamara' was played in the beginning and that of 'Vande Mataram' at the end of the programme.

The location of the secret radio had to be kept highly confidential, and to prevent the police from finding out, Printer had advised the group to keep on changing the places of operation from time to time. After a few days at Sea View, Printer, Mehta, Mirza, Killewala and Ushaben again began the process of looking out for another suitable site. They selected Ratan Mahal opposite the lower gate of the Government House on Walkeshwar Road. Printer and others approved of the place. They rented the flat (the fee was less than Rs 100) on 10 September 1942. According to Printer, Babubhai had said that he would pay the rent, and then R.A. Mehta paid the rent (amount). After they moved in, Mirza and Mehta fitted the transmitter and the aerial, Printer gave the final touches, and broadcasting began immediately. Subsequently, Babubhai brought the programmes that were to be broadcast. Printer claimed that Ushaben or Babubhai or himself or a Parsi lady used to speak into the microphone.[10] Killewala said that he had known the landlady, Kasturbai Hansraj Shroff, who lived in that building. He had gone once to hire a flat from her for a friend, who was Printer, in September 1942.[11]

When questioned, Kasturbai was cautious in her replies. As a witness she said that she had known Killewala for many years and he taught her Hindustani. Five or six men had come to rent the flat on the third floor of her building but nobody had introduced them; she had put up a sign board saying that the flat was to be let out and several persons had come to inquire. She had rented the flat to a person who, as far as she remembered, gave the surname of

Gandhi. She did not remember the exact amount, but the rent was Rs 80 or Rs 85 and it was paid on the spot. She fell ill two or three days later and went out of Bombay (to Vile Parle, now a suburb of Bombay). When she returned, the tenant had left. She had no record of the receipt as she had been unwell. She thought that Killewala had come to see her on the day on which she rented out the flat. He used to come to see her often, and on that day he came at the same time as those five or six men.[12]

Years later, Ushaben warmly recalled how the landlady had, in her own way, tried to protect the identity of Ushaben and her colleagues. She also remembered the obstacles that stood in the way of their enterprise. In her words, 'It was a Herculean task to get the necessary materials for the transmitter. Babubhai had to stretch his imagination to the farthest limit to get them. Both Vithalbhai and I banked on his resourcefulness. Many a time, gadgets used to drop out of Babubhai's hat or from his pocket and quite often from his tiffin carrier. It was really exciting.

'Each time, we had to move from one place to another. Once, Babubhai and I found a very safe place in Mulund. We were extremely happy at the idea that we would be able to carry on at least for a month or two from there. So we went to the owner to pay the rent. A strange apparatus was lying there. "Sethji, what is this supposed to be?" we asked. "A detecting machine to catch illegal radios!" came the reply. "A detecting machine!" I was taken aback, but took care to see that my face did not betray any alarm. Babubhai's reaction was: "Behn, we are saved from the tiger's jaws." He had warned me not to wear a white khadi sari that day, but I had not listened to him and had insisted on doing so. From that day, however, I changed my dress slightly so as to be less conspicuous.'

She continued talking in a gentle but determined voice: 'It was no joke to evade an ever-vigilant police and their detective van. One day, while discussing ways and means to safeguard ourselves, we decided that one volunteer should wait outside the building in a car, and in case of any danger, continuously blow the horn. Our programme started just after the decision was taken and the horn began blowing continuously as soon as the 'Saare Jahan Se Achha Hindustan Hamara' was over. We, our technician Mirza and I, just did not know what to do. Since the programme had already begun, we could not talk. So it was only through gestures that we could communicate with each other. He was beckoning me to leave the programme and escape and I was asking him to wait till the programme was over. Ultimately he ran away and I was left alone. I left the radio station after completing the programme only to be told on reaching the ground floor that the horn of our car had got stuck and there was no danger.'[13]

While the Congress Radio group was engrossed in its work of communicating the news to the people, the city was restless and uneasy. People, especially the students, were being swept away by the wave of patriotism. The city witnessed incidents of disturbances and outbreaks of violence, like distribution of unauthorized leaflets, stoppage of vehicular traffic, blocking of roads, cutting telephone wires, damaging municipal property like lamp posts, uprooting trees, throwing stones at the police and burning of police chowkies. The attendance at schools and colleges declined: there was a marked upsurge and unease among the students.[14]

Special appeals to the students were issued. A leaflet especially for the students of Wilson College pronounced that 'Now it is our duty of the first importance to continue struggle with doubled vigour and energy and to calm the burning blazing hearts of our kinsmen now behind the prison bars.'[15]

A printed copy of the leaflet 'Carry On' in September by the Students' Action Committee of the BPCC displayed their combative mood:

> In yet another mighty and memorable round with the Gangster government, the students of Bombay have fully vindicated their historic role in this final REVOLUTION FOR INDIA'S FREEDOM. By their iron resolve and concerted action they have dealt a smashing blow to the fascist British Raj and driven yet another nail in its coffin.[16]

The youth in the city had embraced the movement with wholehearted zeal. They were unafraid of what the future held for them—be it imprisonment and torture, or loss of professional security and comfort. Their ardour was kept alive by the leaders working from the underground. 'Bulletin No. 8 War of Independence' congratulated the Bombay students and advised them to go ahead with their activities and ensure that no school or college remained open until the national struggle came to a victorious conclusion. The powerful message given was: 'Education can wait but not the freedom'. It was suggested that women and children work as secret messengers collecting, collating and disseminating the detailed information about the struggle. People were exhorted to 'act as citizens of free India.'[17]

Ushaben and her colleagues in the radio project sympathized with the people's anger and uprising. Ushaben used to talk about how the students of Wilson College, where she studied, were involved in the movement and how Principal Mackenzie would tell the British soldiers not to enter the campus of the college. She supported the students of her college in their protest against the British rule, and at the same time had to maintain complete secrecy about her involvement in the activities of the underground radio.[18]

On 25 September 1942, the Congress Radio team shifted the transmitter to Ajit Villa, a three-storey building in Gamdevi, where R.A. Mehta was living. R.A. Mehta claimed that initially he was not willing to allow Printer to use his place, but ultimately he agreed. Mirza, Printer and a girl (not Ushaben) used to go there for broadcasting.[19] Mirza and Mehta erected the aerial. Most of the programmes were broadcasted by Mehta, though occasionally Babubhai and Printer went there and spoke into the microphone once or twice.[20] Mehta lived with his mother on the first and second floors; as a result he was anxious and wanted to remove the transmitter set from his place. Since Printer did not seem inclined to do so, Mehta went out in search of a place. He found Laxmi Bhuvan on Sandhurst Road and hired the top floor for a month. According to Mehta he paid Rs 100 for the rent. He did not want to give his name and hired the flat under the fictitious name of Thakore.[21]

This was corroborated in the court by Siddheshwar Vishnu Pandit, the managing trustee of Laxmi Bhuvan building. In his evidence, he deposed that a gentleman who introduced himself as C.R. Thakore, on 2 October 1942 paid Rs 100 as rent for the flat on the third floor; he said that his uncle was to come from Ahmedabad or some such place. He brought some kit on 4 October. Pandit thereafter went out of Bombay. When he returned around 24 October, he learnt that the flat had been vacated. He identified tenant C.R. Thakore at the identification parade.[22]

Efforts for Improved Transmission

The transmitter was taken to Laxmi Bhuvan on 4 October 1942. Until then the members of the Congress Radio group used to read the programmes directly into the microphone. However, when they realized that they were not being heard as clearly as the records of the songs 'Hindustan Hamara' and 'Vande Mataram', they thought of broadcasting recorded programmes. Vithalbhai, from this time onwards, was to play an important role.[23]

According to Printer, Vithalbhai was introduced by Babubhai at the latter's place (office). Pinter was told that this person was also interested in their broadcasting work. Then they discussed the safety of the persons speaking into the microphone as they were afraid of being caught red-handed by the police. As a result, the idea of recording the programmes was thought of. Vithalbhai offered to supply the records of the programmes from time to time. According to Printer, Dr Lohia, Mehta and probably Mirza were present when this conversation took place. Printer's transmitter worked better with records and records were heard more clearly than spoken words.[24]

The beginning of the recorded programmes at Laxmi Bhuvan was an important milestone in the journey of the Congress Radio. It seems that from this stage, the group received tremendous support from Dr Ram Manohar Lohia and other leaders. Ushaben fondly recalled the days soon after they went on air: 'On listening to our broadcast, Dr Ram Manohar Lohia was thrilled and made frantic attempts to locate us. To our utter surprise, after a day or two, my uncle Ajit Desai, a radio engineer and a veteran freedom fighter, came to me with a message that Dr Lohia wanted to meet us. Without a moment's delay, we went to him. Not only did we get a very warm reception but almost all our problems were solved as he took both the financial responsibility as well as the responsibility of supplying us with news bulletins, talks and speeches from leaders like Achyut Patwardhan and Jayaprakash Narayan. Coordinating the activities of our group and Vithalbhai's group, he separated broadcasting work from the recording work by entrusting the former to us and the latter to Vithalbhai's group, and advised us to work as one team under the name of Congress Radio—a name associated with many thrilling experiences and mysteries. All of us readily agreed. The Congress Radio was not a radio only in name. It had its own transmitter, transmitting station, recording station, its own call sign and a district wavelength. We used to start the programme with the announcement: "This is the Congress Radio calling on 42.34 metres from somewhere in India." We used to get news from all over India through trusted messengers. We used to be in contact with Sucheta Kriplani who was in charge of the AICC in Bombay. Often Dr Lohia wrote speeches, Achyut Patwardhan also wrote occasionally and I too used to write sometimes. Most of the speeches in English were relayed by Dr Lohia and Coomie Dastur, whereas Hindi speeches were delivered by Moinuddin Harris, Achyut Patwardhan and myself.'[25]

Babubhai used to bring the records of the programmes to the station. Judging from the voice, Printer could gauge that Ushaben mostly spoke for the records. On one occasion he was present when the record was cut. That night he had been brought there by Babubhai in his car.

Mirza and Ushaben were also with them. They were driven to a bungalow in Lamington Road. Printer waited in his car while Babubhai went up. He returned after a long time and said that Vithalbhai had shifted to another place. Then they drove to a bungalow near French Bridge, where Vithalbhai received them; they all sat in the back room. Thereafter, Vithalbhai took out a recording machine from a box or a suitcase. Jagannath Thakor (a radio mechanic in Chicago Radio Company, henceforth Jagannath) was already there.[26]

Vithalbhai connected the recording machine to the main and took a test of Ushaben's voice. It was suitably adjusted, then Ushaben read out something and it was recorded. When the record was complete, Printer and others took it with them. Printer said that he did not know from where the recording machine was obtained, but he had seen the nameplate of Chicago Radio on it. He also said that Babubhai had told Printer that Chicago Radio was giving instruments to Vithalbhai. According to Printer he had a talk with Jagannath there and Jagannath had told him that another transmitter, about which he had spoken, was almost ready.[27] Jagannath, on the other hand, said that he was never on friendly terms with Printer. He never told him anything about any transmitting set built by Jagannath or any activity of Nanak Motwane (henceforth Motwane).[28]

Ushaben reminisced nostalgically about those days. She once said, 'We used to relay news, speeches, instructions and appeals to different classes of people. For this, there was a batch of speakers and writers including Dr Lohia, Achyut Patwardhan, Moinuddin Harris, Coomie Dastur (later Kamal Wood), K.A. Abbas and myself. So records were cut in their voices. Vithalbhai was in charge of this work. Because of the risk involved, we could not take the speakers to the broadcasting section, of which Babubhai was mainly in charge. As in the case of our broadcasting station, we also used to shift our recording station at regular intervals. We started with Sumatiben Morarjee's House at French Bridge, then another place at Malabar Hill and then moved to Thackersey's Bungalow at Peddar Road.'[29]

The members of the Congress Radio group were very keen to make the transmitter more powerful, but the parts required to increase its power were not readily available in the market. The burden of solving this problem was thrown on Babubhai's shoulders. One morning he phoned Printer asking him to be ready to go with him to a certain place. They had suspected that their telephones were tapped, so conversations on the phone would be vague. Babubhai came after half an hour and they went to see Dahyabhai Patel at the Oriental Insurance Company.[30]

Shantilal Bhat, the sound recorder at Circo Talkies, was also with them in Babubhai's car. Babubhai said that Bhat had been sent by Dr Lohia to watch the technical side. At Dahyabhai's room the group talked about the supply of the parts for the transmitter and showed willingness to go to the place he suggested. Babubhai's car was left behind and they all went in Dahyabhai's car to Chicago Radio Company. They were warmly welcomed by Motwane who greeted Dahyabhai very respectfully. Babubhai and Dahyabhai had a talk with Motwane, but the others, including Printer, could not hear what was being said since they were in the waiting room. After a while they went in and then Motwane told them that he would put them in touch with the right man. He phoned someone and after a few minutes Jagannath entered. Thereafter Dahyabhai left. Printer had the list of the parts required for strengthening

An Appeal to the College Students.

———()———

It is a matter of regret and pain to learn that the students of Bombay, the Vanguards of freedom, unlike of the designation have called off the strike. Students, soldiers of independence, must pay their own quota in this mightest struggle of independence.

What should be your quota ? The fundamental one one should be ' the Strike', **GO ON STRIKE**. Thus you serve your country though passively but most emphatically by non-cooperating with university. The idea behind the strike is that each one in his independence capacity is boycotting the slavish education. By not maintaining the strike, you are hampering the work of the sincere workers,— co-students— and indirectly giving a death blow to the progress of congress. This is not the time for the students to lay idle at home or read the silver screen magazines. Do what you can in your individual capacity and serve your country. Most of our senators are of the opinion that the Colleges should be closed down for a definate period and the ensuing examinations should be postponed following the footsteps of sister universities of India.

The task and responsibility be on you Be worthy of it. Keep out of you colleges and convince the senators that at this criticial hour, the stunents of Bombay cannot be the mere spectators but shall fulfill the pledge, which they have taken under the congress banner ' DO or DIE "

' *Students Organisation.* '

An appeal to college students in 1942

the transmitter, including some transmitting valves. The group wanted about 400–500 watts power. Jagannath saw the list and said that all the parts were not available. They were, however, expected within a few days. He was ready to give immediate delivery of those parts that were available. He consulted Motwane and told the group that the parts would be kept ready at 1 p.m. the next day. According to Printer, Jagannath told the group that he used to listen to the programmes at Borivali, but they could not be heard clearly. He also said that he himself was building a powerful transmitter for the Congress Radio. When it was ready, the difficulty of reception would disappear. (All this took place before Vithalbhai was introduced to Printer). Later on, Babubhai and Jagannath told Printer that Vithalbhai was having a transmitter on parallel lines and later on they would share the programmes between the two transmitters; one transmitter was to broadcast the Hindi programme and when that was switched off, the other transmitter would broadcast the English programme.[31]

The next day, Babubhai told Printer that he had gone to the shop but could not get the parts from Jagannath because they had the name of Chicago Radio on them which had to be removed before being handed over. Some days later Babubhai phoned Printer and told him that he had received the parts. Printer went to see Babubhai in his office on the third floor at Noble Chambers. Mehta, Babubhai, Ushaben and Mirza were already there. Printer was taken into the inner room and shown a box containing the parts, but he could not see any transmitting parts; there were resistances, condensers, six crystals and some other small parts. The specification plates had been removed from the crystals, and the frequency had been written on them in ink. There were also porcelain valve holders used for transmitting purposes, and some insulating pillars. These parts were taken to Laxmi Bhuvan, and Printer fitted in

the crystals and changed the frequency from 41.78 metres
to 42.34 metres.[32] There was broadcasting of programmes
regularly every day from 27 August 1942 to 12 November
1942, except on 15, 16 and 17 October 1942, when,
according to Printer, the set was being strengthened.[33]

The original strength of Printer's set when he
purchased it from a person called Dharap was 100 watts,
but he had reduced it to 10 watts by means of a voltage
divider. Printer's crystal was fractured, but he avoided
buying another one because it would then become known
that he wanted to build a transmitter. Moreover, on his
own admission he had lied to Babubhai by saying that
he had increased the power to 1500 watts.[34] Some parts
required for strengthening Printer's set were procured and
the strength was increased, ostensibly to 100 watts, but
actually 30 watts, according to the evidence of Deputy
Inspector Fergusson.[35]

A wireless receiver set was required to test whether the
transmitted programmes could be heard clearly or not.
According to Printer, the Philips radio receiving set, an
exhibit in the case, was used by him and colleagues to test
the broadcasting, and Babubhai had brought it. Printer did
not know who purchased it.[36]

It is important to keep in mind that the radio was a
powerful means of communication during the days of the
Second World War, when the news was heavily censored.
Now this radio set that was bought for the enterprise also
had a story of its own. Jamnadas Ratansi, the radio dealer
with a shop on the New Queen's Road near Royal Opera
House, said that he dealt in Philips radio receiving sets.
He purchased some sets from Precious Electric Company
on 9 October 1942. Bipin S. Inamdar (Inamdar) who
was working with Star Radio Engineering Ltd said that

he wanted a small receiving set and the Philips radio set was sold to him for Rs 255 with a concession of Rs 15. Inamdar did not mention for whom it was bought. He promised to give details about it, but never did. Jamnadas gave him the guarantee cards two or three days after he bought the set, but it was never returned to Jamnadas. (Both the guarantee cards were to be signed by the owner; one of them was to be sent to Philips Radio India.) They were taken away by Inamdar and not signed in Jamnadas's presence. Later it was discovered later that they were signed by one Maganlal T. Dalal.[37]

According to Inamdar, he sold the radio set (produced before the court) on cash payment to Maganlal T. Dalal who had come to him, even though he did not know him. When Inamdar asked for the licence number required to possess the radio set, Maganlal T. Dalal promised to give it to him, but never did. Two days later Inamdar went to find him at the address he had given (Block A, Soonawala Building, Tardeo), but could not trace him. Since Inamdar had to go out of Bombay, he did not inform the police. Later Inamdar showed the police the signed guarantee cards returned by this customer who had left in a hurry. Interestingly, Inamdar said that he had never listened to the Congress broadcast and he did not know Babubhai. He did, however, know Ushaben who was his relative.[38]

It could not be proved who had given that bogus name of Maganlal T. Dalal. Though the judge found Inamdar's conduct suspicious, Printer's allegation that Babubhai had supplied the radio receiving set (found in Parekh Wadi) was not borne out by any other evidence.[39]

In Printer's statement he said that he, Dr Lohia and Babubhai had talked about the payment for the apparatus, when they were broadcasting from Laxmi Bhuvan. Babubhai had wanted Dr Lohia to give more money to increase the power and build a new transmitter and it was settled that Dr Lohia would advance about Rs 15,000–20,000; Printer had confirmed the estimate as a technician. Printer learnt later from Babubhai that Dr Lohia had paid the money, but he did not get the amount he expected. He said that he received only Rs 2,000–3,000 towards the price of the parts sold by him; he got nothing for his services.[40]

The judgment mentions that according to Printer, Babubhai admitted that he received money from Dr Lohia, but there was no independent corroboration on this point. Some parts were required for strengthening of the set, and these parts were procured and the set was strengthened. But Printer's story that Babubhai procured these parts remained uncorroborated.[41]

Jagannath had built several transmitters. He used to build transmitters continuously to meet military requirements (because of the war) and did not know for whom a particular transmitter was built. He built one a month after Gandhi's arrest. He said that Motwane sent him to Vithalbhai's house (Bhaskar Bhavan, Lamington Road) to repair a recording machine in October 1942. That was the first time he met Vithalbhai. Motwane had told Jagannath that Vithalbhai was a friend who was having some difficulty and that he should help him solve it. Vithalbhai showed him a recording machine and asked him to repair it. There was no name of the dealer on it. Neither had he seen the machine before. There were similar machines in Chicago Radio Company as well. Jagannath thereafter repaired the machine and took a test by cutting a record of his own voice.[42]

Vithalbhai once took Jagannath with him in his car to the second floor of a bungalow in Banganga, where he saw some transmitting parts like chokes and condensers, and some parts fitted on a chassis. Vithalbhai said that he wanted to test and study the different parts and asked Jagannath to teach him how to handle them. Jagannath advised him how to assemble them, but they were not assembled in his presence. About a month before he went to Banganga with Vithalbhai, Jagannath had seen some of these parts in Chicago Radio Company and had mounted them on a chassis in the company's office at the insistence of Motwane. He did not know why or for whom Motwane had asked him to mount the parts of the chassis. He prepared the design for the chassis according to the instructions given by Motwane. Vithalbhai did not tell Jagannath why he had the transmitting parts in that bungalow, or why he wanted to study them. An amplifier was required for a transmitter, but there was no amplifier when Jagannath went to Banganga with Vithalbhai, nor did he take one there.[43]

Jagannath said that he had repaired the amplifier that was produced before the court, and had obtained the necessary parts from the godown on the strength of the slip signed by the manager. (He had said that Motwane was the sales manager, in charge of the ground floor and the shop and also in charge of indenting goods and allowing the goods to go out of the godown. Jagannath worked under his orders.) After the repair that took just a day, he handed over the amplifier to Motwane. Jagannath did not know whom Motwane had delivered it to. However, he saw it later in Khandke Building, when the police took him there.[44]

After transmitting from Laxmi Bhuvan for a few days, the group shifted their location to Parekh Wadi on Girgaum Back Road. According to Printer, Inamdar had found this place and Printer had approved of it. Babubhai, Mehta

and Printer brought the apparatus there in a car. Killewala
(accompanied by Mehta) took the money for the rent
from Babubhai and paid for the rent (for rooms 103–106
on the fifth floor of the building). Babubhai, Mehta and
Printer shifted the apparatus there in a car.[45] According to
R.A. Mehta, Printer had told him that he could not rent
the rooms in Parekh Wadi as they were to be let out to
Hindus only. Thus Mehta was asked by Printer to take
them on hire for him. So Mehta went there, paid the rent
of Rs 120 and hired the rooms under the fictitious name of
Mohanlal R. Desai (this was also the case when they had
rented the previous places).[46] This was later corroborated
by Ramsaran Dube and Fulchand Jethabhai. Ramsaran
Dube, the rent collector at Parekh Wadi, said that Rs 120
was paid as rent by 'a Gujarati Hindu boy' who had come
to look for a flat.[47] Fulchand Jethabhai, the accountant
in Amritlal Nathuchand Trust, Parekh Wadi, confirmed
after checking his book that rooms no. 103–106 were let
out on 15 October 1942 to one Mohanlal Rasiklal Desai
for his uncle from Jamnagar, who was expected after eight
or ten days.[48]

Mirza, Mehta and Inamdar erected the set in Parekh
Wadi (room no. 106). Mehta and Inamdar (Printer
called him by his first name Vipin/Bipin as he said that
he did not know his full name.) used to broadcast from
the records brought by Babubhai.[49] Printer, Mirza and
R.A. Mehta had purchased a bedding with a holdall, a hat
box, two suitcases and a water bottle to be taken in the car
in which the transmitting set was to be taken from place
to place in order to give them the appearance of bonafide
travellers. This is borne out by the fact that the kit (of such
articles) was found in Parekh Wadi when it was raided
by the police.[50] Remembering those days, Ushaben said

that usually the transmitter and the other paraphernalia
were shifted from place to place in Babubhai's car. The
Congress Radio team had to be very cautious about their
work and movement as they were always worried about
being apprehended by the police. In addition, as Ushaben
said, 'Another great obstacle in our way was the mischief
played by AIR (All India Radio but Anti-India Radio to
us) to jam our broadcasts. When everything was ready
and we were absolutely sure about a good reception, they
would start their tricks. It was really disgusting. So, our
technicians decided to try the same trick—to jam AIR—
and we were partly successful.'[51]

According to R.A. Mehta, after remaining in Parekh
Wadi for a few days, Printer told him that the transmitter
would have to be shifted as it was dangerous to keep it
there for much longer. Printer had found a place on Warden
Road near Mahaluxmi temple, and asked Mehta to hire
it for him. Mehta did so, paid the rent of Rs 90 for this
place (Paradise Bungalow) and gave his name as Pandya.[52]
The bungalow was hired in the name of S.B. Pandya on 23
October 1942 and its possession was taken on 3 November
1942.[53] According to Badlu Ramcharan, the rent collector
for Mr Vakil for Paradise Bungalow at Mahaluxmi, he was
present when the police came to make a search of the flat
on the second floor. The tenant had come there only once.
He would not be able to recognize him.[54]

Concurrently, the public was becoming increasingly
restive. Ushaben and her colleagues witnessed how the
city reacted. There were the outbursts of the anger of
the people, acts of destruction and disturbances. Stray
arrests for shouting Congress slogans and pelting the
stones continued. Attendances at the colleges had reduced
to nearly 50 per cent. Since the commencement of the

हरेक हिन्दुस्तानी के कर्तव्य

Duties of Every Indian—a Hindi pamphlet in 1942

disturbances on 9 August 1942, the total number of arrests was 2,701. Thirty-six people had died and 478 had been injured. However, many innovative programmes including flag salutation ceremonies and processions were planned from 2 to 9 October to celebrate the 'Gandhi Week' and the government had received information about them.[55]

Women too were captivated by the magic of the Mahatma. In an enthralling letter dated 5 October addressed to 'Every Government Officer and Servant' from 'yours, in sisterly love, more than 500 women of Bombay' they stated in a determined way that

> The British Govt. has deftly killed our spirit and self-respect. Mahatma Gandhi instilled the same into us and showed us the path of deliverance through suffering. The Congress exhorts you to shed all fear and observe complete HARTAL on 8 October. Will you respond to the call in token sympathy for the national cause of FREEDOM?[56]

It can be inferred that the young team operating the Congress Radio was painfully aware of the oppressive steps taken by the government in Bombay that included arrests, curfew, whipping anyone convicted of rioting, use of tear gas and banning processions, flag ceremonies and picketing. In retaliation, there were some disruptive activities displaying the anger and frustration of the people.[57] On 18 October 1942, Congress Radio announced that a separate English programme would be broadcast on 39 metres. But before the apparatus could be shifted to Paradise Bungalow, the police raided Parekh Wadi on 12 November 1942 when the broadcast was on. Ushaben and Chandrakant Babubhai Jhaveri (henceforth Chandrakant) were present on the site and were caught red-handed.[58]

3

Arrests and Institution of the Case

On 3 September 1942, the Bombay Congress Bulletin said that the Congress Broadcasting Station would be on the air at 8.45 p.m. on 41.78 metres. This was most probably the earliest announcement in the Congress Bulletins about the broadcasts. According to Kokje, it was divulged on 14 October that the Radio would be off the air till 18 October.[1]

However, the report on 3 September was highly significant as it alerted the police about the existence of the underground radio. Deputy Inspector Fergusson was entrusted with the task of keeping a watch and finding out the location of the radio station. He was then the deputy inspector of police and in charge of the police wireless in the city. His office and main central station were at Shepherd Road, Byculla. He was a competent officer and was experienced in the working of the wireless; he himself had built the police wireless. He monitored the Congress Radio with perseverance and diligence. After tuning into the station he would ask the reporters to take down notes, and he himself would drive around listening to the broadcast. He located the areas as lying between Chowpatty and C.P. Tank. Thereafter the area was further narrowed down to Sandhurst Road, Girgaum Road, Queen's Road and Chowpatty. He believed that the transmitter was kept moving.[2]

The Trajectory Followed by the Police

Ganesh Keshav Kokje (Kokje) played a key role in the arrest of the persons involved in the operation of the Congress Radio. He was the inspector of police, CID Special Branch, and had been in charge of the War Branch since 1940. He was also one of the officers responsible for arresting the Congress leaders on 9 August; later he detained the members of the Congress Radio team. The rigorous probing and stern examinations of Printer, Mirza and others by the police opened the floodgates of the evidence required, and the secrets of the Congress Radio collapsed like a house of cards as Printer betrayed his colleagues. He revealed the whereabouts of the important places from where the Congress Radio operated. He and Deputy Commissioner Taylor went to Parekh Wadi and also to Sea View, Ajit Villa and Laxmi Bhuvan. Babubhai pointed Ratan Mahal to him, while R.A. Mehta showed him Paradise Bungalow. The police soon descended upon these other sites. Once there, Kokje called the various landlords and held identification parades, which led to S.V. Pandit and Ramasharan Dube identifying R.A. Mehta, and Daraskhan, the watchman of Sea View, pointing out Babubhai and Printer.[3]

Keeping in mind that the Congress Radio started soon after the AICC meeting on 7 and 8 August 1942 in Bombay, the police had begun making detailed inquiries into the filming of the sessions. As a result, the persons

who were involved with various tasks were called as
witnesses. After Jagannath's statement, Kokje went to the
Famous Cine Laboratory and took charge of twenty-two
tin boxes containing reels from Abdul Karim Kazi. They
contained the sound and picture film of the AICC meeting.
Kokje held an identification parade, where Majid Karim
Kazi (Majid), the chief technician in the Famous Cine
Laboratories, identified Vithalbhai and Jagannath in the
identification parade.[4]

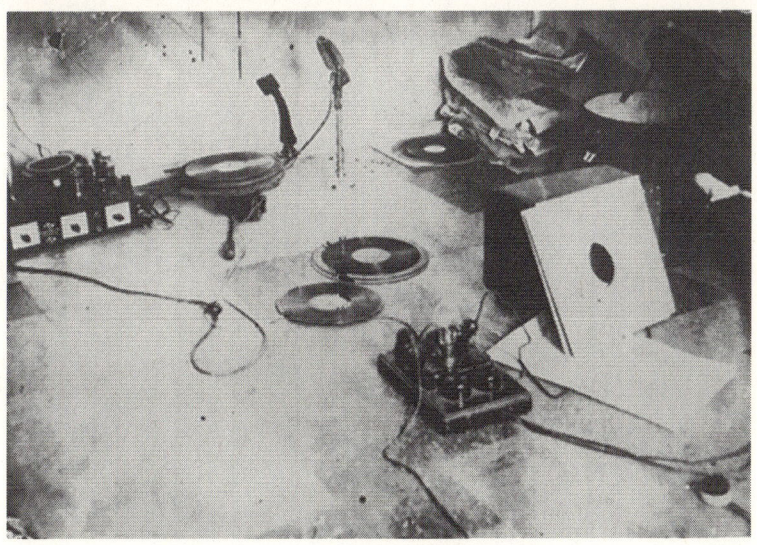

The seized Congress Radio apparatus

Kokje explored Motwane's involvement in the filming of the
AICC sessions. According to Jagannath, the Chicago Radio
Company had installed ten or twelve loudspeakers inside
the pandal and outside it for the meeting. Three amplifiers
had also been supplied. Deshpande and Jagannath had
been put in charge of the operation of the loudspeakers
and amplifiers by Motwane who was present throughout

the meeting. Films of the session were taken by the Famous Cine Laboratories under Motwane's instructions.[5]

Two sound recording trucks had also been parked at a distance of 10 feet away from each other, but Jagannath did not know to whom they belonged. Motwane later told him that one of them belonged to Famous Cine Company.[6] Jagannath had provided the electric supply (current) to both the trucks under Motwane's instructions. The Famous Cine Company's truck received the sound from the microphone near the speaker, and not from the loudspeaker outside. Jagannath believed that with a sensitive microphone, the sound from the loudspeaker could be recorded in a house even at a distance of 25 feet; all sound emanating from the vicinity would in that case be absorbed in the recording. In fact, if the loudspeaker outside the pandal was sufficiently near a house, a record could be cut inside that house.[7]

Jagannath was familiar with the premises of the Famous Cine Laboratories. He had been sent there by Motwane to check on how the photographs of the AICC meeting had come out. On his way he met Vithalbhai who expressed his wish to see the AICC film. So together they went to Vithalbhai's residence, had a meal there and then left in Vithalbhai's car for the Famous Cine Laboratories. Here, they met Majid, who had been instructed by Motwane to show the film to them. They had reached there around 10 p.m. and were there till 3 a.m. They saw the film till midnight. The sound and the picture films were separate. At that time no records were cut. On the next day he reported to Motwane that the film had come out quite well.[8]

Later when the Congress Radio station was seized at Parekh Wadi, 120 records were also found there. Among these were two sides of a record that had been cut from the sound films taken by the Famous Cine Laboratory

during the AICC session on 7 and 8 August. According
to the prosecution, this had been done by Jagannath and
Vithalbhai in the editing room of Famous Cine Laboratory.[9]

Jagannath, however, said that though he knew how to
cut a record, he did not see any record-cutting machine
in the editing room. Nor had he ever seen any record cut
about the Congress Radio broadcast. He also expressed
his ignorance of any blank records being supplied to
Vithalbhai from their shop. He went on to say that he
had never been friendly with Printer and claimed that he
never talked with Printer about any transmitting set being
built by him or Vithalbhai or about any of Motwane's
activities. Moreover, he had never told Jagannath Joshi
(senior clerk at the godown of Chicago Radio Company)
that a transmitter was being built for the Congress Radio;
he himself did not know about this. In addition, he had
never mentioned that blank records were needed for the
Congress Radio.[10]

Majid said in his statement that Motwane had entered
into an agreement with them for filming the AICC session;
he had hired the apparatus for Rs 300 per day and had
asked Majid to take the truck to the pandal, which Majid
did. Motwane supplied 7,000 feet of the raw film. He also
controlled the recording of the session, and they took the
shots according to his instructions. These instructions were
conveyed to Majid by buzzers. Majid shot about 7,000 feet
in two days. The sound film was taken by Majid and the
picture film by a cameraman. The films were developed
at Majid's place and kept with Majid as per Motwane's
instructions. They were ready within seven or eight days.[11]

Some days later Motwane sent word to Majid that
somebody from his firm would come at night to edit the
film. This was some time about the end of September or

two or three days before Gandhi Jayanti. According to
Motwane's message, Jagannath and Vithalbhai had gone
to Majid at about 9.30 or 10 p.m. Majid gave them the tins
containing the reels and took them to the editing room on
the first floor. They had carried nothing with them. Majid
showed them how to function the operating machine and
left them there. The following morning he found some
scrapings on the ground in the editing room. These could
have been the scrapings of the film, but he was not sure.[12]

The evidence of Abdul Karim Rashid Kazi, the manager,
Famous Cine Laboratories, was not very different from that
of Majid's. According to Abdul Karim Rashid Kazi, the
sound films were not synchronized with the picture film.
They were separate and were processed in his laboratory.
His book showed 6,700 feet of sound film and 7,000 feet
of picture film.[13]

As Kokje delved deeper into the case, a strand of the
inquiry brought up the name of Khandke Building on
Walkeshwar Road. Kokje had first questioned Printer
and later Jagannath who gave Kokje some information
and took him to the building on Walkeshwar Road on 18
November. The police inspector wanted to find out more
about Jayachand Tarachand Sheth.[14]

In his statement as a witness, Jayachand Tarachand
Sheth, managing director of Commin Company, said that
on 17 November 1942 he received a telephone message in
his office saying that some radio parts and radio articles
were lying on the third floor of Khandke Building on
Walkeshwar Road, and that several arrests had been made
in connection with the Congress Radio broadcasts and
that he should remove the articles from there. He could
not recognize the voice; neither did the caller give his name
even after being asked. He assumed that someone was

pulling his leg. But the caller persisted and Jayachand went
home, unlocked the rooms (on the third floor) and in the
corner of the rear room found these articles, some in boxes
and some wrapped in paper. According to him, neither he
nor anyone in his home knew how they had made their way
into his house. The discovery made him very nervous and
he did not know what to do. He was so agitated that he did
not immediately report his findings to the police. Instead,
he moved them to his godown where he kept his heavy
chemicals. He used to keep his costly dyes, small tins and
small cases in the two rooms on the third floor of Khandke
Building. The next day (18 November), Kokje and Sub-
Inspector Desai called on Jayachand Tarachand (who was in
his office and was asked to open the locked room on the top
floor of Khandke Building). When they searched the place,
they found nothing suspicious. Jayachand told the police
what had happened. He was then taken to the CID office
(where Kokje questioned him). Jayachand admitted how
the articles were found and how he had removed them.
He was only released after he promised to produce certain
articles.[15] Kokje conceded that if he had arrested Jayachand,
he would never have got hold of those parts. He further
clarified that there was no special reason to oblige or trust
him. On 19 November, Kokje went to Khandke Building
with Desai and as promised, Jayachand produced the
articles in the presence of the witnesses.[16]

Kokje showed the articles to Jagannath and he identified
all of them. Kokje took charge of them after making a
statement of the witnesses. On 18 November, before going to
Khandke Building, he had called Motwane as a consequence
of Jagannath's statement and had arrested him.[17]

Questioning Jayachand brought some facts to
light. Jamnadas Devkaran Chandriani (a partner in the

International Radio Company) said as a witness that he knew Jayachand; they were co-directors in a motor company that closed its business in about 1938–39. According to him he sold the amplifier (produced before the court) to Jayachand sometime in October 1942 for Rs 900 (a duplicate bill for the same was also produced), but Jayachand did not reveal why he wanted the amplifier.[18] However, Jayachand did say that he had gone to the shop of Jamnadas Devkaran in October 1942 to buy a radio set, which he purchased for Rs 1,700 or so. He never paid Rs 900 for any amplifier, neither did he ask for any amplifier to be repaired. When he was shown the office copy of a bill dated 9 October 1942 for Rs 900, he said that he had never received such a bill.[19]

The matter was examined by the police and at a later stage by the judge in detail. It is stated in the judgment that the incomplete wireless transmitting set produced by Jayachand Tarachand Sheth from Khandke Building was not the subject matter of the present case.[20]

Inspector Kokje was following all the major and minor characters carefully and meticulously in a thoroughly professional way. Around the middle of October 1942, Fergusson reported to Kokje that he had located the Congress Radio station in the zone between Chowpatty and C.P. Tank. This led Kokje to keep watch on the shop of B.M. Tanna, the proprietor of Tanna Radio Accessories on Lamington Road. He was suspicious of Tanna, having arrested him in 1940 while he was transmitting news about cotton features via a radio transmitter. He started his surveillance on him from 15 October onwards, but Tanna didn't turn up at his shop for four or five days. His absence coincided with the closure of the Congress broadcast on 15, 16 and 17 October. This further aroused Kokje's suspicions so he continued to keep Tanna under close observation. On 31 October, he received some additional information which led him to keep a watch on Dinbai Petit Street, off Balaram Street. He arrested Manukumar Madhavji and Madhavji Sunderji just as they were carrying a complete transmitter unit in a taxi.[21]

He took them to the CID office and was given the names of B.M. Tanna and Mansukhlal Nihalchand, the manager of the Lamington Road branch of the Chicago Radio Company. Both of them were close friends and their shops were in the same building. They were arrested on 5 November and their shops searched. Their residences were searched as well, but Kokje did not find anything incriminating in them. At the CID office, the two of them were questioned about the Congress broadcasts. On the basis of their information, he brought Jagannath to the CID office and questioned him on 11 November. On the information given by Jagannath he arranged for the arrest of Printer, Babubhai and Vithalbhai on 12 November. He had also been keeping a watch on Vithalbhai's residence since 6 November.[22]

Kokje had deputed Sub-Inspector Ismail to arrest Printer. He with Kothare went to arrest Vithalbhai but the latter was not found at home. Kokje had sent Dinanath Krishnarao Pednekar, deputy inspector of police, CID, to arrest Babubhai in Noble Chambers. Babubhai was arrested with Printer at his office on 12 November.[23] (Ushaben and Chandrakant were in the hall outside the office room. She had been arranging papers on the desk where there was a typewriter. But when Pednekar came out of the office, both of them had left.) Printer said that he was apprehensive about the situation that day and had phoned Babubhai, who said that everything was all right and asked him to come over. When Printer went to Babubhai's office, he found Pednekar there. Pednekar had known that Kokje had wanted Printer, so he arrested him as well.[24] Vithalbhai was arrested on 13 November, and Motwane on 18 November.

Kokje questioned Printer, who offered to show to the police Parekh Wadi, the place where the transmitter had been installed; it was just as the evening programme was coming to an end. Kokje telephoned Deputy Commissioner Taylor. Printer took Taylor and Kokje (on 12 November) to the fifth floor of Parekh Wadi on Girgaum Back Road to the flat comprising the room numbers 103–106 on that floor.[25]

When they reached the building, they found that the door was closed from inside. At about 9.05 or 9.10 p.m., they forced the doors open. One led into the gallery and the other into room no. 106 where the apparatus had been installed. By then the Congress Radio had already started its broadcast and the programme was coming to an end. Kokje found Ushaben and Chandrakant playing the record of 'Vande Mataram'. The record was being played on a gramophone motor, which was connected to the amplifier, power pack, transmitter, etc. A holdall was spread out on the floor in front of the door. Ushaben was sitting near the gramophone and Chandrakant was standing near the holdall; the distance between them was about two paces. Kokje had made preparations for a formal panchnama. After they entered the room and the panchnama was started, the fuse blew out and kerosene lights had to be brought from outside. This took about twenty to thirty minutes and until then they used an electric torch. The panchnama was written at about 9.30 p.m. Kokje assumed that the playing of the song

'Vande Mataram' stopped because the fuse blew out. Kokje arrested Ushaben and Chandrakant, and locked and sealed the room. Everything else was left as it was, including the aerial connection.[26]

Kokje had not known Ushaben before he arrested her. He spoke with her ten to fifteen times during the course of his investigation, and even though he was not familiar with her, he recognized her voice later from a record. Inspector Kokje took Ushaben and Chandrakant to the CID office and left an armed guard at Parekh Wadi. The next day (13 November), he took Deputy Inspector Fergusson and two wireless experts, Mistry and Majumdar, to Parekh Wadi and made a detailed panchnama. The articles in the room were photographed. Among these were: a transmitting set in working order with the aerial, 120 gramophone records, a Philips wireless receiving set, a bedding, a hatbox and a suitcase. Kokje took all these articles to the CID office.[27] Manuel Morrison Fergusson, deputy inspector of police, examined the transmitter and discovered that it was a complete phone transmitter in working order. He tested it by speaking on the microphone, and the speech was heard on the receiver in the same room. They also played the record 'Hindustan Hamara' that was found, and it was heard on the receiver. Before dismantling the set, Kokje had a photograph of the room taken. The transmitter was then dismantled and removed to the police office. Manuel Morrison Fergusson said that the transmitter found in Parekh Wadi was capable of an output (a voltage) of 100 watts, though actually it had an output (a voltage) of about 30 watts. According to Morrison Fergusson, this transmitter must have been worth about Rs 3,000.[28]

All the 120 gramophone records (found by Kokje at Parekh Wadi) expressed patriotic feelings and nationalist thoughts. Out of them seven were commercial records and other were home-cut records, 17 of 10 inches and 96 of 12 inches. Kokje thought that two records were cut only on one side. However, he clarified that the records in Parekh Wadi were not counted on the night of 12 November; at that time some were in the hatbox, some in the suitcase and some lying about. In his opinion, records nos. 44 and 61 of 12 inches were in Ushaben's voice. He had prepared a comparative statement of the police monitoring report and the records found at Parekh Wadi, and after he played them, he found that 35 of them tallied with the monitoring reports.[29] Some of the records were played in the court and compared with the corresponding monitoring notes. The judge, in his judgment, cited Kokje's statement that out of 120 records, 35 tallied with the monitoring reports.[30]

The Day of Arrest as Remembered by Ushaben[31]

Ushaben remembered the day of the arrest as clearly as if it was yesterday. Recapturing that exciting time she said, 'On 12 November 1942, the day of our arrest, all those involved with the Congress Radio held a meeting to discuss what we would do in case we were arrested. A number of prominent radio dealers in the city had been picked up just a week before. Through them the authorities learnt that Babubhai and Vithalbhai were the main persons behind the Congress Radio. We decided that at no cost would the names of any colleague or any other secrets be revealed to the police.

'On 12 November at noon, the police raided Babubhai's office. Many of us workers, including Chandrakantbhai Jhaveri and I were there. When we learnt that the police was arriving, we quickly cleared the office of all the files.

I then entered Babubhai's office and innocently asked, "Bhai, what shall I tell Doctor (Dr Lohia) about Mother's (transmitter's) health?" He replied, "Tell him I cannot come today even though I know that Mother is serious. He may decide whether to change the prescription or continue with the same medicine."

'When the police asked Babubhai about me, he said, "She is my neighbour's daughter. Her mother is sick and since there's no male member in her family to look after her, I have to pitch in." The officers seemed to be satisfied with the explanation and allowed me to leave. I rushed to the recording session where Vithalbhai was busy recording the day's programme and the speeches of Dr Lohia and Harrisbhai. I apprised them of the latest events. We discussed the situation. Dr Lohia said, "The work must go on . . ." And I said, "Yes, the work must go on."

'In the meantime, news arrived that one of the technicians had been arrested. At first we thought we would not broadcast any programme that night. However, on second thought we decided to run one station and change the location of the other transmitter overnight. We felt that it was our duty as disciplined soldiers to face the impending danger. I left the recording station with a firm resolve that the programme would start on schedule. I went home and informed my mother and brothers about the possibility of the radio station being raided that night. My brothers, Janakbhai and Chandrakantbhai, were both active in the struggle.

'When I was leaving for the broadcasting station as usual, Chandrakantbhai Jhaveri accompanied me. He was fully aware of the risk, but came with me in spite of my repeated requests not to do so, saying, "How can I allow you to walk straight into the tiger's open jaws?" I was deeply touched by his act.

'I asked him to stand outside, near the entrance, and knock three times in case he sensed any danger. I then entered the broadcasting room, switched on the transmitter and relayed the whole programme. Ultimately when I was putting on the "Vande Mataram" record, I heard hard knocks on the door. I thought Chandrakantbhai was warning me, but instead of him, I saw a big battalion of policemen headed by the deputy commissioner of police entering the room with triumphant smiles on their faces. They were accompanied by some military technicians, and our own chief technician, Printer. When they entered, the "Vande Mataram" record was still on. So, they asked Printer as to who was operating the transmitter. On his pointing at me, the police chief said in a commanding tone, "Stop the record." I not only refused to obey the order but mustering all the courage at my command, firmly replied, "The record will not stop. This is our national song. So all of you stand at attention." And lo and behold! One and all of them, including the chief, did stand at attention.

'We wanted to announce the news of the spectacular raid, of being betrayed by our chief technician who led the police to this station and of our arrest at the post of duty. But this traitor of the technician came to the rescue of the police by tampering with the fuse. Of course, our colleagues, who were listening to the radio, did get a hint of what was happening when they heard the breaking open of the doors. When the fuse blew, the lights went out, making the police extremely edgy. They took quite some time to get hold of a hurricane lamp and then began the arrest formalities. A list of all the equipment found on the premises was prepared and the panchas were called in. The watchman of the building was summoned as one of the panchas. He protested to the police, "*Saab, hum toh garib log hain. Hum kya samjhe in baaton ko?*" (Sir, we are poor people. How do we understand these things?) The police tried to coerce him, but he refused to believe that there was a transmitter in the room.

'"How do I know what a transmitter is?" he said. The policeman shouted back, "You fool, don't you realize that it can blurt out some songs?" Amidst laughter the dear old man said, "How can a wooden piece sing?" It was only when I told him that there was no harm in his signing that he put his initials on the panchnama, albeit very reluctantly.

'The arrest formalities took nearly three and a half hours. When Chandrakantbhai and I finally stepped out of the room, we found that there were policemen waiting for us at each and every step all the way down. I said to Chandrakantbhai, "Bhai, we do not know whether we will ever get such a reception again, but today we are getting a Guard of Honour—and that too from the rifled policemen!" He was equally unperturbed and reacted saying, "Yes, this is certainly a memorable day for us."'

Charges Against the Accused

When the investigations were complete, the government directed that Special Judge N.S. Lokur should try the case against the five accused, and on 2 April 1943 accorded sanction under Section 196A of the Criminal Procedure Code for their prosecution for the offence of criminal conspiracy punishable under Section 120-B of the Indian Penal Code (IPC). A prima facie case having been made out, a charge was framed under Section 120-B of the IPC, Section 20 of the Telegraph Act (XIII of 1885) and Rules

16(5), 16(7), 39(6), and 121 of the Defence of India Rules.[32] The case was heard and decided in the Court of the Special Judge appointed under Section 4 of the Special Criminal Court Ordinance, 1942. On 22 April 1943, Special Judge N.S. Lokur charged Vithaldas alias Babubhai Madhavji Khakar, Vithaldas Kanthadbhai Jhaveri, Usha Mehta, Chandrakant Babubhai Jhaveri and Nanak G. Motwane, as follows:[33]

Firstly, between 14 August 1942 and 12 November 1942, at Bombay, they agreed and conspired among and between themselves and others to do or cause to be done illegal acts—possessing, establishing, maintaining and working illegally wireless telegraph and wireless telegraphy apparatus; and committing, without lawful authority or excuse, prejudicial acts and spreading prejudicial reports through the said wireless telegraph and apparatus, and thereby committed an offence punishable under Section 120-B of the IPC read with Section 20 of the Telegraph Act (XIII) of 1885 and Rule 16 of the Defence of India Rules read with Government Notification No. W16(22)/40-II, dated 10 September 1941 and with Rule 38 (1) (a) and (c) of the Defence of India Rules.

Secondly, in pursuance of the said conspiracy they, at Bombay, did illegally establish, maintain and work wireless telegraph in contravention of Section 4 of the Indian Telegraph Act and in contravention of Rule 16(3) read with Government Notification No. W16(22)/40-II, dated 10 September 1941, and aided and abetted each other in establishing, maintaining and working the said wireless telegraph in the manner aforesaid and thereby committed offences punishable under Section 20 of the Indian Telegraph Act (XIII of 1885) and Rule 16(7) read with Rule 16(3) and 121 of the Defence of India Rules.

Thirdly, in pursuance of the said conspiracy Usha Mehta and Chandrakant Babubhai Jhaveri at Bombay, on or about 12 November 1942, did possess a wireless apparatus—a transmitter and other transmitting parts—without a licence and in contravention of Rule 16(5) read with Government Notification No. W16 (22)/40-II, dated 10 September 1941; and Vithaldas (Babubhai) Madhavji Khakar alias Babubhai, Vithaldas Kanthadbhai Jhaveri and Nanak G. Motwane did aid and abet them and each other in possessing the same in pursuance of the said conspiracy and thereby committed offences punishable under Rule 16(7) read with Rule 16(5) and Rule 121 of the Defence of India Rules.

Fourthly, in pursuance of the said conspiracy, Usha Mehta and Chandrakant Babubhai Jhaveri, at Bombay, on or about 12 November 1941, had without lawful authority or excuse in their possession documents containing prejudicial reports—reports of broadcasting; and Vithaldas Madhavji Khakar alias Babubhai, Vithaldas Kanthadbhai Jhaveri and Nanak G. Motwane did aid and abet them and each other in possessing the same in pursuance of the said conspiracy and thereby committed an offence punishable under Rule 39(6) read with Rule 39(1) (b) and Rule 121 of the Defence of India Rules; and

Fifthly, in pursuance of the said conspiracy, they at Bombay, between 14 August 1942 and 12 November 1942, without lawful authority or excuse, committed prejudicial acts and spread prejudicial reports by means of wireless apparatus, intended or likely to (1) cause disaffection among and interfere with the discipline of, and the performance of their duties by, the members of His Majesty's forces and other public servants;

(2) induce members of His Majesty's forces and other public servants to fail in the performance of their duties as such; (3) prejudice the attendance of persons for service in His Majesty's forces and the police force; (4) bring into hatred or contempt and excite disaffection towards the government established by law in British India; (5) bring into hatred or contempt and excite disaffection towards His Majesty's forces; (6) impede, delay and restrict work necessary for the efficient prosecution of the war; (7) undermine public confidence in the national credit and in government currency notes which were legal tender in India; (8) encourage and excite the public generally to refuse and deter payment of land revenue and taxes payable to the government; (9) influence the conduct and attitude of the public or a section of the public in a manner likely to be prejudicial to the defence of British India, and; (10) otherwise prejudice the efficient prosecution of the war and defence of British India and the public safety and interest generally, and aided and abetted each other in the commission of the said prejudicial acts and in the spreading of the said prejudicial reports and thereby committed offences punishable under Rule 38(5) read with Rule 38(1)(a) and (c) and Rule 121 of the Defence of India Rules.

The Special Judge N.S. Lokur said that these offences were within his cognizance, and he directed that the accused be tried by him of the said charges.

The Case: Points for Determination and Findings of the Judge

According to the judge the points for determination before him and his findings were as follows:[34]

(1) Whether there was a criminal conspiracy to do or cause to be done the illegal acts mentioned in the first clause of the charge. It was found in the affirmative.

(2) Whether any and which of the accused had joined in that conspiracy, and

(3) Whether in pursuance of the said conspiracy, the accused illegally established, maintained or worked a wireless telegraph and aided or abetted each other in doing so. The findings were in the affirmative against Vithaldas (Babubhai) Madhavji Khakar, Usha Mehta and Chandrakant Babubhai Jhaveri and in the negative against Vithaldas Kanthadbhai Jhaveri and Nanak G. Motwane.

(4) Whether in pursuance of the said conspiracy Usha Mehta and Chandrakant Babubhai Jhaveri were in illegal possession of a wireless transmitter and other transmitting parts without a licence. It was found in the affirmative.

(5) Whether Vithaldas (Babubhai) Madhavji Khakar, Vithaldas Kanthadbhai Jhaveri and Nanak G. Motwane aided and abetted them in doing so. The findings were in the affirmative against accused Vithaldas (Babubhai) Madhavji Khakar and in the negative against Vithaldas Kanthadbhai Jhaveri and Nanak G. Motwane.

(6) Whether in pursuance of the said conspiracy Usha Mehta and Chandrakant Babubhai Jhaveri were without lawful authority or excuse in possession of home-cut gramophone records containing prejudicial reports, and

(8) Whether Vithaldas (Babubhai) Madhavji Khakar, Vithaldas Kanthadbhai Jhaveri and Nanak G. Motwane sided and abetted Usha Mehta and Chandrakant Babubhai Jhaveri in doing so. Interestingly these issues were found to be irrelevant as gramophone records were not considered documents in the judgment.

(7) Whether those records were documents. The judge's deliberation led him to decide this in the negative.

(9) Whether in pursuance of the said conspiracy the accused with the aid and abetment of each other without lawful authority or excuse committed prejudicial acts and spread prejudicial reports, by means of a wireless apparatus, such as were intended or were likely to cause the mischief described in the fifth clause of the charge. The findings were in the affirmative against Vithaldas (Babubhai) Madhavji Khakar and Usha Mehta, and in the negative against Vithaldas Kanthadbhai Jhaveri, Chandrakant Babubhai Jhaveri and Nanak G. Motwane.

* * *

In his opening sentence of the judgment, the judge said: 'This case has brought to light the daring with which a broadcasting station was illegally established and worked in different populated localities in Bombay and the cunning which, for nearly three months, baffled the attempts of the police to trace it.'[35]

The judge observed that after the arrest of the Congress leaders on 9 August 1942, a conspiracy came into existence to establish a wireless transmitting apparatus for broadcasting programmes such as those contained in the records found in Parekh Wadi. These programmes were broadcast from the transmitter found at Parekh Wadi on 12 November. To establish an unauthorized transmitter without a licence was an offence and it was also an offence to broadcast prejudicial reports. And a conspiracy to do so was a criminal conspiracy. The judge observed that the actual programme to be broadcast would naturally be prepared from time to time and could not have been present before in the minds of the conspirators from the beginning, but the very idea must have been conceived for the purpose of broadcasting such prejudicial matter.[36]

Needless to say, the case had generated a lot of interest and excitement. The government was determined to be tough with 'the offenders', while the people were filled with respect and admiration for the young team of the Congress Radio. Some eminent lawyers appeared for both sides: Sohrab D. Vimadalal with C.B. Velkar instructed by the public prosecutor, N.K. Petigara, appeared for the Crown. P.L. Thakkar with Wamon Thakore appeared for the first accused; K.M. Munshi with Nanubhai Desai instructed by A.C. Krishnamurti and Messrs Matubhai, Jamiatram and Madon appeared for the second accused; S.R. Tendolkar with M.M. Jape for the third accused; Tendolkar with H.P. Thakore for the fourth accused; and M.C. Setalvad with A.B. Thakur for the fifth accused.[37]

The judge was certain that 'in pursuance of the said conspiracy', a transmitting apparatus was set up and was broadcasting such programmes regularly every day, from 27 August till 12 November 1942, except on 15, 16 and 17 October, when, according to Printer, the set was being strengthened. Police reporters monitored the broadcasts from 9 October to 2 November 1942, and they produced the original shorthand notes, the transcripts in longhand

and the reports they made to their superiors from day to day. (Very often the programmes could not be heard distinctly.) According to the judge, there was sufficient proof that these programmes were broadcast from the transmitter found in Parekh Wadi.[38] However the defence lawyers, who had marshalled their legal acumen to defend the young members of the Congress Radio, doubted this, putting forth logical and impressive arguments.

Tendolkar raised a doubt as to whether the programmes that were being monitored by the police reporters were actually being broadcast from the transmitter at Parekh Wadi. According to Inspector Kokje, when the door of room no. 106 was broken open, the time was 9.05 or 9.10 p.m. and the song 'Vande Mataram' was being played. The transmitter was working at that time, and when the fuse burnt out, the electric current was cut off just after the police and the panchas entered the room. The panch, Dube, said that before entering the room he heard what seemed to him as the tune of some stringed instrument. The prosecution suggested that that must have been the sound emitted by the transmitter. On the other hand, Deputy Inspector Fergusson who had been listening to the broadcast that night from the beginning, said that he heard the broadcast on the same wavelength as on the previous night, and that it went off the air after the opening song 'Hindustan Hamara' had finished and the usual announcement was made in Hindi. This indicated that the radio station went off the air at about 8.50 p.m. or so. Taking this point, the defence argued that the transmitter at Parekh Wadi, which according to Inspector Kokje went on till the end of the programme and was playing 'Vande Mataram', could not have been the same transmitter broadcasting the programme heard by Deputy Inspector

Fergusson. The counsel for the prosecution, however, explained this contradiction by suggesting that Fergusson might have made a mistake. But, according to the judge, even when cross-examined, Deputy Inspector Fergusson repeated that on the night of the 12 November the first song was played, and while the Hindi announcements were being made the radio went off the air, and it was difficult to believe that he could have made a mistake.[39]

The judge maintained that unfortunately when the detailed panchnama of room no. 106 was made on the night of 12 November, the description of the record on the gramophone motor connected to the transmitter was not mentioned. If it had been done, there would have been no doubt as to which record was being played when the police entered the room. Kokje had said that though the room was left untouched on the night of 12 November, it was kept under observation until he went there the next day for a panchnama. On the next day, before entering the room, a photograph was taken showing the placement of things lying around. If this was so (according to Kokje the fuse had gone off while the record was being played), the pick-up needle should have been found resting on the record on the next day, at the time of the panchnama. Instead, the photograph clearly showed that the pick-up needle was not on the record; it had been raised by some person. There was nothing to show that the record was of the song 'Vande Mataram'.[40]

Moreover, what was difficult to believe was that if the broadcast was going on when the police reached the room, would Dube have only heard the humming sound of a stringed instrument and Inspector Kokje the playing of 'Vande Mataram'? A Philips radio receiving set was also in the room, which was used to receive the broadcast from the station, and it was not unlikely that it had been tuned in to so that those who were working the transmitter could check if the broadcasting was going on satisfactorily or not. In that case, both Dube and Kokje should have heard the broadcast clearly. Therefore, the judge surmised that the fuse must have gone off before Kokje broke open the door of the room, which was why Dube did not hear anything being broadcast at that time. This, according to the judge, fitted in with the testimony of Deputy Inspector Fergusson which stated that the station went off the air at about 8.50 p.m. when the Hindi announcement was being made. When the electric supply went off, the pick-up needle must have been raised from the record, and the inmates of the room must have been expecting someone, whom they may have sent out to fetch lights or another fuse. It was during that interval that Kokje raided the room. When the lights were brought in, he saw that there was a gramophone record on the disc of the motor and, as the time was 9.05 p.m., he may have imagined that the record must have been that of 'Vande Mataram'. The judge preferred to believe Fergusson's evidence since he had actually heard the broadcast at that time. This, however, did not mean that the station Fergusson was listening to was different from the station located in Parekh Wadi.[41]

Another argument the defence lawyers put forward to prove that the transmitting set at Parekh Wadi was not the one broadcasting the programmes the police heard was related to the frequency of the crystal, which was being used for the transmitter set. The basis of this argument was that it was fitted with a crystal having a frequency of 7075 kc (kilocycles). The function of a crystal was to fix the frequency of a transmitter to a pin point and the frequency of 7075 kc corresponded to 42.40 metres (the formula being 3,00,000 divided by the frequency in kc. gives the wavelength in metres). But the monitoring reports showed that the reporters always heard the broadcast on a wavelength of 42.12 or 42.34 and never on 42.40. Thus, there was no satisfactory evidence to show that the frequency of the crystal fitted on the transmitter in Parekh Wadi was 7075 kc. The inscription plate usually fixed on the crystal giving the specification had been removed and the frequency 7075 kc. was written on the inner plate in ink. It was not known who wrote it and when. When Inspector Kokje had the frequency of the crystal on this transmitter tested by Tanna, it was found to be 7094 kc to 7096 kc.[42]

This showed that the frequency written in ink on the crystal as 7075 kc was not correct. The metre wavelength that corresponded to frequency 7094 would be 42.28 metres. In Deputy Inspector Fergusson's opinion there generally was a margin of error up to 7 kc, and even allowing for that margin, 7087 kc corresponded to the wavelength 42.33 metres which is close to the wavelength on which the broadcast was actually heard by the police reporters. The judge therefore opined that, from the frequency written on the crystal, it could not be said that the transmitter in Parekh Wadi was not broadcasting the programmes which were heard by the police reporters.[43] Thus, this argument put forward by the defence lawyers was set aside.

Further, Printer's testimony and other facts had provided sufficient evidence to show that the transmitter had been working from Sea View, Ratan Mahal, Laxmi Bhuvan and Parekh Wadi. Deputy Inspector Fergusson said in his deposition that he used to hear the broadcast coming with the same strength at the same place for two

or three days, and then it would become weaker, and
that towards the end, that is, before 11 November, it
came with the same strength for five days. Based on this
it was argued that the transmitter that was broadcasting
the monitored programmes was being shifted from one
place to another within two or three days and before
the police raid it was working in the same place for five
days. This contradicted Printer's version regarding the
shifting of the transmitter from place to place—that the
transmitter was never shifted within two or three days
from any place. But the judge did not attach much weight
to Fergusson's evidence on this point. Fergusson had been
trying to locate the broadcasting station, moving through
the city in his motor car with a receiving set in it, and it
was only his surmise that the strength of the broadcasting
used to become weaker after every two or three days.
No inference could be drawn from the strength of the
broadcast, neither could he track down the exact location
of the broadcasting station. If the station were really
different from the one in Parekh Wadi, it would not have
gone off the air as soon as the police attached the set in
Parekh Wadi. According to Fergusson, he had again heard
the Congress Radio in the end of February 1943 (after
the members of the team were arrested), and it was then
announced that the radio had been off the air for three
months. But, according to the judge, that must certainly
have been a different transmitter and it was not working
before the end of February 1943. This clearly showed that
the monitored broadcast came from the radio station that
the police seized on 12 November 1942.[44]

In addition, the very presence of the records at the
building was convincing proof that the Congress Radio
station had been located there at that time. But the defence

lawyer argued that all the records that were attached at the panchnama on 13 November 1942 might not have been there when the police raided the room. All the 120 records were described in detail in the panchnama, though it did not state where the different records were lying. It appeared as if the hatbox was there for the purpose of keeping the records in it—in fact, Kokje maintained that there were some records in the hatbox and some in the suitcase. However, Tendolkar argued that the contents of the hatbox were given in detail in the panchnama, but there was no reference to the records having been found there. The photograph also clearly showed that some records were lying on the floor, one record was on the gramophone motor and some were lying near the hatbox. Yet, the panchnama did not state that there was any record on the gramophone motor. The total number of the records found was mentioned and the description of each was given in detail. Though the panch, Dube, claimed there were fifteen to twenty records, he must have seen only those records when he entered the room. The panchnama was done the next day and the independent panchas were experts in radio engineering. The judge maintained that it was inconceivable that some records could have been brought there from outside and incorporated in the panchnama. He agreed with Inspector Kokje that there were some records in the hatbox and some in the suitcase. It was unlikely that when the transmitter was in use, all the records would be taken out and thrown about on the ground. The judge had no hesitation in holding that all the 120 records were found in that room and at least those 35 of them were played into the microphone and broadcasted and the corresponding monitoring notes were substantially correct.[45]

A few gramophone records with speeches and information contained some matter critical of the British rule. The question that arose was whether the gramophone records could be considered as 'documents'. One of the arguments put by the defence was that the gramophone records were not documents. This brought up another interesting issue which revolved around what the definition of a 'document' really was. Rule 39(1) (b) prohibited the possession of 'any document containing any prejudicial report' without lawful authority or excuse. Interestingly in Section 3 Clause 16 of the General Clauses Act, 1897, a document was defined as including 'any matter written, expressed or described upon any substance by means of letters, photographs or marks or by more than one of those means which is intended to be used or which may be used for the purpose of recording that matter'. According to the judge, 'The marks cut on a gramophone record do not convey any sense unless it is played on a machine. It is not to be read or seen, but heard. In fact, it is a record of sounds with a view to their subsequent reproduction.'[46]

According to Section 3 Clause 58 of the General Clauses Act, 1897 'expressions referring to "writing" are to be construed as including references to printing, lithography, photography and other modes of representing or reproducing words in a visible form.' The argument from the prosecution was that this definition showed that it is only a 'writing' which has to be in a visible form, while in Clause 16, a document is defined as including matter not only 'written' but also matter 'expressed or described' and therefore it is not necessary that a document should contain visible matter. Even if the matter can be made audible and understood thereby, the substance containing such matter would be included in the definition of a document. According to the judge, there was some force in this contention, but the Defence of India Rules themselves appeared to have taken a different view and added an explanation to Rule 40 to the following effect: 'In this rule, "document" includes gramophone records, soundtracks and any other articles on which sounds have been recorded with a view to their subsequent reproduction.' If a document, as defined in the General Clauses Act, 1897, included a gramophone record, it was not necessary to add this explanation to Rule 40. There was no such explanation added to Rule 39, with which the court was concerned.[47]

Vimadalal, the lawyer for the prosecution, put forward one more argument, which pointed out that in Section 131 of the Indian Penal Code, an explanation was added that the words 'officer', 'soldier' and 'airman' used in that section included any person subject to the army, navy, etc., and that though no such explanation appeared in the subsequent Sections 132 to 138, the words 'officer', 'soldier' and 'airman' in those sections would include any person subject to the army, navy, etc., and that in a similar manner the explanation to Rule 40 of the Defence of India Rules would apply to other rules in interpreting the word 'document'. It was not necessary to consider whether the explanation to Section 132 of the Indian Penal Code applied to the subsequent sections. But, assuming that it did, yet the meaning of the words 'officer', 'sailor', 'airman' was given in the earlier section, and the same words might be taken to have been used in the same sense in the subsequent sections. However, according to the judge, the interpretation of the word 'document' given in Rule 40 could not be taken as applying to that word used in the preceding rules. Otherwise, the explanation would have been added to

Rule 39 instead of to Rule 40. The judge, therefore, held that the word 'document' used in Rule 39(1) (b) was not intended to include a gramophone record. Hence, the possession of the gramophone records would not be in contravention of that rule.[48] So the gramophone records were not considered 'documents'.

Conclusion

Though most of the primary facts can be tied together while tracing the account of the Congress Radio, some fragments are still missing. Much of what had been done by so many leaders and patriots—both underground and publicly—had been noticed, yet still some fragments remain untraceable. One such segment is the details about the financial resources. Years after the case of the Congress Radio, Ram Manohar Lohia in his statement to the CID stated that the money for the radio project was provided by a committee comprising Purshottam Trikamdas, Shantilal Shah, Uma Shankar Dixit and Giridharilal Kriplani. Khakar and Achyut Patwardhan also collected funds. In addition, donations came mainly from cotton merchants, grain dealers, share market men, business houses and trade associations in Bombay.[49]

It is interesting to note that the Congress Radio welcomed people's contributions. In one of its broadcasts it was announced: 'We are poor, very poor and, if you are rich and like our work, go to the accredited Congress chief of your town and give him as much as you can earmark for Congress Radio Calling.'[50]

The Congress Radio operation involved the participation of highly committed young freedom lovers as well as the contribution of technical experts. It had originated and thrived when the movement in Bombay was at its height and when the involvement of the students was intense. Undeterred by the possible consequences if arrested, Ushaben and her colleagues worked tirelessly to contribute their time and energy to the colossal task of achieving freedom. Along with the games of hide-and-seek, collating news and speeches and the drama of planning and organizing, their guiding spirit was the intense love for the nation, unquestionable and all-pervasive.

4

The Accused and the Trial

The dramatic arrest of Ushaben and Chandrakant paved the way for the arrest of other members of the group of the Congress Radio and a flow of information to the police. N.K. Lokur, the special judge appointed for the case, worked with efficiency and precision. Testimonies of more than fifty persons were collected. The case generated a lot of excitement and interest among the people, but due to severe restraints on the press, its details could not be published. However, word of mouth proved to be as effective and reliable.*

The trial of the five accused in the Congress Radio case remains an important chapter in the history of India's freedom struggle. The judge and the lawyers meticulously tried to sift the facts from the evidence collected and the accused witnessed the drama in the court with equanimity. All the five accused, coming from diverse backgrounds,

---

* It has been a pleasure to hear octogenarians in the city talking excitedly about the case.

were inhabitants of Bombay. Years later, when I asked Ushaben, 'Don't you think you all were wrongly accused and sentenced?', she answered in her nonchalant way, 'The judge was doing his duty. The government was sure that we had committed a crime. We knew that we had not. However, we were ready to face the consequences.'[1] The police had collected the information about each of the accused in minute detail, and the lawyers, both of the prosecution and the defence, were all set to argue the case.

The Accused

(1) Vithaldas alias Babubhai Madhavji Khakar (27–28 years old)

There were strong arguments proving Babubhai's involvement in the case. The testimony of Printer, Mirza and others as well as additional corroborations proved that he was at the helm of the whole scheme. He managed the required resources and equipment and coordinated with various supporters of the project. However, Babubhai pleaded not guilty and refused point blank to accept any of the charges levelled against him. He said that he did not ask Printer to build a transmitter, neither did he discuss with Printer any project regarding the setting up of a transmitter. He had never bought any transmitting parts and given them to Printer. It was Printer who bought the amplifier, etc. from Chicago Radio Company; he had just given him a lift to Chicago Radio Company. He had not shown Printer any place for the purpose of broadcasting and had not supplied programmes for the Congress Radio broadcast. He did not ask Killewala to help Printer in buying anything. He could not say why Printer and Mirza gave evidence against him. He did not buy the radio receiving set. He went to Ratan Mahal only when Kokje took him there. He did not know whether there was any transmitter at Ajit Villa or Laxmi Bhuvan and he never went to Parekh Wadi. He had gone to Sea View when Printer invited him, Mirza and Ushaben for an ice cream party. He denied knowing Vithalbhai before he met him in jail, and the labels on the records were not in his writing. Neither did he know Dahyabhai Patel or Bipin Inamdar and he had never seen Dr Ram Manohar Lohia.[2]

The judge did not accept these arguments. It had been proved that he had gone to Sea View to rent it for the running of the transmitter. In an identification parade, held by the police, in which Babubhai and Printer also appeared, Daraskhan, the watchman at Sea View, picked them out correctly and identified them as the persons who had hired the flat. According to the judge, the panchnama clearly showed that Babubhai and Printer were among a group of fourteen other persons from different communities, and that they had been correctly identified. If a dishonest panchnama had been made, then Ahmed Umarkhan might also have been asked to identify them. The judge found no reason to doubt Daraskhan's honesty. Since Daraskhan used to see Babubhai, Ushaben and Printer, he would have remembered their features. Babubhai's story was that he had gone to Sea View when Printer had invited him, Ushaben and Mirza for an ice cream party, towards the end of September. According to the judge, this story appeared to have been put forward to explain why Daraskhan had identified him.[3]

It had also been proved that the handwriting of the captions on some records was Babubhai's. Each home-cut record had a label in the centre displaying a written caption

IN THE COURT OF THE SPECIAL JUDGE APPOINTED
UNDER SEC. 4 OF THE SPECIAL CRIMINAL COURTS
ORDINANCE, 1942.
Case No. 7 of 1943.

Emperor

Vs.

1. Vithaldas _alias_ Babubhai Madhavji Khakar.
2. Vithaldas Kanthadbhai Jhaveri.
3. Miss Usha Mehta.
4. Chandrakant Babubhai Jhaveri.
5. Nanak G. Motwane.

Coram: LOKUR, J.

Friday, 14th May 1943.

Judgment:-

    This case has brought to light the daring with which
a broadcasting station was illegally established and worked
in different populated localities in Bombay and the cunning
which, for nearly three months, baffled the attempts of
the Police to trace it.

    The main story of the case for the prosecution is to
be gathered from the evidence of Printer, his assistant
Mirza, Jagannath and the investigating officer, Inspector
Kokje. Printer is an expert in radio engineering and was the
principal of the Bombay Technical Institute, Byculla, where
students were given training in radio and electrical --
engineering. In 1937 he went to England with five of his
students, including Mirza. On his return from England in
1938 he secured a licence for amateur transmitting and
purchased a transmitter for the purpose of giving lessons
to his students. On the outbreak of the war in 1939
Printer's amateur transmitting licence was cancelled, and
he was bound to surrender his transmitting apparatus to the
authorities concerned. But instead of doing so, he dismantled the apparatus and secretly and unauthorisedly
retained the parts with himself. He then invented a

The judgment, 14 May 1943

mentioning the subject of the record. Since the police suspected that Babubhai and Vithalbhai wrote these labels, they decided to have the handwriting verified. This led to a diligent scrutiny of both their handwritings. The specimens of their handwritings were sent with twenty-five records to the deputy inspector general of police, CID, Poona (now Pune).[4]

In February 1943, the records were sent for checking to Thakurdas Jekisondas Gajjar, who was the handwriting expert attached to the CID, Poona, along with the specimens of the handwritings of Babubhai and Vithalbhai. The expert identified the handwriting on two sides of one record, and one side of one record as Babubhai's handwriting.[5] As Babubhai was not proficient in English, his spelling was weak—he had spelt 'cultivators' as 'cultivaters' and 'appeal' as 'apeal', both in the labels and in the specimen handwriting. Babubhai stated in his written statement that when the specimen handwriting was taken in the presence of the panchas, it had been dictated to him by Inspector Kokje, and as he did not know the correct spelling of 'appeal' and 'cultivators', he asked him how they were spelt and wrote out those words according to Kokje's instructions. But Inspector Kokje said that both Babubhai and Vithalbhai wrote to his dictation at the same time and Vithalbhai committed no such spelling mistakes.[6] According to Kokje he took specimen handwritings of Babubhai and Vithalbhai in the presence of the panchas. And when the specimen writing of Babubhai was taken, Sub-Inspector Desai dictated what was to be written and no spelling was told to Babubhai.[7]

According to the judge, it was unlikely that Inspector Kokje would purposely give incorrect spellings to Babubhai. He was more concerned with the handwriting than with the correctness of the spelling, and it was unlikely that Babubhai would have asked for the spelling of these words while the passage was being dictated to him. The letters 'c', 'a', 'd' and 'f' were found to have the same peculiarities in both the specimen handwriting and the writing on the labels; especially the way in which Babubhai wrote the letter 'f'. Gajjar also took into consideration relative heights of letters, slants, sizing, spacing and curves, and general characteristics. The defence counsel, however, pointed out that the initial 'S' in 'Starvation' written on the label was not similar to the initial 'S' appearing in several words in the specimen handwriting.[8]

The judge conceded that there was some force in this contention, but there was a similar 's' in the word 'troops' appearing in the specimen handwriting; and although that 's' was not the initial letter of the word, yet it was separated and appeared to be written in the same way as the initial 'S' in 'Starvation' on the label. The judge carefully compared the two writings and was satisfied that Gajjar's conclusion was correct and ought to be accepted. If Babubhai was not involved in the conspiracy, he had no reason to write the captions on the records which were actually broadcast. Babubhai's handwriting was found on the record relating to the air raid on Chittagong, stating that it was played on 27 October 1942, though the monitoring report showed that it was actually played on 30 October. It may have been meant to be played on 27 October, but for some reason was actually played later. The record relating to the appeal to cultivators was played on 1 November 1942 and the monitoring report also showed the same date.[9]

Thacker, the defence lawyer, argued that it was not proper for Inspector Kokje to compel Babubhai and Vithalbhai to write down his dictation in order to obtain specimens of their handwritings. The judge, in this context, referred to the statement of Wadia J., in *Emperor v. Ramrao Burde* (1932) 34 B.L.E. 589; and pointed out that in this case Babubhai had admitted that the specimen handwriting sent to Gajjar was his and that he had no complaint to make against the police.[10]

The judge stated that it was true that no typed programmes, said to have been supplied by Babubhai before the recorded programmes were broadcast, had been found with him. They might have been destroyed or concealed somewhere. There was, however, no corroboration of Printer's statement that Babubhai had supplied the typed programmes, though Printer's allegation that Babubhai had supplied the records from time to time could safely be believed from the fact that the captions of at least some of the records seemed to have been written by him.[11]

Another piece of evidence presented by the police was that a tablecloth with Babubhai's initials 'B.M.K.' was found at Paradise Bungalow. According to the judge, it was possible that others might have the same initials, but it was a strange coincidence that a tablecloth bearing the same initials should be found in the room which was intended to be used for the transmitter. Babubhai said that he could not say whether it belonged to him or not; he did not even remember if he had a tablecloth of that type. The judge found it 'a very evasive reply' and said that if Babubhai really had nothing to do with the tablecloth, he could have immediately said that it was not his. It was true that no other clothes belonging to Babubhai bearing such initials had been produced by the prosecution, 'but this very coincidence is a circumstance which may be taken into consideration as a piece of evidence against Accused No. 1 (Babubhai).' Taking all these circumstances into

consideration, the judge found that Babubhai had joined
the conspiracy to establish, maintain and work a wireless
transmitting apparatus for the purpose of broadcasting
prejudicial reports. Babubhai was proved to have been an
active member of the conspiracy from the very beginning
and it did not appear that he ever ceased to have anything
to do with it. There was no doubt that he carried out
certain acts preparatory to a contravention of the Defence
of India Rules.[12]

(2) Vithalbhai Kanthadbhai Jhaveri (27 years old)

Vithalbhai too pleaded not guilty. He had been actively
involved with the activities of the Congress and was
convicted in the earlier Civil Disobedience Movement in
Bombay. Printer had alleged that Babubhai had introduced
him to Vithalbhai, but the judge felt there was no evidence
to corroborate that accusation.[13]

Vithalbhai stated that he did not have a record-cutting
machine; he had never met Jagannath in any room or house
at Banganga. He did not take Jagannath in his car from
Banganga and drop him at Grant Road Station. He did
not want to study parts of a transmitter and Jagannath did
not explain it. Jagannath did not explain (the working of)
a record-cutting machine in Vithalbhai's house at the
latter's instance; he had only repaired a radiogram in his
house. Vithalbhai further denied ever cutting a record in
Jagannath's presence or writing captions on the records.
However, he acknowledged, he had accompanied
Jagannath to Famous Cine Laboratory to see the picture
of the AICC session and no record was cut there. He had
gone to Chicago Radio Company to purchase radios,
radiograms and loud-speaking telephones but not for any

transmitting parts. Babubhai did not introduce Printer to him; he had met Printer only in the CID office and he did not know Ushaben. Further, he did not know Jayachand personally and had never been to Khandke Building.[14]

Nevertheless, Printer still maintained that after the record about the atrocities by the British troops on the villagers in Chimur cut by Vithalbhai was ready, Vithalbhai wrote the caption on its label in Printer's presence. (It was a record in Ushaben's voice and narrated the horrendous incidents of atrocities committed by the British troops on the villagers and the rape of women in the village of Chimur in the Central Provinces.)[15] But Printer's story that Vithalbhai had cut this record was uncorroborated. While it was proved that Babubhai wrote some captions on the labels of the records, it could not be proved that the writing on the labels of some records was that of Vithalbhai. The judge maintained that the record could have been cut by anybody; there was sufficient corroboration to show that Printer must have been present when the record was cut and that Ushaben must have read out the typed manuscript for the record. Moreover, Gajjar had honestly stated that he could not identify Vithalbhai's handwriting on any of the records because the specimen writing of Vithalbhai was dissembled and could not, therefore, be used for comparison. It was also suggested that Vithalbhai was concerned with the cutting of another record with the song 'Hindustan Hamara' sung by Master Krishna at the AICC session on 7 and 8 August 1942 on one side and two speeches at that session on the other side. The judge had no hesitation in holding that it had been cut from the film taken by the Famous Cine Laboratory, but Vithalbhai's connection with the cutting of that record could not be proved. Moreover, there was no evidence that Vithalbhai was building a transmitting set in the bungalow at Banganga. If, at all, any such set was being built in pursuance of the conspiracy, Printer would not have remained aloof. Printer was in the dark regarding the construction of such set. If any such set was being built in the bungalow at Banganga, it was not in pursuance of this conspiracy. Further, it was not alleged that Vithalbhai participated in the hiring of the flats for the location of the Congress Radio Station, nor was he present in any of the flats at any time.[16] Ushaben remembered this with a twinkle in her eyes while telling me how Vithalbhai had managed to get away with his handwriting from the expert's eyes.[17]

(3) Usha Hariprasad Mehta (22 years old)

Ushaben was an active member of the group, efficiently managing important as well as odd jobs like compiling news, writing messages and instructions to the people from freedom fighters, and typing the programmes spoken into the microphone. The judgment recorded that Usha Mehta was found to have joined the conspiracy from the beginning and to have continued taking active part in it.[18] Ushaben and Chandrakant had been caught red-handed with the illegal wireless transmitter and other transmitting parts. Ushaben had offered no explanation as to why she was there in the room with the wireless transmitter.

When asked, 'What do you want to say regarding the evidence adduced against you?', her answer was, 'Nothing.' When asked, 'Where were you arrested?', she answered, 'I do not want to answer any question or offer any explanation of the evidence adduced against me.' Again, when asked, 'The evidence for the prosecution is closed. Do you want to make any statement now?', her answer was 'No.' She did not want to make any statement in her defence. To the question 'So you do not want to make any statement in your own defence?', her answer was 'No.' When asked if she had ever gone to Sea View, she said, 'I do not want to answer any question at this stage.'[19] According to the judge, there was ample evidence to prove that she had joined the conspiracy almost from the beginning. She had accompanied Printer and Babubhai to hire the flat in Sea View. She had been identified by the watchman of that building, Daraskhan, as he had seen her going to the flat several times.[20] Her courage and determination must have touched a chord even in the most diehard of loyalists to the British rule. She pleaded Not Guilty. Years later she would often explain how working for our nation's freedom could never be a crime, hence she never felt guilty for participating in the project of the Congress Radio.

Printer had pointed out that Vithalbhai had cut a record (in Ushaben's voice about the atrocities in Chimur) in the building near French Bridge, and Ushaben had read the typed speech (in Hindi) before the microphone. He recollected and identified this record because he remembered the words, 'I was pregnant' ('*Mai garbhavati thee*'), which sounded strange coming from the mouth of Ushaben.[21] The judge believed that Printer must have been present when the record was cut and that Ushaben must have read out the typed script for the record.[22]

Years later she would tell us how the news of the rape of helpless women had disturbed her immensely.[23] Many of us had also seen and heard her delivering charged speeches in the meetings held on the issues of rape and violence against women.

Printer said that Ushaben mostly read out the typed scripts for the records, but the monitoring notes showed that out of 35 records (35 out of the 120 records found at Parekh Wadi tallied with the monitoring reports), only 8 were in a female voice. At least two of these records were recognized as being in Ushaben's voice. Mirza also said that he had heard several female voices, and swore that he recognized Ushaben's voice when he heard the broadcast. He, however, did not mention that he had ever recognized Printer's voice, even though Printer had admitted that he spoke into the microphone sometimes. It may have been that Mirza had not listened to the broadcasting at that time and may not have noticed it. The judge was cautious, having noted that both Mirza and Printer were accomplices, and by itself, their evidence of recognizing Ushaben's voice could not be accepted without corroboration. Inspector Kokje heard the records and recognized Ushaben's voice. When asked whether he was familiar with her voice, he felt that the word 'familiar' was too strong; at the same time he asserted that he knew her voice and could recognize it. Taking all this into account, the judge was satisfied that on some occasions Ushaben read out the scripts for the records and broadcast.[24]

The judge observed that Ushaben deserved all the credit for refusing to state a 'falsehood to save herself'. He was, however, quick to admit that no adverse inference needed necessarily be drawn from her reticence, and in this context he referred to the case of *Emperor v. Basangouda* (1940), 43 Bom.L.R.144 and Rule 16(2) of the Defence of India Rules and the Sub-rule 8. Instead, the burden of the proof lay with the prosecution and was not shifted to the accused by her refusal to offer any explanation of the circumstances appearing against her. However, the circumstances in which Ushaben and Chandrakant were found in the room with the transmitter justified a presumption being raised against both of them that they were in possession of the wireless telegraph apparatus.[25]

Another argument the defence put forth was that no key to the room was found in their possession. But as Chandrakant himself had stated, a third person was also present who may have left the room when the lights went out, to get another light or another fuse. The absence of a key in the possession of either Ushaben or Chandrakant could not lead to any conclusion; therefore, both of them were to be held with having possession of a transmitter in violation of Rule 16(5).[26]

Printer had also said that Ushaben used to type the programmes on the typewriter in the Noble Chambers. (He said that he had gone there while she was actually typing something and had taken a peep.) This story, however, could not be proved as there was no evidence/corroboration supporting it. 'But,' according to the judge, 'there is sufficient corroboration to hold that she used to speak into the microphone of the transmitter frequently, before the recorded programmes began to be broadcast.'[27]

The judge noted that there was no evidence showing that the presence of Ushaben and Chandrakant in Noble Chambers on 12 November—when Pednekar came to arrest Babubhai—had 'anything to do with the conspiracy or broadcasting'. (At that time Ushaben was sitting near a typewriter with some papers spread out on the table, but by the time Pednekar came out of the room after arresting Babubhai, both Ushaben and Chandrakant had disappeared.) The judge also remarked that there was no corroboration to Printer's statement that Ushaben had accompanied him to Ratan Mahal when they had gone there to hire the premises. The landlady, Kasturbai, had clearly said that all those who had come there were men.[28]

Ushaben and Chandrakant were not tried for possessing home-cut gramophone records containing prejudicial reports, as the records were not considered as 'documents'.

(4) Chandrakant Babubhai Jhaveri (23 years old)

Chandrakant also pleaded not guilty. According to Printer, Chandrakant used to be present at Babubhai's office. Chandrakant, however, said that he had accompanied Ushaben to Parekh Wadi only to keep her company, and five minutes after he entered, the police arrived. He admitted that he had closed the door as Ushaben had instructed and that there was another person already there, and that when he left, he closed the door. He did not recognize that person. It was the first time he was present at Noble Chambers and later at Parekh Wadi on 12 November 1942. When the police entered the room at Parekh Wadi, the lights went out within a couple of minutes; it was dark for more than half an hour. There was no broadcasting going on while he was there. When asked whether there was a transmitter at Parekh Wadi, he answered, 'Some gramophone records and other apparatus were lying in the other room.' No record or musical instrument was played while he was there. When asked, 'What were you doing there?' he answered, 'I was doing nothing but sitting there.' When he was asked, 'Were you in Noble Chambers when Babubhai was arrested?', he answered, 'I had gone there to his office in the afternoon to meet Ushaben. We are friends and I had gone to meet her there casually. I waited there for five minutes and then went away; I do not know when Babubhai was arrested.'[29]

There was hardly any argument in defence of Ushaben and Chandrakant, as they were caught red-handed with

the wireless transmitter on 12 November. Possession of a
wireless transmitter and other transmitting parts without
a licence was illegal as per the prevailing law. The judge
noted that it was highly improbable that if Chandrakant
were not part of the conspiracy, why would he go there
with Ushaben and remain with her after the fuse had burnt
and the electrical supply was cut off. However, there was
no evidence about his participation in the conspiracy before
he was found at the transmitting station on 12 November
1942. So he could not be held guilty of the offences which
were committed in pursuance of the conspiracy before he
joined. It was apparent that he had joined the conspiracy
at a later stage, but before he could take a more active part,
the activity had been exposed and the transmitter seized.[30]

(5) Nanak Gainchand Motwane (41 years old)

It was not easy for the court to prove the case against
Motwane. He was a partner and sales manager at
Chicago Radio Company, a well-established and well-
known company that had a large merchandise, including
amplifiers which could be used for various purposes, such
as for transmitters, loudspeakers and theatre equipment. It
also built transmitting sets.

Because of Jagannath's statement, Kokje started
investigating Chicago Radio Company, particularly about
items like transmitting valves, crystals, blank records and
suchlike. He checked the books, cash memos and other
papers, and recorded the statements of several employees,
including Gopal Ramchandra Joshi, Shivram Vinayak
Khandekar, Shantaram Harishchandra Kubal and Shantilal
Chandulal. As a consequence of Shantilal's statement,
he questioned Shivram Raman (who worked at Chicago

BLITZ, April 20, 1946

Behind the Freedom Radio...

This is the photograph which gave prosecution pinpricks in "Freedom Radio Case" when Inspector Kolje, chief witness, tried to avoid the imputation that material evidence was tampered with. Jist much as he asserted, on oath, that "nothing has been touched" when the photographs were taken, the off-disc needle poised on "Vande Mataram" record gave the lie to his story.

A jeweller, a businessman and a student (Usha Mehta) thought of the idea of sending out Freedom Broadcasts on two powerful transmitters, operating quite independently of one another. This completely baffled the CID's vigilant listening-post and led its officers into a wild goose chase. Here's one of the transmitters: its simple construction belies the power of its range.

Not the least feature of the Freedom Radio's mechanism was its complete mobility. Camouflaged under travel-beddings and bedding, the component parts of the transmitter could be safely hidden away. Sometimes even a bed and a table carried were pressed into service. Such dexterous ingenuity held the best brains of CID at bay and GOI's radio-experts guessing.

"QUIT INDIA"—ON THE AIR: FULL STORY OF CONGRESS RADIO

"VOICE OF FREEDOM" BROADCAST INDIAN REVOLT THROUGH THE MOUTH OF INTREPID GIRL

★ By Kumud C. Khanna

AMONG some hundred political prisoners who, since the advent of the Congress Ministry, have proudly come out of the Yeravda Jail, two stand out in a category by themselves. For a while the "crime" of every political worker meriting incarceration at the hands of the British Raj was patriotism, these two and another colleague were literally guilty of surcharging the atmosphere with revolution.

With their release, the curtain rises on what is perhaps the most inspiring and not a little intriguing episode of our revolutionary history.

Startling facts can now be revealed which, torn from their political contexts make the story of the "Congress Radio" read like a modernised fable complete with an evil genius and a roving transmitter. In its true perspective, however, it is a stirring saga of supreme daring, ingenuity and resourcefulness displayed by two young men and a woman at a time of extreme national storm and stress.

Two Transmitters

Characteristically enough the prime-movers in this "Criminal Conspiracy" (Section 120A I.P.C.)—Babubhai alias Vithaldas Jhaveji Khakhar (jeweller), Vithaldas Kantabhai Javeri (businessman) and Miss Usha Mehta (student)—conceived the idea of establishing and working an "underground transmitter," when they

Printer, who in addition to having a nimble mind had a nimble conscience. Later, when he turned approver, he was of little use to the prosecutor for, as Special Judge Lokur said of him, "Unfortunately he is not a witness in whose words implicit reliance can be placed. Besides being an accomplice is in, on his own statement, a needy and unscrupulous adventurer who does not care for honesty and has scant regard for truth."

As principal of Bombay Technical Institute, Printer had an amateur transmitter for his purpose of giving lessons to his students. In 1939 his licence was cancelled, but instead of surrendering his apparatus, he secretly dismantled it and retained the parts. Thereafter he produced a tumor but a brilliant invention, called "Kerogas"—a mechanism for running motors on kerosene.

When the use of "Kerogas" was prohibited by the Government, owing to the scarcity of kerosene, he went on to manufacture

"RADIO-BEN" USHA MEHTA

The main purpose of the sponsors of the Congress Radio was not to put it on the front page of newspapers—which by the way they did—but to really serve the people and their movement by bringing home to them news and views which they had no other means of getting.

Defeated Censorship

Those days the press was gagged—telegrams, telephones and postal matter was subject to rigorous tapping and lynx-eyed censorship. THE CONGRESS RADIO HAD ITS OWN NETWORK OF REPORTERS AND MESSENGERS SPREAD ALL OVER THE COUNTRY, WHO BROUGHT FOR IT THE LATEST NEWS FROM ALL FRONTS OF FREEDOM'S BATTLE. THUS IT COULD BOAST OF EXCLUSIVE BROADCASTS ABOUT THE MILITARY-POLICE ATROCITIES IN ASHTI AND CHIMUR, AND NEWS-SCOOPS ON THE PATRI SARKAR OF SATARA, THE PEOPLE'S REVOLT OF JAUNPUR, BALLIA AND MID-

A page from *Blitz*, 20 April 1946

Radio Company under V.G. Motwane, Nanak Motwane's brother). He perceived some discrepancies in the number of articles such as crystals, tubes and valves in the register and the ledger in which the records were kept. He also found a cash memo showing that a complete microphone was sold to Messrs Baburao and Co. (mentioned as Babubhai & Co. in the judgment), Laxmi Building, Fort, Bombay. But on inquiry he found that no such company existed in that building.[31] He also took possession of some documents and had the company's Lucknow office searched, because Rupani, the manager of that branch, had come to Bombay and had taken some controlled parts from Chicago Radio Company. V.G. Motwane, Nanak's brother, was also arrested on 1 December 1942, but was soon released.[32]

Interestingly, Chicago Radio Company was never on the radar of the police despite its proximity to these activities. Deputy Inspector Manuel Morrison Fergusson said that he had known Motwane for several years. He often used to go to the company to purchase parts for the police wireless. Between August and November 1942, he went there almost every day to buy something or place some orders, and used to find Motwane in the showroom, very busy and surrounded by army and navy officers and customers. He also used to go to the workshop to see Jagannath and had seen him making parts of a transmitter or repairing the transmitters. Sometime in August he had a talk with him about the Congress Radio and had cracked a joke, saying that if anybody had a hand in the Congress Radio Station, it would probably be Jagannath. (That was the time when the Congress Radio station was operating.) Fergusson generally went to the godown to search for the parts and sometimes they were delivered to him in the showroom. He said that besides Chicago Radio Company, there were other firms dealing in controlled radio parts; a crystal was a controlled part.[33] Dinanath Krishnarao Pednekar, deputy inspector of police, CID, had also gone to Chicago Radio Company in November 1942 to find out how many recording sets they had. He had looked at their books and had found the stock correct.[34]

Motwane was examined and also gave a written statement in which he said that he was not guilty of the conspiracy regarding Printer's set. He did not know Printer intimately; Printer might have come to his shop. He did not even know that Printer wanted to build a transmitter after the AICC session. The amplifier and the gramophone pick-up, the volume control and the microphone were sold by his shop on 14 and 24 August 1942 in the ordinary course of business. It was not true that Dahyabhai, Printer, Babubhai and some others had met Motwane at his shop to obtain some transmitting parts, as Printer had stated in his evidence. Moreover, none of the parts that were said to have been used for strengthening the transmitter (including the crystals) had been supplied by his shop or under his instructions. He further stated that he did not send Jagannath to repair a record-cutting machine at Vithalbhai's house or to any building in Banganga in connection with a transmitter. He added that he did not instruct Jagannath to build the amplifiers or power packs; nor had he instructed Jagannath Joshi to supply blank records or parts to Jagannath Thakor. He had at no time supplied any recording machine or records to Vithalbhai or Jagannath. He acknowledged that he had engaged two sound trucks for recording the speeches at the AICC meeting on 7 and 8 August, but both of them were not working simultaneously. Subhedar's truck was only a stand-by truck. The sound film records were given to

Majid for developing and he had not seen them afterwards. Motwane had supplied loudspeakers for the AICC meeting and the film was taken with his machine, while the sound recording machine was hired from the Famous Cine Company. He clarified that he had not sent Jagannath to see if the picture and the sound record had come out well. Neither had he sent a word to Majid Kazi that somebody from his firm would come at night to edit the film. His shop had a theatre and if he wished to see the film, which belonged to him, he could have sent for it and seen it in his theatre, which was fully equipped with an editing table.[35]

Motwane said that his shop sold a number of recording machines and records in the ordinary course of its business to various customers. He had not known Babubhai, Ushaben and Chandrakant before coming to the court, and only knew Vithalbhai as a customer. Motwane had occasionally sent his men to his house or shop, like he would do for any other customer, for repairs of his radiograms and telephones. Regarding the issue of giving articles to Rupani for the Lucknow branch of the company, he made it clear that those articles were against orders received in the ordinary course of business. He further elucidated that no parts were supplied by his shop or under his instructions for the set at Khandke Building or that he had anything to do with that set. Jagannath's story about that set having been built at Motwane's shop and under his instruction was false.[36]

Some doubts about Motwane's innocence were raised over a parcel containing records and a cutting machine. It was lying on Motwane's table and was taken away by Lakha (a member of his staff). Motwane's defence was that this parcel was for a military officer who had called at his shop during the day for some records and cutting needles. Before he decided to purchase them, he asked for a demonstration. He also agreed to pay for this. Accordingly a record was partly cut and shown to him. Then he ordered all the records to be packed with the needles and the cut record and kept ready for him to be taken away sometime later. After that he never called at Motwane's shop. He had not left his name or address with Motwane.[37]

Motwane specified that he was not a member of the Congress. His shop had, in the ordinary course of its business, done work for the Congress, as for other customers, and had been paid its proper charges. In addition, his shop had also supplied materials and done large amounts of work for the military, navy and air services and the police. His shop had also made donations for purposes connected with the war and had rendered free services in regard to several works connected with war.[38]

A strong argument against Motwane was that he had supplied the required parts to the team of the Congress Radio. Printer had increased the power of the transmitter to 100 watts (presumably with the parts brought by Babubhai, who in turn might have got them from Motwane). The judge said that on this point there was only the evidence of Printer, Mirza and Jagannath, all of whom were accomplices. He stated that there was no satisfactory evidence to show that the parts required by Printer came from Motwane. In this context, the crystal used in the transmitter was important.[39]

The crystal had its specification plate removed and the frequency of 7075 was written on the inner plate in ink. An attempt was made to prove that Chicago Radio Company did possess a Bliley crystal of the type B5, having the frequency 7075, and that it was not sold to anyone and that had not been accounted for. From this it was inferred that it must have been given to Printer for being fitted in the transmitter. The judge was aware of the fact that the old crystal that Printer possessed was out of order and that he had fitted it as a dummy to deceive Babubhai. Printer changed it before increasing the power of the transmitter and changing the wavelength from 41.78 to 42.34 metres.[40]

After going through the evidence, the judge found that at least three crystals in Chicago Radio Company's stock had not been satisfactorily accounted for. Shivram Raman had prepared a statement showing the number of crystals received and disposed of. In September 1941, after the government notification, a list of controlled parts in stock was prepared and sent to the Commissioner of Police—158 crystals were mentioned in it.[41]

On 7 September, Shantilal Chandulal, the assistant to the godown keeper at Chicago Radio Company, had prepared a list of crystals in the godown to be sent to the Burma Posts and Telegraphs Department, Calcutta, for their information. In that list the frequencies of all the crystals in stock were mentioned. After taking into consideration thirty crystals subsequently received and sixteen found in excess in the godown, it was shown in the list prepared by Shivram Raman that there should have been sixty-five crystals in the stock. Of these, sixty were taken by the police from the Lucknow branch of the company and the remaining five were shown in Shivram Raman's list (out of these three were of type HF2 and two of type B5), and they were produced in the court. But the judge compared the frequencies of the three of type HF2 with the frequencies of the crystals of that type in the stock mentioned in the list sent to Burma Posts and Telegraphs Department, Calcutta, and found that the three produced in the court were never in the company's stock.[42]

According to the judge, there was a good deal of force in the prosecution's contention that these three must have been obtained from somewhere else and produced to make up the five which should have been in the stock—the three crystals had gone somewhere and were not accounted for. On the other hand, the list of transmitting crystals in stock sent by the Chicago Radio Company to the Burma Posts and Telegraphs Department, Calcutta, showed that there was in stock a crystal of B5 type having the frequency 7075 kc, and it did not appear from the records that the crystal was sold to any customer. It must be in the stock of Chicago Radio Company when the list sent to Burma Posts and Telegraphs Department, Calcutta, was prepared.[43]

This argument appeared to be plausible on the face of it. But according to the judge, this was not sufficient to prove that Motwane gave the crystal for the use of the transmitter. Moreover and most importantly, there was no evidence to prove that the crystal used in the transmitter was a Bliley crystal of type B5 and that its frequency was 7075 kc. Its specification plate had been removed and somebody must have written 7075 on the inner plate. But this was obviously incorrect. When the new crystal was fitted, the Congress Radio Station announced that it was broadcasting on 42.34 metres wavelength. This wavelength did not match the frequency written on the crystal. Printer, an expert technician, must have calculated the metres wavelength from the frequency of the crystal.[44]

It might be inferred from this that the figure written on the crystal was 7086 and not 7075. Inspector Kokje also admitted that he got this crystal tested by Tanna and its frequency was found to be 7094 or 7096 kc. It was not proved that the frequency was ever 7075 kc. It was not proved who wrote that figure on the crystal or when it was written, but it was certainly inaccurate. If so, it could not be said that it was the same crystal that was described in the list sent to Burma Posts and Telegraphs Department, Calcutta, as the crystal of type B5 with the frequency of 7075 kc. Thus, it could be assumed that Motwane could not have sent that crystal for being fitted in the transmitter. According to the evidence, there were some crystals with the set in Khandke Building and the unaccounted crystals might have been sent there.[45]

The judge referred to the list of crystals in the godown, prepared by Shantilal. It showed that after 7 September 1942, six crystals were supplied from the godown in accordance with Motwane's instructions and one of those crystals was mentioned to have been of the type B5 with the frequency 7075 kc. Shantilal did not know to whom it had been supplied and therefore he had put a mark of interrogation in his note. This note was kept in a file that was attached from the Chicago Radio Company in the presence of the panchas and was signed by both the panchas at the time of the panchnama. The defence challenged the genuineness of this document, pointing out that it was an unusual document and should not ordinarily appear in that file. The judge refrained from any opinion about its genuineness as he found it unnecessary. The important issue was the frequency of the crystal that was fitted on, which had been written in ink on its plate as 7075, and as the judge had pointed out, this frequency was different. So even if Motwane had given away a crystal of that frequency to some unknown person, as shown in the note prepared by Shantilal, it was not given to be used for the Congress Radio transmitter.[46]

The only other evidence against Motwane was his conduct in dispatching all the crystals and blank records

to the Lucknow branch of his company with Rupani,
the manager of the Lucknow branch of Chicago Radio
Company. The correspondence relating to the circumstances
under which Rupani was summoned, and all the crystals
taken away, was produced. It showed that there was an
order for fifty-six transmitters for the military and as all
the controlled parts were kept in the head office, it was
necessary to send the crystals to Lucknow. There was no
propriety in concealing the existence of those crystals, as
the Police Commissioner had been already notified and an
account had been regularly kept. In addition, the police had
seized all those crystals and the fact that they were sent to
Lucknow under those circumstances did not indicate that
Motwane had a guilty conscience. Moreover, there was
no evidence that Motwane had made available the home
recording machine or blank records for cutting of records for
the Congress Radio. The blank records from his company
bear the name of Chicago Radio Company, whereas the
records found in Parekh Wadi were R.C.A. records.[47]

Dahyabhai Patel, who was said to have been introduced
by Babubhai to Motwane, had not been called (it was not
shown what influence he had on Motwane). Printer's
testimony on that point could not be corroborated by any
other evidence and could not, therefore, be accepted.[48]

On the evidence produced, it could not be proved that
Motwane had joined the conspiracy or had done anything
to carry out its objectives further. According to the judge,
'He must therefore, be acquitted of all the charges.'[49]

Witnesses for the Prosecution

Printer's testimony was of vital importance for the
prosecution. He had taken the side of the establishment,

and had agreed to help the police in its investigation. He presented the complete story of the operation of the Congress Radio in his testimony, and also identified various parts of the apparatus and the Philips radio receiving set. He also said that the records produced in the court were similar to the ones he and his colleagues played at the broadcasting stations, with similar descriptive captions noted on them. He had no hesitation in giving statements about the roles played by Babubhai, Ushaben and others, even though all of them were members of the same group.

The judgment mentions that Printer was the mainstay of the conspiracy and it may be said to his credit that he had not tried to save his own skin and had unhesitatingly admitted the part he had played from the beginning to the end. At the same time, the judge was aware of the fact that though Printer had given a consistent and detailed story of the conspiracy from the beginning to the end, he was 'not a witness on whose word implicit reliance can be placed'. And, 'Besides being an accomplice, he is, on his own statement, a needy and unscrupulous adventurer who does not care for honesty and has scant regard for truth.'[50]

In this context, the judge pointed out certain issues: his track record of work, working of his institute, cases against him, pledging all his articles to Malupchand Shantidas, using Mirza's name for renting the house he lived in, hiding the name of the Parsi lady who spoke into the transmitter's microphone and making false representations to Babubhai at least on two occasions (once by fitting up his cracked crystal as a dummy to the transmitter and next by lying that he had raised the strength of his wireless transmitter). Printer had lied to Babubhai that he had raised the strength of his wireless transmitter to 1,500 watts, though he had not raised it to more than 100 watts. Later, Deputy Inspector Fergusson found that its strength was only 30 watts.[51]

In addition, the judge noted that shortly before the trial of this case commenced, a case had been set up against him for an offence under Rule 16 (7) read with Rule 121 of the Defence of India Rules and Section 20 of the Indian Telegraph Act read with Section 109 of the IPC. He had appeared before the chief presidency magistrate and that case had been adjourned to 15 May (the judgment of the Congress Radio case was delivered on 14 May). Although he had claimed that he wasn't given any promise that if he gave evidence in favour of the prosecution in this case, the other one would be withdrawn, the matter must have weighed on his mind.[52]

The judge, therefore, did not rely only on Printer's story but took care to corroborate it with the other witnesses' statements and the findings of articles like the transmitter and records. Mirza verified Printer's story, while R.A. Mehta admitted the part he had played. The judgment records that: 'All these three witnesses (Printer, Mehta and Mirza) are accomplices, but their story regarding the construction and the strengthening of the wireless transmitter and its removal from place to place is sufficiently borne out by other unimpeachable evidence.'[53]

The judge stated that besides Printer, several other witnesses for the prosecution were actively concerned in the conspiracy; the counsel for the prosecution, however, frankly conceded that Mirza, Killewala, Bipin Inamdar, Jagannath, Shantilal, Jaychand and R.A. Mehta should be considered as accomplices. Hence the testimony of all these must be regarded as tainted evidence.[54]

According to the judge, it was unfortunate that men like Printer, Mirza and R.A. Mehta—who played very prominent parts in the conspiracy and actively carried out its objects in various ways—had to be examined as witnesses for the prosecution instead of being placed in the dock to be tried with the accused. Many witnesses (who came after Printer and Mirza) seemed to have sympathized with the accused.[55] The judge also noted that R.A. Mehta and several other witnesses who were connected with the conspiracy refused to give any incriminating answers unless they were compelled to do so under Section 132 of the Indian Evidence Act. This ensured that any statements they made would not be used in the future against them. His safety assured, Mehta did not hesitate to take all the blame on himself, possibly to screen the accused. Babubhai was his business partner and, therefore, he was an interested witness.[56]

The Judgment

The arguments and the judgment of Case No. 7 of 1943, *Emperor Vs. 1. Vithaldas alias Babubhai Madhavji Khakar 2. Vithaldas Kanthadbhai Jhaveri 3. Usha Mehta 4. Chandrakant Babubhai Jhaveri 5. Nanak G. Motwane* in the Court of the Special Judge N.S. Lokur were not covered in detail by the press because of restrictions. More than fifty witnesses were examined and the judgment was delivered on 14 May 1942.

The journey of the Congress Radio was neatly traced in the judgment. While Babubhai, Vithalbhai, Chandrakant and Nanak denied their connection with the Radio Station and the alleged conspiracy, Ushaben refused to make any statements or offer any explanations of the facts appearing in the evidence against her.

Taking all the details into consideration, the judge ruled that Babubhai, Ushaben and Chandrakant were found to have been concerned in the conspiracy to establish, maintain and work an unauthorized wireless transmitter. This in itself was a serious offence, but to use it for broadcasting prejudicial reports intended or likely to spread disaffection and hamper war efforts was, to say the least, greatly heinous and deserved a deterrent sentence. Babubhai took a leading role not only by financing the project but also by taking part in it at every stage, and the judge saw no reason why he should not be given the maximum sentence of imprisonment under Rules 16(7) and 38(5) of the Defence of India Rules. Ushaben seemed 'to be equally guilty'. She was playing 'the second fiddle' and had 'not stooped to put forward a false defence to escape conviction'. The judge opined that she would, therefore, be dealt with more leniently. Chandrakant had recently joined the project, and before he could take a more active part in carrying out its objects, the conspiracy was exposed and the transmitter seized. The offence of criminal conspiracy was by itself separately punishable under Section 120-B of the IPC, even though the offences which had formed the object of the conspiracy were not committed at all. However, in this case, the offences which constituted the object of the conspiracy were actually and had in fact been carried out. A separate sentence for the offence under Section 120-B of the IPC was, therefore, not called for. (*Harsha Nath Chatterjee v. Emperor*, I.L.R. 42 Cal. 1153 and *Punjab Singh v. The Crown*, I.L.R. 15 Lah. 84.) The sentences for the offences in the charge would, therefore, be ordered to run concurrently.[57]

The judge convicted Vithaldas Madhavji Khakar alias Babubhai (a) under Section 120-B of the IPC, (b) Rule 16(7) read with Rule 16(3) and 121 of the Defence of India Rules along with Section 20 of the Indian Telegraph Act 1885,

(c) Rule 16(7) read with Rule 16(5) and Rule 121 of the Defence of India Rules, and (d) Rule 38(5) read with Rule 38(1)(a) and (c) and Rule 121 of the Defence of India Rules, and sentenced him to undergo rigorous imprisonment for a period of five years for each of the four offences, the sentences to run concurrently. He was acquitted of the charge under Rule 39(6) read with Rule 39(1) (b) and Rule 121 of the Defence of India Rules. The judge convicted Usha Mehta (a) under Section 120-B of the IPC, (b) Rule 16(7) read with Rule 16(3) and Rule 121 of the Defence of India Rules along with Section 20 of the Indian Telegraph Act 1885, (c) Rule 16(7) read with Rule 16(5) of the Defence of India Rules and (d) Rule 38(5) read with Rule 38(1)(a) and (c) and Rule 121 of the Defence of India Rules and sentenced her to undergo rigorous imprisonment for a period of four years for each of the four offences, the sentences to run concurrently. She was acquitted of the charge under Rule 39(6) read with Rule 39(1) (b) and Rule 121 of the Defence of India Rules. The judge convicted Chandrakant Jhaveri (a) under Section 120-B of the IPC, (b) Rule 16(7) read with Rule 16(3) and Rule 121 of the Defence of India Rules along with Section 20 of the Indian Telegraph Act 1885, and (c) Rule 16(7) read with Rule 16(5) of the Defence of India Rules and sentenced him to undergo rigorous imprisonment for a period of one year for each of the three offences, the sentences to run concurrently. He was acquitted of other charges. Vithaldas Kanthadbhai Jhaveri and Nanak Motwane were acquitted of all the charges and discharged.[58]

The Congress Radio broadcasting station was monitored at the monitoring station, Shepherd Road. The CID monitored the Congress Radio bulletins (in Hindustani and English) with the help of a few persons, including

Mahomed Ashroff Fiz Ahmed Choudhary (police sub-inspector, CID Special Branch), Raymond Ben Raymond (shorthand reporter), Hansraj Sardarchand Ghaia (police sub-inspector, CID), Bhagsing Sardar Hajara Singh (reporter in CID) and Harischandra Shrivastav (reporter, CID) and Rama Harittar Iyer (police stenographer).[59]

The judge appreciated the intelligent investigation of the case by Inspector Kokje and acknowledged the help he received from the learned counsel on both the sides throughout the protracted trial. He had a word of appreciation for Vimadalal, the counsel for the prosecution, also. According to him, Vimadalal made 'the best of the materials available and conducted the case with conspicuous fairness and equanimity, conceding every point that his witnesses had rendered untenable and giving every facility asked by the defence.'[60]

Conclusion

Later, I would often ask Ushaben what it felt like to have a case against her and to sit through the trial. She would smile warmly, her thoughts going back to those thrilling times. Once, sitting in her little office at Mani Bhavan, watching the rain falling on the leaves outside the window and experiencing the soothing feeling after the first rain of Mumbai's famous monsoon, we slipped into talking about the days gone by. By then I had read the papers about the case against the five accused and the judgment. I requested her to tell me more about those experiences. In her words, 'Though we were reluctant to engage lawyers for our defence, we had to ultimately yield to the pressures of friends and party workers, who were afraid that the Congress would come into disrepute if we were not defended. A Citizens' Defence Committee was formed with Chhotalal Mehta as the convener. It engaged a battery of the topmost lawyers of the country including Shri Kanhaiyalal Munshi, Shri Motilal Setalvad, Shri S.R. Tendolkar (who later became a judge of the High Court), Shri Jape and Shri Thacker. Shri Vimadalal was appointed as the public prosecutor. Both Tendolkar and Vimadalal were my teachers in the Government Law College.

'As you know, a special court presided over by Justice Lokur was instituted. The trial for the case against us continued for nearly six weeks. All witnesses were examined and very ably cross-examined by the defence lawyers who left no stone unturned to see that we were acquitted. I still remember how Munshiji in his imitable style once argued that all the accused far from being criminals and conspirators were patriots and selfless soldiers motivated by the highest and noblest ideals in fighting for the freedom of Mother India which could be claimed as an inherent right of every Indian.

'Vimadalal tried his best to prove our guilt. All possible evidence was produced. The inscriptions on our records were in Vithalbhai's handwriting. He, however, acted so efficiently that the police could not identify his handwriting. Due to this and the powerful defence put up by our defence lawyers, especially Munshi and Setalvad, Vithalbhai and Nanak Motwane were acquitted. Chandrakantbhai and I were caught red-handed; we were prepared for the severest punishment, and Babubhai too could not escape.

'During the trial in the Court, all five defendants—Vithalbhai, Babubhai, Chandrakantbhai, Nanakbhai and I—had to sit in the dock for about seven hours at a stretch. We, however, did not feel tired or bored. Instead, we felt relaxed and enjoyed the trial, especially when there was repartee between the Public Prosecutor Vimadalal and our defence lawyer Tendolkar, as well as those between Vimadalal who wanted us to be treated as conspirators and criminals, and Munshi and Setalvad who showered praise on us for having the courage to rise in revolt against an unjust government. Vithalbhai, an accomplished artist, kept himself busy drawing sketches of important personalities in the courtroom, including of the judge. On the last day, we presented these sketches to the judge, the public prosecutor and the defence lawyers. The judge was deeply moved by this gesture and in an emotionally choked voice said, "I am reminded of Mahatma Gandhi who presented a pair of sandals to General Smuts who prosecuted him."'[61]

5

Broadcasts from the Congress Radio

The Congress Radio was on the air for almost two and half months, at a time when the fervour generated by the Quit India resolution was at its height. People were starved for news, and eagerly awaited the broadcasts. In fact, decades later, Captain Lakshmi Sahgal, the legendary revolutionary and the chief of the Rani Jhansi Regiment of the Indian National Army, recollected how eager they were to hear the Congress Radio.

The bulletins and news filled a huge void created by the authoritarian measures taken by the British government. In 1942, there was a move to suppress all news about the people's agitation for freedom: the government, in fact, was in the process of doing so in order to isolate the people from the nationalistic activities before the August Resolution.[1]

The National War Front was launched in May 1942 to muster support for the government's war effort and to foster anti-Congress propaganda. The authorities very worried and concerned, so much that they were even contemplating deporting Gandhi to Aden or Nyasaland, and the other main Congress leaders to Uganda or elsewhere in East Africa. During wartime, the Defence of India Rules permitted the government to take any arbitrary action against persons and property in the name of the war effort. As pointed out by Hutchins, martial law had not been declared because civilian officials continued in nominal— and often actual—command of operations to suppress the uprising. The actions taken were no less severe than what would have been taken under martial law.[2]

Press ordinances, which had been prepared in advance of the 9 August raids and arrests, warned editors against publishing articles in support of the Congress's call for a mass movement. Editors were also forbidden to report or comment on any of the measures taken by the government to avert or repress the movement. These prohibitions only added to a series of wartime press controls already in effect.[3]

Moreover, two important notifications were issued from Delhi on 8 and 9 August 1942: (i) to prohibit the printing or publishing of any news relating to the mass movement sanctioned by the AICC or to the measures taken by the government against that movement, and (ii) to declare the AICC, the Working Committee of the All India Congress and the Delhi Provincial Congress Committee unlawful.[4]

The controversial Revolutionary Movements' Ordinance, which was intended to crush the Quit India Movement, was signed by the Viceroy on 12 August 1942. It was withheld from being issued in the *Gazette of India* because all the provinces, except the Central Provinces, argued that they could make do with the powers under the Defence of India Rules (DIR). The government also brought into force the Special Criminal Courts Ordinance II of 1942, which was applied to cases arising from the disturbances from 26 October 1942 onwards. This enabled the authorities to try offences and award severe punishments without following the usual court procedures.[5]

The government's harsh and autocratic policy towards the Congress and the arrest of its important leaders disrupted the links of communication with the people. As pointed out by Paul R. Greenough, not only did the internal communication within the Congress hierarchy abruptly cease, but also the flow of directives from leadership levels to the mass of followers; these were regularly conducted through the medium of the nationalist press, but were halted by severe censorship.[6]

For the British rulers, the situation was getting increasingly uneasy. World War II was at its height, the Japanese were at the doorsteps and the simmering internal crisis brought about by the Quit India movement were all making the government more and more determined to block out all the news about the movement.[7]

K.C. Neogy, member of the Central Legislative Assembly of India and later a member of the Constituent Assembly, declared boldly in the Central Legislative Assembly in September 1942 that:

The Press has been gagged so successfully that nothing but officially approved news can be published either in India or abroad . . . The magnificent achievement of the Press censoring policy is indicated by the fact that for some time 96 Indian newspapers, including some of the most leading and influential dailies, voluntarily ceased publication. Out of this number, about 22 have later resumed publication. The rest continue their voluntary suppression as a protest against the illogical and dictatorial control exercised over the publication of news which does not, even according to foreign journalists present at New Delhi, permit a balanced picture of the situation to be given.[8]

The tight control exercised over the press gave rise to the underground publications, and it became a thrilling adventure to publish patriotic pamphlets and bulletins.[9]

The already charged political atmosphere in 1942 became more volatile because of World War II and the advance of Subhash Chandra Bose's Indian National Army in Burma. The public, anxious to learn more about the political turmoil and turbulence, naturally turned to any medium they could. The radio at that time seemed to be a powerful medium to disseminate news. The authorities realized the gravity of the situation, and in a letter Amery referred to 'the extent and power of the ether war raging in India every night'. He further stated: 'The usual question when an Indian buys a wireless set, I was told by big dealers in Bombay, is "Can I hear Germany and Japan on this?" That was long before the troubles. Nine large stations batter at India every night.'[10]

Because of the political unrest, a curfew order was promulgated in Bombay on 9 August.[11] On the afternoon of 10 August, the Government of Bombay issued an order making picketing unlawful both in Bombay city and in Ahmedabad.[12]

* * *

The stage was, thus, set to receive the news from the underground Congress Radio, and the broadcasts fulfilled their expectations—the frequent disturbances, the

dislocation of railways and the destruction of other means
of communication, such as the telegraph and the telephone,
all formed part of their coverage; even the interior regions
of the country were not neglected. Ushaben's eyes would
beam with joy and pride when she remembered the times
when she would announce: 'Speaking from somewhere in
India, this is the Congress Radio on 42.34 metres.'

For her, those were hallowed days. In her words, 'We
used to receive news from all over India through special
messengers. We were the first to give the news of the
Chittagong bomb raid, of the Jamshedpur strike and of the
happenings in Ballia. We broadcast the full description of
the atrocities in Ashti and Chimur. The newspapers dared
not touch these subjects under the prevailing conditions;
only the Congress Radio could defy the orders and tell the
people what was really happening. Our listeners helped
us in spreading the news to the people at large. The news
bulletins were supplied by Sucheta Kriplani and Aruna
Asaf Ali, the records were carried from the Recording
Station to the broadcasting station by Bipin Inamdar and
Ravindra Mehta.

'We used to relay news, speeches and appeals to different
classes of people. For this, there was a batch of speakers
and writers including Dr Lohia, Achyut Patwardhan,
Moinuddin Harris, Coomie Dastur (later Kamal Wood),
K.A. Abbas and myself. It was not safe to take all of them
to the broadcasting station, which is why we thought of
getting the speeches recorded. The recording place was
different from the broadcasting station. This lessened
the risk considerably. Vithalbhai Jhaveri was responsible
for this section and Babubhai mainly in charge of the
broadcasting station. As in the case of our broadcasting
station, we also used to shift our recording station at regular

- 17 -

POLICE WIRELESS MONITORING REPORT.

Date: 21st October 1942.

Name of Station: Illegal Congress Radio.
Wavelength: 42.12 Meters.
Frequency: 7.12 K.C.   = 7120 M.C.
Time of starting: 8.30 a.m.
Time of ending: 9.10 a.m.
==

M E S S A G E.

Language: English   Speaker: Male.

This is the Congress Radio calling from somewhere in India. You will now listen to a talk on the nature of the Indian Revolution.

What we are witnessing to-day is indeed a revolution but not of the traditional pattern. All previous revolutions of the past 200 years in whatever part of the world they took place were the work of an active minority. One of the two chief aspects of the Russian Revolution has placed it on record that barely one per cent of the Russian population actually carried out the Bolshevik Revolution. This act of minority was indeed supported by the passive sympathy of the majority and the indifference of the rest. The French Revolution was made by Paris and the fire swept over the entire country. These acts of minorities of revolutionaries in France or in Russia succeeded because the regime they were trying to destroy was collapsing through internal decay and was not able to hold the loyalty of its own paid men. In fact the loyalty of troops and the whole garrison dwindled when the revolutionaries could persuade them to join their fight. It was the patriotic garrison that enabled the Russian Bolsheviks to capture power. Revolution and capture of power are synonymous terms but the way in which the capture of power has hitherto been understood is mere transfer than capture it was slipped from old hands unable to retain it into new, eager and vigorous to handle it. There have been uptil now no revolutions in the world where the hands of power changed during the revolutionary process itself. All vital changes of power were made only after the Revolution was a success and an accomplished fact. For a number of reasons, India cannot go the traditional revolutionary way. In the first place, we have been disarmed for a very long time and neither her revolutionaries nor her people are prepared for an armed insurrection. Secondly, the British State has of necessity evolved a method whereby concentrated armed might in the way of tanks, artillery and aeroplanes is centred in the hands of the British soldiers and the Indian army, infantrymen and subordinate ranks. The racial barrier between the British soldiers and the Indian people makes it impossible for us to impair their loyalty to the existing administration. What we can do best hope for is a conflict between the British and Indian section which may, to some extent, neutralize the strength of the Indian army. Thirdly, our long tradition of peace and our continued disarmament and the great teachings of Mahatma Gandhi have combined to produce a grand new weapon of war against injustice and tyranny. Our weapon claims to show a new way to the world so our revolution cannot be based on a traditional pattern or known example. It is its own model and pathfinder. It is a strike of the whole people resolved to do no work other than what is necessary to exist. The strike of the nationalists is neither complete nor continuous. There are ups and downs. A nation on strike is a nation existing. It invites upon itself the full anger of the machine that it is determined to break. The machine --forces it to work and in its refusal to do so, it breaks up the unity of the machine. The British machine in India like any other machine is a unity whose parts are related to one another.

Police Wireless Monitoring Report, 21 October 1942

intervals. We started with Sumatiben Morarjee's house at French Bridge, then went to another place at Malabar Hill and then moved to Thackersey's bungalow at Pedder Road. Vithalbhai would not only record the speeches and the news bulletins but also indicate in invisible ink on the record the names of announcers.'[13]

Collating the news, speaking into the microphone, playing the records, typing the programmes and bulletins and making notes (a trait that stayed with her during her academic career) were rewarding experiences for young Ushaben. She would often talk to us about such work as well as about the views of the intellectuals outside India who were sympathetic to India. Among them were Bernard Shaw, Harold Laski, Albert Einstein, Romain Rolland and Louis Fischer.

Reception and Transcripts of the Broadcasts

The Congress Radio went on air at the end of August 1942; however, the police only began making transcriptions of the bulletins from October—the day they started listening to and taking notes from them. The police found it difficult to hear the bulletins clearly, and reports on the reception varied: bad reception,[14] the reporter's conviction that the actual broadcasting was made entirely from gramophone records due to very good reception on about 43 metres for Hindustani and 39 metres for English,[15] clear reception only at times[16] and uninteresting programmes.[17]

The announcers on the Radio were polite, courteous and keen to maintain a rapport with their listeners. The evening broadcast of 14 October requested for 'leave for a couple of days. We shall be again on the air on the 18 October at 7.30 in the morning.' (There was no transmission on these days as the equipment was being upgraded.) Sometimes if the broadcast was not clear, the announcers politely asked the listeners to bear with them. On 25 October they had said, 'This is the Congress Radio calling from India on 42.34 metres. We beg to be excused by our listeners. Our radio will be silent for five minutes and we shall be again on the air. Don't switch off your radio. Our programme will restart after five minutes.' On 26 October, at 8.45 p.m., they announced: 'We regret that due to some reasons we could not speak to you yesterday. Azad Hindustan will come to know with what great difficulties we are making arrangements to give true news to the world. Everybody should know that the Congress Radio gives news collected from their own sources. Congress Radio gives correct news.'[18]

The process of presenting the 'correct news' and the news 'collected from their own sources' was not easy as there was no formal machinery nor any regular paid staff or a well-set office. The broadcasts were daily bulletins, made of compilations of news from different places in the country. The nationalist workers and volunteers would collect the news/information, pass them on to the leaders like Dr Ram Manohar Lohia and Sucheta Kriplani, who in turn would get them to the Congress Radio team. In their urgency to relay the information at the earliest, the team had little time to put the news in a coherent format. Consequently, the broadcasts at best present a collage of the happenings in the country. Each broadcast was an independent unit, full of its own thrill of collating with care the news that was suppressed by the British authorities. Each unit brought its own political perspective that was passionately patriotic and nationalist. Ushaben talked about how she would sit quietly in a corner, taking care to appear casual, and would hurriedly put the information (that was received) together, would write on a paper and be ready for the broadcast. Her handwritten copies of the broadcasts are silent witnesses to that process. The records, mostly containing the speeches of the leaders, would be played as and when required. In her words, 'Presenting an engaging programme on the radio with the "correct news" was the only concern.'[19]

The Congress Radio attempted to broadcast news about the happenings in the country from the Congress/nationalist perspective. The listeners heard about police and military brutalities as well as people's protests. The news also advocated self-sufficiency of villages and advised the people on various issues like stopping work for factories and railways. The bold broadcasts, ardently announced, remain an important source for learning more about the course of the Quit India movement in various parts of India and reflect the intensity of the efforts of the patriots to achieve independence.

It is difficult to group or categorize the broadcasts as they were meant to cover the contemporary happenings on a daily/weekly basis, though this depended on procurement of the information/news. However, the broadcasts can be viewed in two groups to give an idea about what was happening in the country: the news about (i) disturbances and the dislocation of means of communication (discussed in the next sub-section) and (ii) criticisms of the government, guiding ideas, messages to some specific groups such as students or peasants and speeches of leaders (discussed in the sub-section 'The Perspective of the Congress Radio' in Chapter 6).

This is the Congress Radio Calling from somewhere in India on 42.34 meters.

CONGRESS RADIO CALLING.

It is over a week since we received news from Bombay that a powerful transmission set used for Congress broadcasts had been seized by the usurper administration. The Bombay administration has apparently doled out conflicting reports. This set, we are told, is only one of many and the Congress is almost running a factory for the manufacture of secret senders. But we have also been told that this set was seized, while in operation and along with the announcers. It is not our intention to unravel this mystery. It shall remain a mystery until India is free. And to our people we say, do not bother about us, do not talk about us, let us carry on our work. Should anyone of you get to know or guess the persons doing this work or places where this work is done, God damn you if you talk about it to the best of your friends.

Had it not been for the high and strong walls of popular sympathy that protect us, we would have died long ago. We have been careless. We have done things far too openly. But India is our land, bt the British usurpers sneak about, if we do things at all, it will be with a bang and not a whimper. It is not for nothing, that Congress Radio Calling is the best secret sender the world has so far seen. The reason does not lie in our competence; we know know we are not competent enough, though slightly less incompetent than the British. The reason does not lie in our money-resources; we are far too poor. Congress Radio Calling is the best secret sender of the world because it is the voice not of a minority, not of a mere majority, but of an entire people, the voice of the Indian people.

To the British usurper we say, leave off trying to find this voice. You may find a set in Bombay, but what of the sets in Calcutta, Delhi, Allahabad, Bangalore, Nagpur and other places. You may find one set in Bombay, but in its place will spring up two still more powerful. Where will you escape this voice, it will haunt you wherever you go, to the right of you, to the left of you, above you, behind you, in front of you, this voice of truth and freedom and democracy and peace, it will go through you and show you up in all your nakedness of beastly terror until you are made to quit this fair country of ours.

We wish to address a word to our British comrades in the air force, the xxx navy and all other detection squads of the usurper government. Please do not help the Maxwells and Linlithgows; they are the enemies of freedom and peace. To the Indian policemen, what shall we say except that we count on their support. If you, our brothers in the police force, help in detecting the Congress Radio, it will be like killing your own parent or brother or xxxxkkxng smothering your own child.

To our listeners, to the Indian people, we admit our inadequacies. But do not forget that we are a secret sender. Certain technical difficulties we can never overcome. And yet we will continue to bring you the voice of truth and freedom, it may sometimes falter or break, but we give you our pledge, it will never die out. But we demand two returns from you. We are poor, very poor and, if you are rich and like our work, go to the accredited Congress chief of your town and give him as much as you can earmarked for Congress Radio Calling.

A Broadcast Bulletin, 9 and 10 November 1942

Broadcasts about Disturbances and Dislocation of Means of Communication

During its almost two and half months' operation, the Congress Radio's broadcasts captured the mood of the times—the exhilaration and enthusiasm generated by a country caught up in the fervour of the Quit India movement. They were also fearless, commenting on the ruthless behaviour of the British officials and making biting jibes at the practice of cruelty adopted by the British officials towards the Indians.[20] One pointed out the financial difficulties faced by the government and cited an experience of Alladi Krishnaswamy Ayyar, the accountant general of Madras.[21]

The following broadcasts for September, October and November 1942 give us a sense of the major happenings and unrest in the country.

September 1942

One of the earliest and most detailed bulletins in September described the government's repression of the people's movement in certain places where large numbers had mobilized. It brought to light the power of the people's protests in Nagpur, Ballia and Monghyr. The British authorities were completely absent in Nagpur for two days except for the central police station, which looked like a beleaguered fortress, and a few other centres of power. The people of Nagpur had understood the main tactic of the revolutionary struggle—they staged mass demonstrations, destroyed communications and spread propaganda among the families of policemen and other government servants. Perhaps the most successful example of coordination

NEWS 20TH OCTOBER, 1942. *to Evening*

N.W.F.P.

Here is the latest news from the Frontier Province.

PESHAWAR:- In a previous Bulletin we gave you a brief account of the brutal lathi and bayonet attack that was made on the Red Shirts, when they picketted the Peshawar Courts on the 5th of October. Here are some further details of that incident, along with news of other brutalities that the usurper administration in the N.W.F.P. is perpetrating to crush the brave resistance of Badshah Khan's army.

On the 5th of October, 280 Red Shirts were seriously wounded, the total number of injured being 400.

6-10-42:- The City observed complete hartal as a protest against the arrest of the President of the City Congress Committee and other workers.   Unable to pursuade the merchants to break the discipline of the Congress and open their shops, the Collector under his orders, had the doors of a large number of shops broken open.

MARDAN:-(5-10-42):- Government offices and courts were picketted at Mardan.   The police opened fire several times and some workers were killed.   Details have not yet been received.

Methods of Torture that would shame the Gestapo!

The work of crushing the movement in this province has now been entrusted to the wild and ferocious border police, as the Government cannot rely on the ordinary police to use the required amount of brutality in dealing with the non-violent civil resisters.   The new police use all kinds of methods to torture the Red Shirts, for instance, they inflict blows on them in such a way that serious internal injury is caused without there being any outward bruise or hurt; As a consequence many of the Red Shirts are now suffering from serious bladder trouble.

A Magistrate ~~drove his~~ *ran* car ~~knocking~~ *knocked* down and ~~over-running~~ *passed over* the Red Shirts.

Though the Red Shirts do not themselves take part in any dislocation activities, the public at Peshawar and other parts of the province, have uprooted telephone and telegraph poles, cut off wires and raided the police stations.   Students and boys who are arrested on suspicion for taking part in these activities are not tried by the usual channels of law and justice but are taken to the nearby canals and ducked or drowned.

BIHAR.

SEHAN (Muzaffarpur):- Collective fines of Rs. 6,000/- have been imposed on the small village of Sehan, 15 miles from Muzaffarpur.   Out of this the local Khadi Bhandar alone has been made liable for Rs. 5,000/- and the whole Bhandar containing stocks worth much more has been confiscated.

In this village people going about wearing white khadi caps have been assaulted by the police and compelled to give up their caps at the point of the bayonet.

In the same village a baby of two years was murdered by a British tommy for no other fault than that of being the child of a Congressman.

On Hajipur, a collective fine of Rs. 90,000/- has been imposed. The total municipal revenue of this town is only Rs. 10,000/- (ten thousand).

UNITED PROVINCES.

ALLAHABAD:- News comes from Allahabad that 144 policemen were suspended and detained in their barracks, and 36 were put under arrest on the 18th of October, as they refused to submit to medical examination preliminary to their being sent abroad.   The administration at Allahabad it seems, has been making more and more use of the newly drafted civic guards as they have no confidence in the old police force.   Therefore, it was decided to send this batch of 180 policemen abroad.   The Civic Guards at Allahabad are notorious for the number of goondas that have been drafted

A broadcast bulletin, 20 October 1942

between the town and the rest of the district was seen in Ballia—all the police stations of the district were occupied; all post offices, government buildings and the officers were brought under control. The district magistrate was persuaded (or possibly forced) to unlock the jail gates and release political prisoners. Railways, roads and telegraph wires to and from Ballia were considerably damaged. The British military was left with only two means of transport— water and air. The bulletin noted that such disturbances took place in Monghyr as well.[22]

Reports from different provinces were collected diligently and read boldly. The radio brought to light incidents of the atrocities committed by the British rule and the disturbances in Maharashtra. In Nandurbar in Khandesh, a police sub-inspector ran after small boys and girls and shot them indiscriminately.[23] The details of the strike of 2,000 workers of Iron & Steel Works in Kirloskarwadi in Maharashtra that lasted several days were also relayed in a broadcast.[24] The people of Mahad gave a brave and tough fight to the British administration.[25] In Shendurni, the people rose in a body and took possession of the police chowki, the post office, the Gram Panchayat and the school buildings. They protected themselves from the police attacks by dislocating the railway lines. In addition, Kolaba district was isolated from the rest of the country for over a week. The telephone and telegram wires were damaged. The roads were blocked with felled trees and bridges, and culverts were broken.[26] Another broadcast informed about the sinking of a ship in the Arabian Sea.[27]

Reports from Gujarat included news of a brutal attack by the police on a huge procession organized by the people of Bardoli to observe Azad Din. The procession was composed of students, people from neighbouring villages and Muslims.[28] Further reports from Gujarat displayed the mood of the people: resignations by policemen and other officials,[29] picketing of courts, burning of the Union Jack; and three hundred Bhils removed one and half miles of rails from the private siding belonging to the manganese mines of Killick Nixon & Co. and threw hundreds of tons of manganese meant for export to America into the forest.[30]

Broadcasts brought to light the frustrations and discontent of the people in Bihar. Four thousand persons attacked a train at Dehri-on-Sone; the police fired and killed eleven. When people started to retreat carrying the wounded, fresh police and military reinforcements arrived and hundreds were killed.[31] The damage of rice fields near Ranchi because of heavy truck and tank movement and other military manoeuvres irked poor farmers who ultimately took the matter into their hands and fought the military with bamboo sticks.[32]

In the United Provinces, some first- and second-class train compartments were burnt or damaged at Agra, while the bridge and culverts on the Allahabad–Jaunpur road were destroyed.[33] Many processions were seen in Delhi on 9 September.[34] Other reports included the burning of the Babatpur aerodrome and a military clothing factory in Agra district and the people taking possession of Gangapur military grain godown.[35] According to a report from the United Provinces, extensive damage was done to the railway lines in east United Provinces and fresh dislocations were taking place daily.[36]

News from the Central Provinces brought an update of the uneasy situation there. In Saugar district about 4,000 people launched a forest satyagraha at Baleh, Kesli, Dalpatpur and Karrapur.[37] In Jubbulpore, at the reserve forest, Bargi people removed or damaged the government teak reserved for military purposes. In Karrapur, people refused to give food or shelter to the visiting magistrate and the police party; public prosecutors of Saugar and Seoni (S.S. Pandya and Gangadhar Rao Kher) as well as 54 constables in Saugar resigned; 290 women were arrested in Saugar district. Moreover, in Jubbulpore a committee of lawyers was established to help the victims of government terrorism and the political prisoners.[38] The police and military continued their repressive policy and opened fire on the processions in Jubbulpore, Saugar, Betul, Mandla and Balaghat, causing three deaths and 173 casualities.[39] A committee was formed in Jubbulpore to help the political prisoners and victims of atrocities.[40]

The broadcasts from the Congress Radio informed the listeners about the repressive steps taken by the government and dislocations in the means of communications. At the same time they gave powerful messages of patriotism and unity. The Congress Radio had proudly declared that happenings in the first month of 'our non-violent revolution' in Nagpur in the Central Provinces, Ballia in United Provinces and Monghyr in Bihar showed 'an underlying unity'.[41] Further, it noted that the Indian police personnel working under the British respected the leaders fighting for freedom. On 10 September the Red Shirts led by Dr Khan and Mr Kazmi went to the court and government offices and exhorted the officers to leave their posts. At the police lines, the police forces heard Dr Khan's lecture with great attention and only dispersed after saluting him.[42]

News from Assam and Bengal revealed the disquiet in those provinces.[43] Bolepur, the seat of Ravindra Nath Tagore University, had become the scene of a stubborn struggle between the people and the government; 6,000 workers of Calcutta Port Trust workshops were on strike for a month; and hundreds of wounded soldiers were pouring into Calcutta from the Assam border every day, indicative of the severe battles between the Japanese and the British forces.[44] The Congress Radio also reported an interesting incident that revealed the people's resistance to the British policy in the district of Birbhum in Bengal. Even though the government had suppressed all the news of this area, the radio had managed to get them.[45] Some interesting incidents of people's resistance to the police action in Bengal were also covered in the Congress Radio bulletins.[46]

The report from Bihar was that as the government did not trust the Indian military to put down their own people, the British soldiers were posted in the province. However, the dislocation of railways and other means was so intense that the regiments found themselves completely isolated. They could not get the food locally due to the hostility of the villagers.[47] The people in Cuttack district in Orissa brought about a complete deadlock of the government machinery, as the village panchayats ruled. The boatmen refused to ply for the government officers and the other approaches to the area were blocked and dislocated.[48]

In Bengal, all Union Board properties in Arambagh subdivision (Hooghly) and the Madariput Civil Court (Faridpur) were burnt down. Work had almost stopped in the Chikandi (Faridpur) and Bolpur (Birbhum) courts due to picketing.[49] In Calcutta, during the course of one month, five air raid alerts had been sounded and eleven planes had been spotted far above the city.[50] There were reports of the removal of quarter-mile rails in Nilganj (between Bhairab and Mymensingh) and burning of sleepers; and an attack by 400 men on the railway line in Parbatipur, resulting in the removal of about one mile of rails and burning of sleepers to ashes.[51] On the Assam Bengal Railway, a quarter mile of rails were removed in Baihata and there were no traces of bolts and fishplates.[52] In Orissa, the people in Dhenkanal were actively involved in this fight for freedom. The Congress Radio narrated an incident in this context. A batch of volunteers, under the leadership of Baishnab Churan Patnaik, had mobilized the people. And when they were attacked by a regiment, Baishnab Churan Patnaik, though injured, was able to escape. The government declared a reward for his arrest.[53]

Despite all the restrictions, Congress Radio continued giving the news about the disturbances. In Karnataka, rails were removed or damaged at Belgaum, Alnavar, Nimbal and Hospet. Telegraph wires were cut at Athani, Akola, Kumta, Kottur, Hadgalli and other places. Roads and bridges were destroyed or damaged at Sindgi Road, Akola, Kumta, Shivnagi and Udupi.[54] At Hubli, the Bar Association passed a resolution asking the government to institute an inquiry into the police firing on 15 August 1942. A large number of the Congress workers, students and citizens were arrested from various places including Belgaum, Gokak, Hubli, Nargunda, Bagalkot, Kundapur, Bijapur and Udupi. Firing was reported at Belgaum and other places.[55] In Dharwar, the wayside stations at Amargol, Kusugal, Hebsur and Byadgi had been burnt or damaged. Telegraphic wires were cut and installations were broken.[56]

News from south India reflected the mood of the people. In Madras province a police outpost was burnt at Kadalangudi and police stations were burnt at Allur and Kovur in Nellore.[57] Students shouted nationalist slogans at some schools in Cochin State. When an Indian soldier was shot down by a 'Tommy' when he refused to carry out the latter's order, the Punjab Regiment retaliated by accounting for not less than seventeen lives of white soldiers.[58]

October 1942

The escalating war situation was driving the British government to adopt oppressive steps against the Indians. The Congress Radio was of the opinion that 'The Britishers are fond of copying Nazi brutality and may think the Nazi may take a lesson from their Anglo-Saxon Britishers.' However, it was quick to notice a ray of hope: 'Despite repression, the Movement throughout the country continues.'[59] It had merrily grabbed the news that during the last session of the Assembly, a procession of donkeys, representing the members of the Viceroy's Executive Council, was organized and paraded through the streets of Delhi.[60]

Covering the news about the people's hardships was important for the Congress Radio. Notorious bullies had been engaged to crush the unarmed people at many places in Bihar. For example, news from Darbhanga informed about a 'European Hitler' who was made the captain of a small band of soldiers and was given a free hand to deal with the local situation.[61] The plight of the poor was acute when a collective fine of Rs 6,000 was imposed on a small village, 15 miles from Muzaffarpur in Bihar, where the police assaulted people wearing khadi caps.[62]

It was further stated that the suffering of villages in the Central Provinces and the United Provinces during the previous two months was unceasing, collective fines were realized and over 50,000 Indians were killed. Reports from Brindaban conveyed that the worshippers were dragged from temples and their ornaments were stolen.[63] Women and persons holding a respectable position were also not spared if a shadow of doubt about their involvement in the movement crossed the minds of the British officers.[64] Listeners were informed that people faced difficulties in getting change against currency notes in Bihar, Calcutta and Travancore.[65]

Ushaben often told us that the Congress Radio was the first to communicate the news of the horrendous atrocities and rapes committed at Chimur in the Central Provinces. The Congress Radio gave a detailed report on these dreadful incidents with courage and conviction.[66] The Congress Radio apprised the listeners that the news gathered by the press reporters was not allowed to be published until they were censored by the censor officer.[67] However the radio managed to get the news and broadcast them boldly, including ghastly incidents like those in Chimur and other acts of oppression by the British authorities.

The Congress Radio brought out the participation and zeal of the workers and the economically deprived sections of the people. Talking about the disorder prevailing in Bihar, Orissa and Bengal, it stated that the workers of Ahmedabad had sustained a loss of 1–1.25 crore of rupees during the last two months. They firmly believed that the revolution of India was the revolution of poor people and it was no use expecting any sacrifice from the rich.[68] The workers at Tatanagar had continued their strike from 20 August to 3 September and the production of steel had come down from 72,000 to 35,000 tons in September. Prominent labour leaders had been arrested.[69]

An incident of the bravery of the people at Malkhachak village in Bihar and the martyrdom of Rajnarain Singh was narrated on the Congress Radio.[70] News of another courageous and patriotic act of people in Bihar was also

इन्कलाब के महामंत्र –

२०-१०-४२ (सत्र)
२१-१०-४२ (सुबह)

अंग्रेजों की गालियाँ देनेका वक्त गया गालियाँ होते हैं जिनकी शक्ति कम है और उन्हें दी जाती हैं जिनकी इज्जत कुछ भी तो बची हुई है। यों तो अंग्रेजों की रंगत का पता हर सच्चे हिन्दुस्तानी को लग ही चुका था। लेकिन लड़ाई के तीन बरसने तो इसे बिल्कुल ही साफ कर दिया। अंग्रेजी हुकूमत डरपोक और जुल्मदिल है, सिर्फ निहत्थों पर वार करना जानती है। निकम्मी और बेवकूफ है। सिर्फ दबे हुओं को दबाना जानती है। आदर्श और मजहब का नाम लेकर कम अस्सम उसे करती है। इस हुकूमत ने पिछले दो महीनेमें हम पर काफी जुल्मो सितम ढाये हैं। नन्हीं नन्हीं बच्चियों, बुढ़ी औरतों और नन्हीं नन्हीं तो गाँव की सभी स्त्रियों पर बलात्कार करवाया। उन्हें मार डाला है और दूसरी क्रिया है। साठ सत्तर हजार निहत्थों हमवतनियों को मार डाला है। हवाई जहाजसे गोले और गोलियाँ चलायी हैं। गाँव के गाँव उजाड़ आते हैं। इस हुकूमत को हम क्या गालियाँ दें। इसे तो हमें तोड़ना है। मिट्टी में मिलाना है। इतना पीसना है कि इसका एक जर्रा भी हमारी पवित्र भूमि को नापाक न करने पावे।

यह हुकूमत तो हमारे लिये क्रोध बन गयी है। हमारे अंग अंग को जलाती है। हमारे आत्मा को दुःखी करती है।

कुछ लोग हमसे नाखुश होते हैं कि हम अंग्रेजों को काफी गालियाँ नहीं देते, चपटी बातें नहीं कहते। यह काम तो हमने दूसरों के लिये छोड़ दिया है। हमारा काम तो आपसे काम लेना है। हम आपको बतायें, आप हमको बतायें कि अंग्रेजी हुकूमत को खत्म करने के लिये क्या क्या करना चाहिये।

अगर हमारा रास्ता हिंसा का हुआ होता और अगर हिन्दुस्तान की पत्तन में अंग्रेज न हुए होते, जिन्हें हम किसी तरह भी अपने साधन न कर सकते। तो मामला माफ था। हमारी कोशिश होती कि अंग्रेजों के हथियार निकम्मे बनें, उनको चलानेवाले हमारे साथ हों और हम कारगर हथियार इकट्ठे करें। लेकिन ये कोशिशें फिजूल हैं, न तो वह हमारा रास्ता ही है और न इस पर चलने से हमें हमारी सफलता ही मिल सकती है।

हमारा तो एक ही हथियार है सत्याग्रह। लेकिन ऐसा सत्याग्रह जिसकी लपटती हुई लपटों में अनीति और जुल्म भस्म हो जायें। हिन्दुस्तान ने अभी की बार सत्याग्रह के रुद्र और तांडव रूप को देखा है। पहले से सत्याग्रह इसकी तैयारियें थीं।

A Broadcast Bulletin (Hindi), 20 and 21 October 1942

transmitted: four jails in Bihar (the Arrah district jail, the Madhubani sub-jail, Hajipur sub-jail and Sitamarhi jail) were thrown open by the people and all the inmates released.[71] According to the Congress Radio, Bihar had declared an 'open rebellion' against the ruthless measures of the government to control the movement.[72]

The situation in Allahabad in the United Provinces also remained uneasy during October.[73] The acts of dislocation of telephone lines and cutting of telegraph wires in the United Provinces continued.[74] Many workers were arrested in Shankarpur in Bihar and the government had put restrictions on the constructive programme. Also many people were fired on in Darjeeling on 9 September.[75] There was further news of cutting the electric wires in many places. The railway lines were damaged in a village near Wardha. On 18 October a military train was derailed at Chalisgaon, where a Muslim sub-inspector and a circle inspector had resigned.[76] The Congress Radio was able to get the news about the restlessness among the textile workers in Ahmedabad,[77] and the disturbances in Gujarat, Bihar, Kolhapur and Bombay.[78]

News from the southern parts of the country also reflected the mood of the people. In Madras an ammunition train was derailed at Trichinopally: 10,000 gallons of petrol and 23 military transport lorries were burnt at Coimbatore; railway coolies were destroying railway lines at Bezwada; a government treasury was burnt in the province of Madras; and in Madura air-raid sirens were sounded to prevent people from gathering under Section 144 to celebrate Gandhi Jayanti.[79] Attention was drawn to the defiance of the students in Travancore[80] and the pathetic condition of political prisoners there.[81] It was reported that in Karnataka the villagers had accepted Gandhiji as their leader. The total number of arrests in Karnataka exceeded 1,600. There was dislocation of traffic and damage to the government property in Bijapur, Dharwar, Hubli, North Karwar and South Kanara. Moreover, many 'kulkarnis' had resigned.[82]

The eastern parts too were seething with revolutionary spirit. Significant damage was done to telegraph poles and railway lines in Bengal and Orissa by a storm.[83] News from Calcutta informed that since the commencement of the war in 1939 no locomotives had been imported into India. Moreover it was feared that during the coming year about 1,700 locomotives would be scrapped out. The jute industry in Calcutta had also been seriously affected.[84] In Bengal the people removed railway lines between the Dashghara and Hooghly stations.[85] The Congress Radio reported that the government in Orissa launched an offensive against the centres of constructive activities: the Khadi Bhandars of some places like Gangapur and Jeysore were declared illegal.[86]

A spontaneous move had sprung up amongst the peasants of Bengal to prevent the export of rice. The Congress Radio reminded the listeners of an earlier broadcast that the people of Bolepur (Tagore's university town), with the help of the Santhals, had prevented the export of 80,000 mounds of rice even though bullets were showered on them.[87] There were other reports of people's uneasiness and resistance. People in Orissa presented brave and fearless resistance. In Balasore, when the police came to arrest some workers at a village, the village leader collected people. Though unarmed, they resisted valiantly. The agents of the administration could not make any arrests but took away with them the bodies of fifteen dead patriots.[88] Unperturbed by the repressive steps, the Congress Radio had announced in a broadcast with deep conviction that 'We have to break the slavery of our country'.[89]

The Congress Radio received reports from Peshawar about brutalities in the North West Frontier Province.[90] People in this area were intensely involved with the ongoing agitation against the British government.[91] Another broadcast showed concern over the alarming situation in that province.[92] Highlighting the women's contribution to the movement, a broadcast announced that the women of an area in the NWFP marched in a procession to protest against the arrests of the Hindus and the Muslims, who had given food and shelter to Khudai Khidmatgars.[93] A broadcast praised the leadership of Allah Bux and criticized the formation of a new ministry by Ghulam Hussain Hidayatullah in Sind that had no support of the people.[94]

November 1942

On 5 November, the Congress Radio announced that it had unearthed a confidential letter dated 23 October 1942 from the provincial press adviser for Sind to all the editors showing how the government was trying to suppress all news concerning the interruptions of rail, road and telegraph communications and the delayed arrival of trains. The editors were asked not to publish such reports unless officially cleared by a competent authority.[95]

The Congress Radio continued dissemination of information about the unrest at the national level and about the gravity on the war front. It confidently declared that 'It is our last struggle and win we must.'[96] A broadcast on 2 November stated that the Japanese had torpedoed a ship near Kerala and Calicut and several dead bodies of American soldiers were found on the

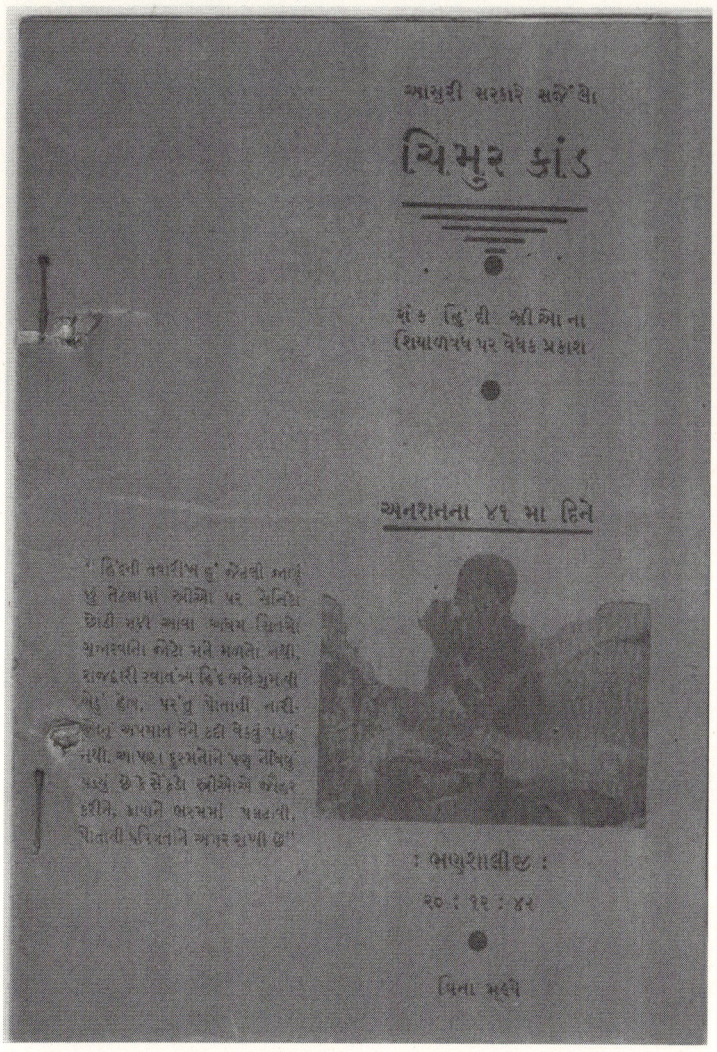

Cover-page of the booklet on Chimur atrocities
(in Gujarati)

seashore.[97] It was said on the Congress Radio that 'The British Imperialism speaks quite untrue while making propaganda against India.'[98]

Information was given about the gutting of three bungalows of government officers at Bardoli. Moreover, four post-boxes in Ahmedabad were set on fire including one at the Head Post Office; a truck carrying military uniforms was looted; telegraphic communication between Madhi and Kadod, between Kadod and Mandvi were also dislocated; many telegraph poles were destroyed and lengths of wire were missing.[99] By this time the positions supported by the government had lost their charm and aura. In Bardoli, eighty patels had already resigned. In Ahmedabad, Pesi Rustomji Jehangir Vakil, a leading businessman, resigned from the District War Committee. In his letter to the collector he explained how bitterly he felt about the atrocities committed by the government in the name of law and order. Incidents of cutting telegraph wires continued.[100]

Resignations continued as people proceeded to follow the path of their conviction: members of the Baripur village panchayat in Dabhoi district as well as nine members of the panchayat in two different villages in Amareli had all stepped down to protest against the repressive policy. As the complete hartal of the Surat market continued, the government was forced to release all the forty-five merchants unconditionally with a promise to withdraw the cases pending against them.[101] Another broadcast announced a positive result of the fast undertaken by the Desh Sevikas.[102]

News from Karnataka highlighted the dislocation of communication, damage to government property in many places and barbaric treatment of students-under-trial.[103] Disorder and agitation were widespread. On 4 November, a goods train was derailed between the Badami and Katgeri railway stations on the Gadag–Bijapur line of Madras and the Southern Maharatta Railway. Chalgeri railway station in Madras and the Southern Maharatta railway was set on fire, the building completely gutted and all records burnt.[104] Further information about the people's movement in places like Arsikere, Shantigrama taluka, Javagal and Shimoga was provided. There were reports from Mysore that the morale of the government officers was fast deteriorating in Hassan and other districts.[105]

A non-violent no-tax struggle had been launched by the rural people in Hassan and other neighbouring districts in Mysore. People refused to pay tolls and octroi duties at the weekly bazaars. The rights of collection at these bazaars were generally auctioned to contractors, but the people refused to pay the duty to the contractors and at places the contractors themselves cooperated with the people in making the bazaars free. The movement had become very popular with the village folk and was spreading from district to district.[106] The agitation continued relentlessly. On the Mysore–Bangalore line, a goods train was derailed at Seringapatam. On 28 October, a bomb exploding on a platform at Bangalore station damaged an engine and the railway line.[107] Burning and destruction of letter-boxes were also reported from Bangalore, other cities of Mysore and several places in Calcutta.[108] Two meetings of the Mysore Representative Assembly held on 19 and 29 October were boycotted by the Congress as a protest against the unwarranted arrest of fifty members. The newspapers had blacked out the proceedings.[109]

The news from Bengal indicated the intensity of the agitation. The telephone and telegraphic connections were destroyed by agitated persons in Ramourhat, many persons were arrested in several villages,[110] and the government rest house in Burdwan was burnt down.

A worrisome fact was that the political prisoners were ill treated in Bengal.[111] In Lokpur and another place, people had stopped the carts full of paddy and carried these away with them. Women also took part in this looting. Several carts full of rice were looted in the village of Shantipura. Such activities took place in almost all parts of India. The Congress Radio lauded women's participation in them.[112]

Harrowing accounts of the distress of people due to the cyclone havoc and military vengeance poured in from Midnapur, Bengal. After the mass uprising in the Tamluk subdivision, soldiers and aeroplanes were sent there: villagers were tortured and their houses were burnt.[113] In the first fortnight of the struggle, mass uprisings took place in almost all the districts of Andhra. These activities were mainly directed at capturing police stations and dislocation of communications. In Guntur and other districts the railway lines were severely damaged despite a vigorous watch by the government. Resignations from the police and other government servants were reported from some places including Cudappa and Bellary.[114]

There were news about unrest among the people in Bengal, Madras and Gujarat.[115] A goods train carrying military supplies was derailed near Lohta station a few miles from Benares and a railway godown was set on fire at a station three miles from Benares Cant.[116]

In Karachi, the boycott of the schools and colleges as well as the repressive actions of the government were intense. The examination of the Diploma of Engineering had to be cancelled as only one student had appeared. His classmates even destroyed his answer paper. The new Ghulam Hussain ministry treated the arrested political workers in a callous and brutal way.[117]

News from Maharashtra informed that the hold of the government was weakening visibly in the districts. To support this, the Radio gave detailed news about the strong resistance of the people in a village in Rajapur. The people's defiance and courage made the Congress Radio comment that this new spirit in the countryside was the undoing of the usurper authority of the government and that it was impossible to hold India's 7 lakh villages by military force.[118]

Ushaben often talked about the Congress Radio broadcasts and how they were able to give first-hand news of the movement and repression by the British authorities. In her opinion, the news about the atrocities in Chimur and the fast undertaken by Professor Bhansali in protest against them were of crucial importance, as such news were repressed. The news bulletins gave a detailed description of this incident.[119]

Conclusion

The Congress Radio advised the listeners to call their friends, neighbours and those who did not own the radio to listen to the broadcasts. It boldly proclaimed that 'Remember, the Congress Radio runs not for entertainment, not even for propaganda, but for giving certain directives to the Indian people in their fight for freedom. Talk of these directives and instructions, talk of our appeals to different classes of the population, talk of the arguments in our speeches, but never talk of the persons behind the Congress Radio. Let the whole country resound with a million voices all trained to talk uniformly by the only voice of truth and freedom in the country, the Congress Radio calling.'[120]

What is more than evident was that the Congress Radio continued to declare the people's firm resolve to attain independence. On the stand taken by the British Prime Minister Winston Churchill that he was not the king's chief minister to preside over the liquidation of the British empire, the Congress Radio posed a question and provided an answer too: 'Why did you, Mr Churchill, preside over the liquidation of your empire in China, Malaya, Burma, East Indies and of your oil and wheat and iron empires in Romania, Yugoslavia and Scandinavian countries? Of course, you did not do it willingly; you were made to do it.' Exhorting the people to cast away fearsome tremors, the broadcast boldly told them: 'Go wind up your trade or business. Leave your factory and go to the village. Throw the sinful war-contract you are still holding in your hands in the face of the Brigadier from whom you got it. Desert the college, the factory where slaves are produced. Let every day be a day of defiance. Yes, Churchill will not liquidate his empire; we will make him do it.'[121]

Ironically, this was the last available broadcast of the Congress Radio. Ushaben and Chandrakant were arrested on the night of 12 November while transmitting the news. Many years later Ushaben said that they were aware of the imminent danger of being caught by the police, but they had decided to voice the message of freedom loud and clear, undeterred by what fate had in store for them.

6

Diverse Perspectives

The extraordinary story of the Congress Radio, inextricable from political realism and patriotic passion, is also a story of various perspectives that came to light with the broadcasts and actions of the British authorities. Gandhi's evocative leadership was acknowledged by the Congress Radio and so were the ways in which disturbances and dislocation were put into action. Empathy for the poor and good for all were the ultimate aims and so were the discourses on protests and disturbances. The political perspective that emerged was enticing, though tangled. Yearning for freedom and power to people was conveyed through the broadcasts of news, sometimes with slamming words and at times through pronouncements couched in idealist romanticism. A fluid mixture of credible news and patriotic fervour made the Congress Radio popular and exciting. In a short span of time it consolidated its reputation as one of the most reliable means to get the news with its proud nationalist core. 'Calling from somewhere in India' accorded it shades of adventure, mystery and romantic

thrill. Its acknowledgement of its technical difficulties
and its direct communication to its listeners must have
endeared it to the people.[1] The short-lived feat appeared
like a shooting star on the national horizon with news and
speeches that aimed to stir the conscience of the nation.

Remembering the thrill of those exhilarating days
Ushaben said: 'In the speeches we mostly used to clarify
and explain the Congress (nationalist) stand, both from
the national and international points of view. The speeches
were mainly delivered by Dr Lohia and occasionally by
Achyut Patwardhan; some of the speeches were written
by eminent journalists, teachers and Congress workers.
Sucheta Kriplani and Aruna Asaf Ali were also helpful.
The broadcasts had news interspersed with songs, speeches
and messages. And of course Gandhi was our undisputed
leader and the British authorities were trying hard to catch
us.' The perspective it offered was obviously different from
that of the British government.[2]

The Perspective of the Congress Radio

The broadcasts from the Congress Radio captured the
mood of the turbulent times. Elaborating 'the nature of the
Indian Revolution', it had proclaimed that India could not
accept the traditional revolutionary way: it was its own
model and path-finder.[3] The Radio accepted the uneasy
and curious coexistence of the tactics of disruption and
disturbances with Gandhi's ideals and his unquestioned
leadership. People were exhorted to action. A broadcast
advised them: 'There are thousands of links in the chains of
this government. Break any link of the chain. Create such
a strength and power in every village and in the streets of
cities that even the shadow of the British may not enter

there.' However, in the same breadth it clarified: 'It is not our principle to throw bombs or stones on human beings. Ours is a new principle which goes to the new world where no one kills another or sucks another.'[4]

The Congress Radio was aware that the Congress was accused of having betrayed its policy of non-violence because of its attempts to paralyse the working of 'this usurper government', and the persons involved in the movement were criticized because of their neglect of Gandhi's ideals. Elucidating the ideal of non-violence in the context of the contemporary times, it pronounced that the dislocation of traffic, burning of government buildings and wrecking of factories were not acts of violence since these had been put to unjust use to perpetuate the slavery of the Indian people. They had, therefore, to be destroyed. It was the grim prerogative of the Indian nation to destroy its wealth in order to paralyse the usurper government, just as it was the grim prerogative of the individual Indian to die at the hands of this same usurper government. In the same breath it also proclaimed: 'In order that freedom be not delayed we are willing as Mahatmaji told—Let the Ganges flow with blood—but Indian blood. Let it be our proud claim that we won our freedom by non-violent means, that we neither killed nor crippled human beings. What we want to kill is human injustice, what we want to cripple is the usurper administration which perpetuates it.'[5]

Along with the disruption and dislocation, Gandhi and his ideas as well as the nature of the movement continued to hold their grip over the operators of the Congress Radio and other underground activities. The youth and the leaders in the movement were swept by the tidal wave of the agitation with its disquiet and trepidation, and yet they did not want to swerve from their allegiance to Gandhi nor was there at any time any question of severing their bond with Gandhi.[6] Gandhi and his message 'Do or Die' were often mentioned warmly by the broadcasters who stressed that the present revolution 'is the revolution of non-violence in which evil is made low and unable to raise its head.'[7] It is important to note that the appeal of the AICC to celebrate Gandhi's birthday (for a week) by organizing nationalist programmes was also read out in a broadcast.[8] The Congress Radio also asked people to observe 'Mahadev Desai Day'.[9]

For Gandhi, Quit India was a movement of crucial importance. Many were with Gandhi in his belief that so long as the British were present in India, it would not be possible to move forward towards the destination of freedom. In May, Gandhi wrote: 'Hitherto the rulers have said, "We would gladly retire if we know to whom we should hand over the reins." My answer now is, "Leave India to God. If that is too much, then leave her to anarchy."'[10] His resolve to protest against the British and to achieve freedom was firm.[11]

Vallabhbhai Patel's speech at the historic AICC session on 7 August at Gowalia Tank and broadcasted by the Congress Radio contained a powerful message of action by the people. According to him, 'So long as Gandhiji remains on the scene, we have only to do his bidding. We must obey his orders strictly and be disciplined. We must follow him strictly at every step that he puts before us. But if Gandhiji and all leaders are rounded up at the very start, there will be no question of going step by step. Then it is the duty of every Indian born in this country to put forth his utmost effort for furthering the cause of freedom. We shall carry out all programmes individually, collectively and simultaneously in whatever way we find useful within non-violence.'[12] These words proved to be prophetic, because Gandhi and other leaders were imprisoned soon after the AICC session and the people felt free to further the movement.

Ushaben often talked about these issues and justified the activity of the underground radio. She had faith in Dr Lohia's leadership while her devotion to Gandhi remained unswerving. She talked about an incident when Dr Lohia, Achyut Patwardhan and she were discussing their working secretly and she had expressed her doubt in this manner of working. In her words, 'Even at the risk of being impertinent, I said, "We are working secretly. There is a battle of wits between the government office and freedom fighters." Dr Lohia interrupted saying, "— such a programme cannot be run openly. Like Bapu we cannot give an advance notice of our programme to the government. So secrecy in this case is not only permissible but is absolutely necessary and completely excusable." Achyut Rao nodded his head and approved the policy of maintaining secrecy.' Many broadcasts reflected the ideas of the Congress socialist leaders who played an important role in the movement and for the collection of the material for the Radio.[13]

Gandhi and the socialist leaders shared warm relations and a deep concern for the deprived. However, they differed in their ways of implementation of these ideals. According to Gandhi, 'I have claimed that I was a socialist long before those I know in India had avowed their creed. But my socialism was natural to me and not adopted from any books. It came out of my unshakable belief in non-violence. No man could be actively non-violent and not rise against social injustice no matter where it occurred.'[14] Ideological differences between Gandhi and his contemporary socialist leaders, however, did not dampen their warmth at a personal level. The socialist leaders like Lohia continued their bulletins on the Congress Radio proclaiming acceptance of Gandhi as their leader. Years later, admitting his earlier criticisms of Gandhi, Jayaprakash Narayan expressed his feelings that '... in spite of our doubts and airs of ideological superiority, we were driven like leaves in Gandhiji's storm.'[15]

The Congress Radio was convinced that the Quit India campaign was not untimely or mistaken; it was, in fact, the only basis for an effective mobilization of the Indian people for a war against the Axis. Talking about the nature of the Indian revolution, it declared with passion that, 'All relationships are broken, all family ties gone, all friendships withered, except the one that arises out of common suffering and binds each Indian to his fellows. There is only one family in the country today, the big family of the Indian nation struggling to form the Free State of India. Once this big family has achieved its aim, but not before that, can the joys of life truly come and the little family ties flower and the friendships grow.'[16]

There were strong messages of the unity of people, especially Hindu–Muslim unity. A broadcast of the Congress Radio offered Eid greetings to the Muslims. It opined that the greatest lie which had been spoken was that the demand for freedom was being made only by some people and 9 crore Muslims were against the independence of India. In fact, the Muslims had always fought for the country's freedom.[17]

Connecting the issue of India's independence with the prevailing international scenario, the Congress Radio brought to the notice of the listeners that the same urge for freedom that was driving the brave Russians or free Frenchmen under Nazi heels to acts of defiance, resistance and sabotage was also driving the Indian people to similar acts of defiance.[18]

* * *

The Congress Radio tried frantically to make its listeners aware of the oppression of the people by the British authorities. It revealed that Lumley, the governor of Bombay, had addressed a signed personal letter to the police officers in the province of Bombay, assuring them that there would be no inquiry for the use of excessive force by them.[19]

The Radio never missed any opportunity to express its strong disapproval of the way the British administration had exploited India. A passionate speech, 'Why is India Dying of Hunger?' on the Congress Radio pointed out the hollowness of the statements of Amery, Secretary of State for India.[20]

There was another strong criticism against the government policy. Jamsaheb of Nawanagar, a member of the British war cabinet, had suggested the Indianization of the Viceroy's Executive Council. But Amery refused to agree. The agitated broadcast on 20 October declared: 'Someday this savage story of brutal repression will be written in letters of blood by Indian martyrs truthfully laid down and are now laying down their blood for their sacred cause.... There are times when repression requires a vigorous answer. That time has come now.'[21]

The Congress Radio was mindful about the British hold over the Indian press and opposed it strongly. In a fervent broadcast it stated: 'One of the most powerful weapons which the usurper administration has marshalled against Free India is the Press, muzzled and controlled to such an extent that it becomes a pitiable tool without will or vision.'[22] The operation of the underground radio itself was a bold initiative of advocacy for freedom of thought and expression.

* * *

The Congress Radio declared in an impassioned way that the government had to be burned to ashes. It advised that the Indians should sever all connections with the Britishers. 'Try to disconnect the communication between cities and villages. Try to abolish the divisions of provinces made by the British government falsely. Try to preserve the grains with the farmers. Try to stop the work in the cities. The citizens can work in villages. They can maintain themselves with whatever they can get in the villages. This is the underlying principle of Gandhi's "Do or die". If the farmers do not sell grains, the government machinery will come to a standstill. The military will not get sufficient food to eat.'[23]

It confidently told the people that in the event of an invasion, an event far from impossible, Indians would have to depend on themselves; the British would not help.[24] In another broadcast it informed that the situation in wartime was volatile and fluid. In Malabar, some Japanese submarines were reported to be operating along the west coast and other areas. In Bengal, five British ships carrying cargo were reported to have been sunk in the Bay of Bengal. There was a fifty-five-minute air-raid alarm in Calcutta. Due to the British vandalism, 550 were dead in Calcutta. The Congress Radio stated: 'Let it be clear that in the event of Japanese invasion, the British administration will be entirely demoralized as was seen before. You should capture the administrative machinery, declare the Free State of India and hoist the national flag.'[25]

The Congress Radio had great faith in the ability of the people. It claimed: 'Without us no government can prevail and no army can march to victory. Let us make our strength felt. Let us do or die.'[26] Eulogizing the sacrifice of the people, it had declared in its special talk on Blackout Diwali: 'Thousands of homes have offered their highest sacrifice so that the light of freedom may burn more brightly in this land.'[27]

The Congress Radio tried to guide the people in their daily life. It enumerated ten duties that every Indian could perform without any risk. These included not transacting business with the British and withdrawing money from the government banks.[28] Indians were advised to picket the offices of foreign goods and factories peacefully. They were further advised to collect funds for national work, achieve Hindu–Muslim unity, keep the *charkha* in homes, and make the villages self-supporting.[29] Through its broadcasts the Radio tenaciously appealed to the people to leave cities and go to the villages, to withdraw deposits from the post offices, and not to visit cinema houses.[30]

A special appeal was made to the businessmen. They were urged to close their factories, shops and offices, to live a life of respect and not to fear.[31] On one occasion, the Congress Radio presented the statement of the AICC regarding government contracts. It said that the government contracts did not mean anything but killing of one's own brothers. The contractors and merchants were asked to stop government work and there was a call to spread the statement of the AICC throughout the country. If the situation did not improve till 15 November, it was proclaimed that it would be the duty of every person to picket those factories that prepared war materials.[32]

The Congress Radio was aware that one of the most glorious aspects of the Indian struggle was the spontaneous resistance that it had evoked from the youth of India. The carefully planned system of education by the British authority had not succeeded in breaking the spirit of the Indian youth. The spirited broadcast advised the students to be friends of peasants and workmen and go to the villages.[33]

It is important to note that the Congress Radio was concerned with women's safety and the issue of rape. When a question was asked: 'How can we prevent mass rapes of our women by soldiers? What should we do?', the response was clear: 'Without hesitation, we answer: do all that you can. You should, of course, try to prevent acts of rape as any other by non-violent resistance; but if you are free and are still alive, then kill or get killed. Rape is outside politics. It is the most bestial thing any Indian can imagine.'[34]

The Congress Radio broadcasted Gandhi's appeal to the soldiers made in his speech on 8 August: 'an order to fire on our own people we shall never obey.'[35]

The Perspective of the British Government

The perspective of the uneasy British rulers, however, was in sharp contrast with the one adhered to by the Congress Radio. In a document prepared by them, *Congress Responsibility for Disturbances 1942–43*, it pointed out in clear terms that 'Only one answer can be given to the question as to who must bear the responsibility for the mass uprisings and individual crimes which have disgraced and are still disgracing the fair name of India. That answer is—the Indian National Congress, under the leadership of Mr Gandhi.'[36]

The British government felt extremely hassled by the severe criticisms levelled by the Congress Radio against its policies and actions. The government of Bombay communicated to the government of India that as the government was probably aware, a persistent attack on the currency in India was being carried on through Congress Radio broadcasts and Congress bulletins. The government of Bombay suggested for the consideration of the government of India the starting of a publicity campaign designed to counter this attack. It offered to make the fullest use of any material supplied by the government of India which could be used for publicity.[37]

After the seizure of the Congress Radio there was an important communication from the government in Delhi to the home secretary to the government of Bombay in December 1942 showing concern about the Congress Radio. It stated,

> We were, of course, most interested to hear of your success in unearthing the Congress Radio Station in Bombay and arresting persons connected with it. We understand that your people monitored the broadcasts from the station pretty fully. It seems to us that a careful collation of these Congress broadcasts with those issued from Japanese or Japanese-controlled stations, and also a full account of the persons responsible for the Congress broadcasts, might have a most important bearing on the enquiry into the responsibility for the disturbances in which we are now engaged and might afford further evidence of what we may call the 'Fifth Column' aspect of those disturbances.'

The Bombay government was asked for a full report on the subject, copies of monitors' records, history sheets of persons connected and general comments.[38] Accordingly, a report was sent by the Commissioner of Police, Bombay, on the Congress Radio Case, with history sheets of the persons connected with the enterprise—Vithaldas (alias Babubhai) Madhavji Khakar, Vithaldas Kanthadbhai Jhaveri, Nanak G. Motwane, Usha Mehta, Chandrakant Babubhai Jhaveri, Jagannath Raghunath Thakor and Nariman Adarbad Printer—to the Home Department.[39]

The fear and anxiety of the government in Delhi about the 'Fifth Column' aspect of the Congress Radio were put to rest by the government in Bombay. H.V.R. Iyengar, additional secretary to the Government of Bombay's Home Department, and C.H. Bristow, adviser to the Government of Bombay, gave their studied opinions.[40] H.V.R. Iyengar, in his balanced and comprehensive note, stated: 'I used to listen to the broadcasts (though it was not always pleasant doing so owing to poor reception) and have now gone through the monitor reports and the summaries prepared by Mr Scott. I used also to listen to Tokyo and Saigon; and though we have not, as the government of India have, the monitor reports of these broadcasts, I have sufficient recollection of them to be able broadly to compare them with the Congress broadcasts. My opinion was and is that these do not furnish any specific evidence of Fifth Column inspiration.'

He further commented: 'Undoubtedly the Congress broadcasts must have brought aid and comfort to the enemy, as indeed must the whole civil disobedience movement. The main themes of the Congress station were, as will be seen from the passages marked in the monitor reports, that people should leave the cities and go back to the villages (an advice repeated time and again); that the villagers should adopt a policy of self-sufficiency and refuse to sell to middlemen; that they should stop working in factories as the goods manufactured there will be used against them; that they should not work the railways as the railways convey the troops which are holding them down, and so on. And of course, there are wild exaggerations of the progress of the "revolution" and the "brutalities" of the British government in suppressing it—stories which Saigon, in particular, repeated with great gusto.'

Iyengar presented a relevant point: 'But the question is not whether the Congress station gave comfort to the enemy, but whether it was inspired by it. I suppose, in a very much smaller way, a parallel case is the *New Leader* of London which inveighs regularly against the Imperialist nature of the war Britain is fighting; the weekly must be of some comfort to Dr Goebbels, but few would say that Maxton or Fenner Brockway was in the pay of the German Propaganda Ministry.'

This well-studied note captured the contemporary politics: 'Apart from repeating stories about the success of the "revolution" and the brutalities of the British, the recurrent theme of the Tokyo and Saigon station was that Japan was coming to give deliverance and independence to India: "We are your friends. We are coming to make you free." The Congress Radio made no such statement; though, being an illegal and secret station, it was in a position to say whatever it wanted to say. On the contrary, what it said was "The British are our enemies, and we must drive them out." There is, of course, to any ordinary thinking mind, a most dangerous lacuna in the argument here, viz. that the British could not be driven out without bringing the Japanese in or that with the British quitting

India, Indian independence at this stage is not worth a moment's purchase. But this lacuna was the big gaping void in the whole of Gandhi's arguments and is evidence of a dangerous hallucination but not necessarily of enemy inspiration.'

Iyengar argued cogently: 'There is much evidence of Congress Socialist philosophy in the broadcasts. I have heard from private sources that Ram Manohar Lohia, an underground Congress Socialist who refused to make common cause with Subhash Chandra Bose, was the main inspiration of these broadcasts, and certainly there is internal evidence in support of this. For instance, on 20 October the station said "We have learnt bitter lessons of democracy of the West—enslavement of the working class and peasantry." On 23 October it stated, "The free India will be of farmers, workers and labourers." Again on 27 October it repeated, "Revolution for freedom is the revolution for the poor. The free India will be of the workers and peasants." There was no wholesale condemnation of the allies and praise of the enemy. On 20 October the broadcast said, "To the world mankind, the Indian people send a message of hope, of peace and goodwill. Let us forget today the violence done by one people upon another. Let us only remember that for the establishment of a truly peaceful and better world we need each country's kindness, each people's individual acts. We need Germany's technical skill, her scientific knowledge, her music. We need England's liberalism, her courage and literature. We need Italy's elegance. We need the old achievements and new triumphs of Russia. We need the gift of laughter—beautiful, laughter-loving Austria. We need her culture, her love of gracious living, and China— what shall we say of China? We need her wisdom, her courage and her new hope. We need the glow and spirit of adventure of young America. We need the knowledge, the childlike simplicity of the primitive people. We need all mankind for the resurrection of peace, for the resurrection of her own dignity." This is in violent contrast to the tone of enemy broadcasts which have never admitted England's "liberalism, courage and literature" or the "culture and gracious living of China".'

After analysing the data, Iyengar concluded, 'In my opinion, the personality and antecedents of the people connected with the Congress station and the nature of its broadcasts suggest that it was the work of Congress and Congress Socialist people and that it derived its inspiration from Congress and Congress Socialist leaders and not from the enemy.'

Commenting on the note, C.H. Bristow, adviser to the Government of Bombay, opined that 'The above seems a fair summary. The Congress Radio is characteristic of the Congress attitude and is essentially anti-British. It attacks what are considered the chief features of British rule viz. capitalism, industrialism and war effort. It encourages all means of bringing that rule to an end, by stopping communications, removing labour from industry by a return to the villages and by boycott. It excuses sabotage by comparing it to the destruction caused in war. As Additional Secretary has pointed out it carefully avoids pro-Jap propaganda, no doubt because the majority of listeners are not pro-Jap. The purpose behind it is to foster anti-British feeling without facing the practical necessity of a choice between the British government and Japanese domination. The authors may have made use of Japanese broadcasts and may themselves be pro-Japs but there is nothing plainly pro-Jap in the broadcasts. The attitude taken is that Congress stands for higher things, peace, a prosperous peasantry, goodwill to the best in all countries and no foreign domination. This is typical of Congress propaganda and fits in with the Congress aim of breaking down British rule in order to establish their own, with deliberate refusal to face the hard fact that India is not in a position to stand alone. There is no sign of fifth column inspiration, however much the propaganda may assist the enemy.'

The government thus settled the issue of the 'Fifth Column' idea behind the Congress Radio.

The Perspective of an Announcer

Details about the announcers and many who in some way or another contributed to the working of the Congress Radio are beguiling but hazy. They did their share of what they thought was patriotic and moved on without any desire for recognition after independence. Interestingly, we find that Khwaja Ahmad Abbas, the eminent journalist and writer, has remembered his experiences with the Congress underground Radio in his autobiography. One of the jobs assigned to him (he never asked by whom) was to record the news bulletins which were then transmitted from somewhere else. Every time they were recorded and transmitted from a different place—on the second floor of a jeweller's shop where there was an arrangement that in case anyone suspected to be a policeman was seen entering the shop, one of the assistants would press a button hidden under his counter to warn those who were busy recording; or on the fourth floor terrace of a building on Walkeshwar Road where there was no staircase, only a lift, which would be taken up and conveniently 'broken down' by the simple expedient of keeping the door open.

Another place which he remembered was a coal cellar, the way to which went through a very orthodox Jain kitchen in a bungalow near French Bridge. This place was almost opposite to Dr Baliga's nursing home, which itself was a hideout for many of the socialist underground workers. Once he dropped in to see Dr Baliga in his nursing home. After a jovial conversation, he told Dr Baliga that he had come 'somewhere near' for recording (he knew exactly where) and thought he would take a chance to call on the doctor. After a while the doctor inquired about Abbas's friends in the Communist Party. And Abbas named several, including Sajjad Zahir, Mehmood-uz-Zafar, Sibtay Hasan and Sardar Zafri, most of whom were also known to Dr Baliga. Dr Baliga then placed before him a new issue of *People's War*, which had a paragraph saying that the Nazis had started broadcasting from somewhere in Germany 'on a powerful transmitter' in the name of the Congress Radio. When Abbas asked what he should do, Dr Baliga said, 'Go there and have a cup of tea. Ask them if they listen in to the clandestine Congress Radio and then enjoy the fun.' Abbas knew what he meant, but he also knew about the bitter communist–socialist feud, each accusing the other of 'betrayal'. And so he asked whether they would pass on the information to the police. Dr Baliga, who seemed to know both the camps, said with conviction: 'They are fools. But they will never do that. I know them.'

Thereafter Abbas went to Raj Bhawan, the CPI office on Sandhurst Road in Girgaum. He met Ali Sardar Zafri and Sibtay Hasan and had tea with them in the Irani restaurant downstairs. Abbas asked them whether they heard the Congress Radio. They replied that they did not, but the monitor did. It was so powerful that it was clearly audible as if it was located in Bombay. When Abbas asked whether it was possible that it was located in Bombay, they said 'impossible'. Then Abbas pointed out that they had not heard it; he urged them to hear it once and then be convinced. He told them: 'You will find no Nazi or fascist propaganda from the Congress Radio.' When Sibtay asked him whether he had something to do with it, Abbas said real conspiratorially that 'Walls have CIDs hidden behind them.' And he left. Three days later Sibtay met Abbas and said 'I heard the Congress Radio last night. I agree with you.' Then lowering his voice, 'But you have to be careful.'[41]

Some of the recordings were played in the court when the Congress Radio case came up to the court. A reporter who was present there later told Abbas that he could clearly identify his voice in one of the records played there, but no journalist would reveal to the judge that he could identify the speaker of that particular recording.

Abbas talked about an interesting aspect of the Congress Radio. Once he went to the Communist Party office where people were discussing that a new radio station called the Congress Radio had started functioning. They said that this radio was supposed to be somewhere in Bombay. But in their opinion they knew very well that it was a Nazi radio that was operating from Germany, Italy or probably from Japan and they just called themselves 'Congress Radio'. K.A. Abbas could not contradict them or say that he had just come from this secret radio station and that it was within a stone's throw of the Communist Party office! Abbas has perceptively observed that such a thing was very usual at that time, because many of them (journalists and writers) were on both sides of the fence; in many economic matters, in many cultural matters they were cooperating with the Communist Party which at that time was supporting the war effort. And on other things they were cooperating with the Congress organization, for instance in the running of this secret Congress Radio. And this was a peculiarity of the national movement, that there was a dialogue, and even cooperation, between people holding different points of view which were so sharply divided at that critical moment.[42]

* * *

The Congress Radio cherished the affectionate support from the people. It claimed to be 'the voice of the Indian people.' It had proclaimed passionately: 'To the British usurper we say, leave off trying to find this voice. You may find a set in Bombay, but what of the sets in Calcutta, Delhi, Allahabad, Bangalore, Nagpur and other places. You may find one set in Bombay, but in its place will spring up two still more powerful. Where will you escape this voice, it will haunt you wherever you go, to the right of you, to the left of you, above you, behind you, in front of you, this voice of truth and freedom and democracy and peace, it will go through you and show you up in all your nakedness of beastly terror until you are made to quit this fair country of ours.'[43]

It is ironic that the underground Congress Radio was seized two or three days after this fiery and fervent warning. However, by that time it had carved a niche for itself in the history of the freedom struggle by its sincere efforts for the dissemination of information about the freedom struggle. In times where the means of communications were limited and restraints imposed by the government were strict and severe, it stands out as an example of courage and conviction to die for the sake of the nation's independence. Its voice evoking freedom of speech and expression, though short-lived, was loud and clear.

Afterword

Interestingly, even after the seizure of the Congress Radio, there appeared to be some unsuccessful, though ardent and earnest, attempts to keep the underground radio alive; most of these efforts took place in Bombay.

In an official note it was stated that the Congress Radio had once again come on the air on a wavelength of 45 metres, and an announcement to this effect had appeared in the Bombay Congress bulletins issued between 6 and 9 January 1943 (both days inclusive). Based on the assumption that the transmission would be heard only on Tuesdays and Thursdays at 8.45 p.m. and on Sundays at 12 noon, arrangements were made to intercept the broadcasts at the Police Wireless Station. At first, nothing could be heard on Tuesdays and Thursdays, except for some suspicious sounds and short announcements to the effect that the Congress Radio was calling and could be heard at the announced time on Sundays on a wavelength of 42.34 metres. However, it was not until 11 February that the Congress bulletins again announced that the Congress

Radio would be on the air at 8.45 p.m. on a wavelength of 42.34 metres. Approximately at 8.45 p.m. every night since 11 February 1943, the Congress Radio came on the air; and the transmissions were between fifteen and thirty minutes in duration. The talks (from gramophone records) were devoted almost entirely to the situation arising out of Gandhi's fast. On account of interferences and distortions, however, it was not possible to receive the station clearly at the Police Wireless Section and so no arrangements could be made to monitor the broadcasts. The original interception of the station disclosed that the station was probably somewhere in or near Bombay Island. Military assistance was requisitioned, and on 13 February 1943, three military wireless detector vans arrived in Bombay. The unit appeared to have established definitely that the broadcasting station was somewhere in the Khetwadi locality.[1] Another report mentioned that there had been no broadcasts from the illegal Congress Radio since 6 March 1943. The Bombay Congress Bulletin of 11 March 1943, however, had announced that the radio would be on the air again that evening.[2]

In this context, a Lucknow report dated 2 December 1942 is important. It refers to a message from Ram Sharma of Agra, who had returned to Delhi from Bombay on 28 November 1942, to Dr K.N. Gairola (a professor at the Benares Hindu University, who played an important role in mobilizing the students). The message from 'AICC' was that Dr Gairola was urgently required in Bombay to help install a wireless transmitting set there to be used for broadcasting Congress news from a soundproof house in Bombay. The report added that Ram Manohar Lohia was in charge of the All India Congress Publicity Office in Bombay which had four or five transmitting sets. Gairola had accordingly left for Bombay.[3]

On 26 January 1944, a government report noted that an illegal Congress Radio broadcast was heard at 9.05 a.m. announcing that Ram Manohar Lohia and Achyut Patwardhan would broadcast from the Congress Radio Station at 8.45 p.m. But at the scheduled time, a couple of national songs were recited and someone read speeches in Hindi and Marathi. These seemed to have been made by Ram Manohar Lohia and Achyut Patwardhan, on the significance of Independence Day, appealing to the people to carry on the Civil Disobedience movement and announcing that the broadcast would be put out every Wednesday and Sunday evening.[4]

* * *

Motivated by the success of the underground radio in Bombay, Ram Manohar Lohia had made efforts to establish a radio station in Calcutta; later, Lohia and Jayaprakash Narayan undertook another venture to incorporate a Congress Radio in Nepal as well. However, these endeavours could not go through. Lohia had taken a transmitting set assembled in Bombay to Calcutta in the beginning of August 1943, but all his labours were in vain because of the non-availability of batteries in Calcutta.[5]

Listening to the news of the people's movement on a radio was a thrilling experience of those times and possession of a radio was considered valuable. A broadcast two or three days before the seizure of the Congress Radio had proclaimed: 'Tune in to the Congress Radio, whatever the consequences. The usurpers have already seized a number of receiving radios in Wardha, Amraoti, Allahabad and several towns of Assam. Compel them to seize all the radios in the country, so that if the voice of truth cannot be heard, the lies sought to be spread by the AIR and the BBC may be smothered before they emerge from their manufactory. But do not surrender your radios whole to the police. Damage them, break them, smash them—these usurpers should not get anything whole from us.[6]

There is also a reference to an underground radio broadcasting station that operated in Poona (now Pune) from the end of August 1942 for two months. It was the initiative of Shirubhau Limaye and his associates, including L.K. Deshpande, Vasant Bapat and S.M. Joshi, and delivered the news of the movement and energetic lectures by leaders like Sane Guruji.[7]

Ram Manohar Lohia's name is often referred to in the context of the underground radio. Ushaben had paid rich tributes to him in her interview with the United Press of India soon after she was released from Yervada prison, Poona. In her words, he was 'the soul behind the whole organization'. While in prison, she had received this message from him: 'History will judge one day whether I was right or wrong in sending you to broadcast on the day of the arrest.'[8]

* * *

To withstand the harsh steps taken by the government to curb the Quit India movement, some leaders who had avoided being arrested went underground to keep the movement alive. There was a central directing organization, the Central Directorate, Central Council of Action or the AICC.[9] According to Wickenden, this central body, with its headquarters in Bombay, comprising both ordinary Congressmen and Congress socialists, directed to the best of its ability the movement throughout the

Cover page of *Quit India* by Mahatma Gandhi

country, issued general instructions, received reports, supplied funds and stimulated where stimulation was required. It was recognized throughout the country as authoritatively representing the Congress and working out the August resolution.[10]

The Central Directorate in Bombay was of vital importance to the movement and the Congress Radio. The underground leaders managed to conduct the movement to such an extent that Bombay was filled with exceptional energy and vibrancy. According to Wickenden, Bombay had as many as eleven members who had managed to avoid arrest. In reality, fifty-three AICC members had escaped arrest in the first instance and all of them remained in concealment with the intention of advancing the movement.[11]

According to K.K. Chaudhari, the story of the underground movement in Bombay city extended over a long period of about thirty-five months from 9 August 1942 up to June 1945. Though all those working underground drew inspiration from Gandhi, their immediate mentors during this phase were the leaders of the Central Directorate: Achyut Patwardhan, Purshottam Trikamdas, Dr M.D.D. Gilder, Khurshedben, Dr Lohia, Aruna Asaf Ali, Jayaprakash Narayan and Sucheta Kriplani.[12]

Wickenden had noted that the Bombay office was located in a rented room. Among the staff were Sadiq Ali and Ram Charan Pande, who had been mentioned as Sucheta Kriplani's secretary under the pseudonym of Satya Prakash.[13] According to T.K. Tope, who had participated in the movement, 'In the 1942 movement the underground Directorate was having its headquarters in Cathedral Street of Kalbadevi; then it was shifted to Govind Building.'[14] Hutchins also stated that an 'AICC office' operated secretly for a time from room no. 30 on the second floor of

Patladhis Mala, No. 69/87 Cathedral Street, Bombay, and later shifted to room no. 16 on the second floor of Govind Building, Khetwadi Main Road, Bombay.[15]

The underground leaders who had great organizational skills and an amazing ability to raise resources (financial and personnel) quickly wove an influential network of workers. The skeleton staff kept on changing. Pseudonyms and false/fictitious names and addresses were frequently used for secret activities as they were essential for effective underground functioning. Chandrakant Mehta, who participated in the movement and underground activities and who was Ushaben's brother, remembered how the underground leaders had assumed different names, so that if a worker were arrested, the police would not get correct names from him/her. Not only that, the leaders used to change their pseudonyms at certain intervals, so that even if the police came to know about them, they would not get arrested. At that time Dr Lohia was called 'Vaid' (Doctor), Jayaprakash Narayan was known as 'Mehta', Aruna Asaf Ali as 'Kusum', Sucheta Kriplani as 'Didi' and Chandrakant Mehta as 'Prabhat'.[16] In his statement, Ram Sevak Mataprasad Pandey, residing in Bombay and connected with underground activities, revealed assumed names of some persons in the AICC office circle—J.B. Kriplani was 'Dada', Sucheta Kriplani was 'Dadi', Ram Manohar Lohia was 'Doctor', Aruna Asaf Ali was 'Kadam', Achyut Patwardhan was 'Kusum' and Sadiq Ali was 'Saty' or Satyaprakash Ji or 'Sushila'. 'Ramesh' was the person who looked after the underground office of the AICC and 'Kikaji' was the person in contact with the underground AICC Directorate.[17]

* * *

Another important component of the movement was the publication of illegal pamphlets and booklets spreading the message of freedom and provoking disturbances. A review of 'the disturbances which followed the sanctioning of a mass movement by the AICC on 8 August 1942' prepared by the Home Department, Government of India, in early 1943 mentioned that soon after 8 August 1942, 'floods of illegal pamphlets appeared in many parts of the country. These inflammatory pamphlets did a great deal of harm in the initial stages of the movement and played an important part in fomenting trouble in rural areas, which followed the first outbursts in towns. Most of the early leaflets were issued in Mr Gandhi's name.'[18] A pamphlet 'ABC of Dislocation' was also circulated. An elaborate plan for the formation of a nationwide guerrilla force called Azad Dastas (Free Bands, in evocation of the name of the Azad Hind Fauj, the Indian National Army then advancing through Burma) was mentioned in it.[19]

The people, especially the youth, were instinctively attracted to such activities. However, of particular interest were Gandhi's ideas. A booklet entitled *Quit India* (a collection of passages from Gandhi's writings and speeches) was compiled by R.K. Prabhu and U.R. Rao and edited by Yusuf Meherally. Three thousand copies of this little book that 'made publishing history', published on 8 August, were sold out in six days. When the second edition was published on 15 August, more than 500 copies were sold in one day and the entire stock of 3,000 copies of the second edition was sold by the end of the second week.[20]

The contraband bulletins and leaflets, published during the movement, are important and interesting. The first leaflet in Bombay, copies of which were seized on 9 August at Shivaji Park, was a student production entitled

No. 1] Wednesday, Aug. 25. 1943 [Four As.

Editorial on International Affatirs
CATANIATED BRITISH.

In the entire Sicilian adventure of the allies, the most notable fact is the total absence of British victories. The British, indeed, took Augusta. held it for a day or so, lost it to the Germans and, for more than three weeks after, stayed put in front of Catania. Meanwhile, the Americans went right round the island clockwise, capturing one city after another, until they and the Canadians pounced upon the Germans from the North and the West. In reality, the Americans took Catania. But with the brazenness so characteristic of their propaganda. the British announced to a now-not-quite-so easily to be-fooled world that their

Inquilab, No. 1, 25 August 1943

'Fight for Freedom' issued in the name of 'Azad Student'. *Quit India* was edited either by Purshottam Trikamdas or Achyut Patwardhan. While 'The Bombay Congress Bulletin' and *Quit India* were circulated from Bombay to various parts of the country, there also were other bulletins in circulation in Bombay such as 'War of Independence', 'Azad Patrika', 'Kamagar Patrika' and 'Vande Mataram'.[21] 'Revolt' was brought out by students in Bombay. 'Ittehad' was edited by Amtussalam. Mohinuddin Harris and Nasrulla Abbasi edited the Urdu edition of 'The Bombay Congress Bulletin'. Some of them continued to appear till as late as March 1944.[22]

Ninth August, the fortnightly journal of the Indian National Congress, priced at 4 annas and edited by Achyut Patwardhan, was a very popular underground publication. Ushaben would often talk about it, even though she was in jail when it appeared. Its first issue had appeared on 9 August 1943 to mark a year of the leaders' arrest and the launch of the movement. In it, Achyut Patwardhan had boldly sent a message to the comrades released from jails: 'A nation of 40 crore can never be crushed. An epic struggle led by a unique leader like Gandhiji must and will succeed.'[23]

The opening line in the journal's second issue dated 23 August 1943 quoted Percy Bysshe Shelley: 'You are many, they are few.' The messages of the valiant and spirited underground leaders in the journal were stimulating and enhanced the morale of the people.[24] Quotes by Gandhi and poets like Lord Byron often would appear on the front page of *Ninth August*. In its issue of 9 January 1944, an appeal was made to remember the pledge of independence, to strike, to fly the national flag on houses and to display in schools, colleges, cinemas or restaurants slogans like

'Britishers! Quit India!', 'Hail Independence!', and 'Do or Die'.[25] Various issues of the journal covered important national and international news like the oppression by the British, miseries of the Indians, unrest in Bengal and the work of Subhash Chandra Bose's army.

Inquilab was another fortnightly that Ushaben fondly remembered. In its issue of 25 November 1943 it proclaimed that 'The country must show visible signs of activity and defiance. The British must know that they cannot get away with weak or lowly terms.'[26]

* * *

It is remarkable that all the five accused in the Congress Radio case, though retaining their nationalist ideas, never attempted to achieve any glory or fame for their work after Independence. Vithaldas (Babubhai) Madhavji Khakar, Chandrakant Babubhai Jhaveri and Nanak G. Motwane pursued their respective businesses.

Vithalbhai Jhaveri continued with his involvement in the activities that promoted Gandhian values and preserved the memories of the independence struggle. He worked hard to collect and preserve photographs and footage as well as films of Gandhi. He documented Gandhi through numerous photographs that were displayed at many exhibitions and used in some books. He collaborated with D.G. Tendulkar for *Mahatma: Life of Mohandas Karamchand Gandhi* (in eight volumes) that remains a significant source of information for scholars and concerned readers. His contribution to making *Mahatma*, the authentic and gripping documentary on Gandhi's life, has been very important. He was awarded the Padma Bhushan by the government of India in 1969.

Ushaben remained committed to the democratic and Gandhian ideals till the end. She received many honours and accolades. The government of India conferred the Padma Vibhushan (the second highest civilian honour in India) on her in 1998. In Ushaben's words, her engagement with the Congress Radio was her 'finest time'. Paying glowing tribute to her contribution in the operation of the Congress Radio, Dr Ram Manohar Lohia, in his letter from Central Jail, Agra, to Professor Harold Laski, wrote a paragraph about her:

> There is a young woman in a Bombay jail, Miss Usha Mehta, perhaps the only woman political in the jails of that province, who is doing a term of four years for running a freedom radio. I am not quarrelling with her sentence, although, had this young woman of rare attainment and rare courage been Spanish or Russian, your countrymen would have glamorised her into a heroine. . . . I might add that her trial and that of her colleagues was banned from the newspapers.[27]

Ushaben remained a great source of inspiration for many, including her friends, colleagues and students. A professor of repute, she was a much-sought figure in public life. Her selfless nature and her genuine concern made people gravitate towards her. Her lifelong concern was towards the service to the nation and working for a better society. She was always guided by a strong sense of duty. Once when I had asked about the motivating factor that led to her working with the Congress Radio, she had replied calmly, 'I just did what I had to. I just rendered my duty to my motherland.'

Image Copyright Acknowledgements

Chapter 1: National Gandhi Museum, New Delhi.

Chapter 2: Usha Mehta Congress Radio Papers, Mani Bhavan Gandhi Sangrahalaya, Mumbai.

Chapter 3: Usha Mehta Congress Radio Papers, Mani Bhavan Gandhi Sangrahalaya, Mumbai.

Chapter 4: Usha Mehta Congress Radio Papers, Mani Bhavan Gandhi Sangrahalaya, Mumbai.

Chapter 5: Usha Mehta Congress Radio Papers, Mani Bhavan Gandhi Sangrahalaya, Mumbai.

Afterword: Mani Bhavan Gandhi Sangrahalaya, Mumbai.

Afterword: Usha Mehta Congress Radio Papers, Mani Bhavan Gandhi Sangrahalaya, Mumbai.

Appendix I: Usha Mehta Congress Radio Papers, Mani Bhavan Gandhi Sangrahalaya, Mumbai.

Appendix II: Usha Mehta Congress Radio Papers, Mani Bhavan Gandhi Sangrahalaya, Mumbai.

Acknowledgements

The journey of writing this book began many years back. Ideas, archival material and conversations with friends and freedom fighters have flowed in, ceaselessly and seamlessly, making the journey fruitful. My sincere thanks to all those who have shared their ideas, information and suggestions.

But for Professor Usha Mehta (Ushaben for many of us), this book would not have been possible. A freedom fighter, a distinguished professor and a wonderful human being, she continued illuminating ideals of service to the society and the nation throughout her life. I owe an immense debt to her. It is she who acquainted me with the sacrifices that our freedom fighters made and hardships they bore happily for the country's freedom. She shared with me various important papers and precious memories in her serene manner and also answered my questions about the Quit India movement and the Congress Radio in her own unassuming way, without accentuating her own role. Ushaben's quiet and effective guidance for my PhD dissertation as well as her equanimity and sincerity throughout my interactions with her left an indelible mark on me. Knowing her very closely was a privilege that I cherish.

I am grateful to Professor Lord Bhikhu Parekh who has taken a keen interest in this book and has been a sustained source of encouragement. It has been a pleasure talking with him about his long association with Ushaben. My heartfelt thanks to him and Dr Ramachandra Guha for meticulously going through the manuscript.

Mr Yogesh Kamdar has extended unstinted support at every stage of this book. His perusal of the earlier drafts and his perceptive comments on them and his sharing of experiences of working with Ushaben have been very valuable.

I acknowledge with pleasure the support received from the staff of Mani Bhavan Gandhi Sangrahalaya. Mr Meghshyam T. Ajgaonkar shared many of his experiences of working with Ushaben. He and Mr Sajeev Rajan willingly extended all administrative help that was needed. Ms Ranjan Bharuchi carefully provided all important material and never failed in finding a book that was required. Mr Samarth Lokhande procured the reading material in the library at a moment's notice. Ms Sandhya Mehta helped in preparation of the images used in this book. The zest and attentiveness of all of them have been a source of encouragement.

I sincerely thank the staff of the library of Maharashtra State Archives and the Mumbai Police Headquarters.

My conversations with the late Professor Aloo Dastur and the late Mr Vasant Pradhan at Mani Bhavan have been enriching.

My sincere thanks to Mr Satish Sahney, Dr Dattatray Padsalgikar and Dr Aneesh Pradhan for their wholehearted support to my work.

All throughout my efforts, I have received affectionate support from my daughter Archisha, her husband Ashok Mehan and my grandsons, Dhruv and Vardhan as well as my sister Dr Jyotsna Tanna.

I thank Ms Uma Narayan, deputy registrar (library, museum, legal research and publications) in Bombay High Court and Dr Shehernaz Nalwalla for making available some useful material for the book and Mr A. Annamalai, Director, National Gandhi Museum, Delhi for permitting to use two images from the collection of the National Gandhi Museum. I am grateful to Mani Bhavan Gandhi Sangrahalaya for permitting me to use images from its collection.

My heartfelt thanks to my literary agent, Mr Kanishka Gupta, for his avid interest and sincere inputs and Ms Aruna Ghose for her helpful suggestions and comments.

Ms Manasi Subramaniam at Penguin Random House has made enormous efforts to make this project a reality. My special thanks to her. Ms Shubhi Surana has been a competent editor who paid attention to all the details. My sincere thanks to her and her colleagues at Penguin Random House.

Appendix I

Judgment[1]

**IN THE COURT OF THE SPECIAL JUDGE
APPOINTED UNDER SECTION 4 OF THE SPECIAL
CRIMINAL COURTS ORDINANCE, 1942**

Case No. 7 of 1943

Emperor

Vs

1. Vithaldas alias Babubhai Madhavji Khakar
2. Vithaldas Kanthadbhai Jhaveri
3. Miss Usha Mehta
4. Chandrakant Babubhai Jhaveri
5. Nanak G. Motwane.

Coram :Lokur, J.
Friday, the 14th May 1943

Judgment:

This case has brought to light the daring with which a broadcasting station was illegally established and worked in different populated localities in Bombay and the cunning which, for nearly three months, baffled the attempts of the Police to trace it.

The main story of the case for the prosecution is to be gathered from the evidence of Printer, his assistant Mirza, Jagannath and the investigating officer, inspector Kokje. Printer is an expert in radio engineering and was the principal of the Bombay Technical Institute, Byculla, where students were given training in radio and electrical engineering. In 1937 he went to England with five of his students, including Mirza. On his return from England in 1938 he secured a licence for amateur transmitting and purchased a transmitter for the purpose of giving lessons to his students. On the outbreak of the war in 1939 Printer's amateur transmitting licence was cancelled, and he was bound to surrender his transmitting apparatus to the authorities concerned. But in instead of doing so he dismantled the apparatus and secretly and unauthorisedly retained the parts with himself. He then invented a mechanism for running motors on kerosene and called it 'Kerogas.' He gave its sole selling agency to accused No.1 and R.A. Mehta. They had their office in Noble Chambers, but the business came to an end as the use of 'Kerogas' was prohibited by Government on account of scarcity of Kerosene. Then Printer conceived the idea of manufacturing 'Hydro-gas' and borrowed Rs. 3,000 from accused No. 1 and R.A Mehta for his experiments. They further advanced Rs. 1,200 or 1,500 to him for manufacturing calcium carbide. Thereafter in July 1942 or so, they refused to join him any longer in the business as they were uncertain of the political future in India. The heavy expenses of the Institute and the failure of his business enterprises landed him into heavy debts to the tune of about Rs. 60,000. Thereafter the office of B. Madhavji & Co was opened in Noble Chambers and, according to Printer, no business was transacted there, but it was used only as a meeting place.

Young Usha Mehta

The meeting of the All-India Congress Committee was held in Bombay on the 7th and 8th of August 1942 and several Congress leaders were arrested on the 9th. Thereafter accused No.1 approached Printer and asked him to build a wireless transmitter with the parts which were in his possession. He agreed and with the help of accused No. 1 he purchased certain missing parts and assembled the transmitter. On August 14,1942 he purchased an amplifier etc. from the Chicago Radio Co. and accused No. 1 paid Rs. 600 for them. He then found that his microphone was not in working order. So on August 24, 1942 he approached accused No. 1 for a new microphone. Accused

No. 1 sent Killewalla with him for that purpose. Killewalla accompanied Printer to Chicago Radio Co. and bought for him a microphone with the money which he had to obtain from his sister. Accused No. 1 paid about Rs. 1,200 or Rs. 1,500 for the parts which Printer had used for the transmitter out of his own stock. When the transmitter was ready, it was to be used for broadcasting in the name of the Congress Radio Station. Printer wanted it to be shifted from his house to some other place. Accused Nos. 1 and 3 and R.A. Mehta saw two or three places and on August 26,1942 the top floor flat of the building called Sea View was hired with Printer's approval. The transmitter was taken there and was fitted up by Printer and Mirza. It was announced in the Congress bulletin of September 3, 1942, Ex-Z-29, that the Congress Broadcasting Station would be broadcasting at 8-45 p.m. on 41.78 metres. Accused No. 1 supplied typed programmes for being broadcast. It is alleged that they were typed in Noble Chambers by accused No. 3 or somebody else. In the beginning accused No. 1 and Mirza worked the transmitter and when, after some days, accused No. 1 and R.A. Mehta became acquainted with its working, they began to work it. Either accused No. 1 or No. 3 or Printer or a Parsi lady, whose name has not been disclosed, used to speak into the microphone and later on that work was assigned to R.A. Mehta. The broadcasting was commenced on 41.78 metres wave length from August 27, 1942.

In a few days Printer suspected that the Police were after them and on his advice the transmitter was shifted to Ratan Mahal on Walkeshwar Road on September 10, 1942. Its rent was paid by R.A. Mehta. Printer and Mirza fitted up the transmitter and aerial there and the programmers supplied by accused No.1 continued to be broadcast as before. Then on September 25, 1942 the transmitter was removed to Ajit Villa where R. A. Mehta was living. There Mehta usually broadcast the programmes and occasionally Printer and accused No..1 relieved him. Mehta was anxious that the transmitter should be taken somewhere else and on October 2, 1942 he secured a flat on the top floor of Laxmi Bhuvan on Sandhurst Road. The transmitter was taken there on October 4, 1942.

Till then typed programmes used to be read into the microphone, but by experience it was found that they were not heard as distinctly as the record of the songs 'Hindustan Hamara' and 'Vande Mataram' which used to be played at the beginning and the end of the programmes. Accused No. 2 then offered to supply home cut records of the programmes from time to time. He had a portable record cutting machine and cut records of speeches usually read out by accused No.3.

Another project undertaken was to increase the power of the transmitter, but the parts required for it were not ordinarily available in the market. Accused No.1 undertook to procure them and is said to have approached Dahyabhai Patel. Dahyabhai took accused No.1 and Printer to accused No.5, a partner and sales manager in Chicago Radio Co. He is alleged to have been persuaded to help the enterprise and he asked his radio mechanic Jagannath to supply the necessary parts to them. Printer was ready with his list, but some of the parts needed were not then in stock. So after consulting accused No.5 Jagannath told Printer that he would keep the parts ready by 1 p.m. on the next day. On the next day, when accused No. 1 went to Chicago Radio Co., the required parts were not delivered to him as the name of Chicago Radio Co. appearing on them had to be removed. When, subsequently, accused No.1 received those parts, he took them to Laxmi Bhuvan and handed them over to Printer. Printer fitted those parts, increased the power of the transmitter from ten watts to 100 watts and changed the frequency from 41.78 metres to 42.34 metres. When this work was being done, the broadcasting had to be stopped for three days from the 15th to the 17th of October 1942.

To test whether the transmitted programmes were heard properly or not, a wireless receiver set was needed and a Philips Radio set No.2983 (Ex. E) is said to have been supplied by accused No.1. It is alleged that it was bought for him in the fictitious name of Maganlal T. Dalal by Bipin Inamdar from the radio dealer Jamnadas Ratansey for Rs.255 on October 9, 1942.

Printer, Mirza and R.A. Mehta purchased a bedding with a holdall, a hat box, two suit cases and a water bottle to be taken in the car in which the transmitting set was to be taken from place to place in order to give them the appearance of bona fide travellers.

On October 15, 1942 rooms Nos. 103 to 106 on the top floor of Parekh Wadi were hired at a rent of Rs. 120 per month and when the transmitting set was strengthened, it was shifted to those rooms. It was set up in the corner room No. 106 and there Bipin Inamdar and R.A. Mehta used to broadcast from the records supplied by accused No.1.

On October 23, 1942 Paradise Bungalow near Mahalaxmi Temple was hired, and its possession was taken on November 3, 1942. In the meantime, according to the evidence of Jagannath Thakor, the radio mechanic in the Chicago Radio Co., another transmitting set was being assembled by accused No.2 in a bungalow at Banganga and Jagannath gave him instructions regarding its construction.

On October 18, 1942 it was announced from the Congress Radio Station that a separate English programme would be broadcast on 39 metres. But on November 12,1942, before the set at Parekh Wadi was removed to Paradise Bungalow, the Police raided Parekh Wadi when the Congress Radio Station was on the air and found accused Nos. 3 and 4 in room No 106 where the transmitter had been set up.

When the Congress bulletin of September 3, 1942 announced that the Congress Radio Station would be on the air at 8-45 p.m. on 41.78 metres, Deputy Inspector Fergusson was deputed to keep a watch and find out where the station was located. The broadcast was monitored by the Police stenographers from October 9th to November 2, 1942. About the middle of October 1942, Deputy Inspector Fergusson reported to Inspector Kokje of the C.I.D. war branch that he had located the Congress Radio Station in the zone between Chaupati and C.P. Tank. This led Inspector Kokje to watch B.M. Tanna the proprietor of Tanna Radio Accessories, who was living in that locality and who had been arrested in 1940 for transmitting news about cotton futures by means of an unauthorised radio transmitter. A watch was kept on him and several suspects were arrested including Tanna and Mansukhal Nihalchand, the manager of the Lamington Road branch of the Chicago Radio Co. On the information given by them Jagannath Thakor was taken to the C.I.D. office on November 11, 1942. On the information given by Jagannath accused Nos. 1 and 2 and Printer were arrested on the 12th. When Printer was questioned, he offered to point out the place where the Congress Radio Station was located and at about 8-45 p.m., when it was expected to be on the air, he took Inspector Kokje to Parekh Wadi and showed where the transmitter had been installed. The door had been closed from inside and at about 9.5 pm it was forced open and accused Nos. 3 and 4 were found inside near the transmitter. Inspector Kokje says that he found accused Nos. 3 and 4 sitting near a gramophone motor with the record of 'Vande Mataram' on its disc, connected to an amplifier and transmitter. Soon after he and the Panchas entered the room, the fuse got burnt, the electric current was cut off and the lights went out. The Radio Station also naturally went off the air and with the aid of some kerosene lamps that were procured, a summary Panchanama was made at that time. Everything was left as it was. The door was locked and sealed and an armed Police guard was kept. Accused Nos. 3 and 4 were taken to the C.I.D. Office.

Inspector Kokje went to Parekh Wadi on the next day with Deputy Inspector Fergusson and two radio experts Mistry and Majumdar to serve as Panchas. As soon as the door of Room No.106 was opened, its photographs were first taken and then a detailed panchanama of the things found in the room was made. An entire transmitting set in working order together with the aerial, 120 gramophone records, a Philips wireless receiving set, a bedding, a hat box, suit cases and other articles that were found there were removed to the C.I.D. office. Accused No.2 was arrested on November 13, 1942 and accused No.5 on November 18th. On the next day another incomplete wireless transmitting set was produced by Jaychand Tarachand Sheth from Khandke Building on Walkeshwar Road, but as that set is not the subject matter of the present charge, it is not necessary to give any details about it .

Out of the 120 records which were found in Parekh Wadi, 7 were commercial records and others were home cut records, 17 of 10 inches and 96 of 12 inches. Inspector

Kokje had them played and found 35 of them to tally with the monitoring reports. At least two of those records were recognised as being in the voice of accused No.3. The two sides of one record were found to have been cut from the sound films taken by the Famous Cine Laboratory during the session of the A.I.C.C. on the 7th and 8th of August and it is alleged for the prosecution that this was done by Jagannath and accused No.2 in the editing room of the Famous Cine Laboratory.

On the label in the centre of each of the home cut records was written a caption to indicate what the record was about and it was suspected that the captions were written by accused No.1 or accused No.2. Hence all such records were sent to the handwriting expert attached to the C.I.D., Poona, together with specimens of handwritings of accused Nos. 1 and 2 taken in the presence of Panchas. The expert, Mr. Gajjar, compared them and found that the captions on three of the labels were definitely in the handwriting of accused No.1.

On the information given by R.A. Mehta, Paradise Bungalow, where the transmitting set was to be next removed, was traced and when it was searched, a table cloth bearing the initials of accused No.1 was found. Inspector Kokje took it into his possession after making a Panchanama.

Inspector Kokje then recorded the statements of several of the employees in the Chicago Radio Co. and seized several documents found there. He also got the company's branch at Lucknow searched, as Rupani, the manager of that branch, was ascertained to have to come to Bombay and taken away various controlled parts from the Chicago Radio Co. V.G. Motwani, the brother of accused No.5 was arrested on December 1, 1942, but he was subsequently released. When the investigation was completed, Government directed that I should try the case against these five accused and on April 2, 1943 accorded sanction under section 196 A of the Criminal Procedure Code for their prosecution for the offence of criminal conspiracy punishable under Section 120 B of the Indian Penal Code.

A prima facie case having been made out, a charge was framed under section 120 B of the Indian Penal Code, section 20 of the Telegraph Act (XIII of 1885) and rule 16 (5), 16(7), 39(6) , 38(5) and 121 of the Defence of India Rules as detailed in Ex. 59. All the accused pleaded not guilty and claimed to be tried. But while accused Nos. 1,2,4 and 5 denied their connection with the Congress Radio Station and the alleged conspiracy, accused No.3 refused to make any statement or offer any explanation of the circumstances appearing in evidence against her.

The points for determination are:-

1. Whether there was a criminal conspiracy to do or cause to be done the illegal acts mentioned in the first clause of the charge.
2. Whether any and which of the accused had joined in that conspiracy.
3. Whether in pursuance of the said conspiracy, the accused illegally established, maintained or worked a wireless telegraph and aided and abetted each other in doing so.
4. Whether in pursuance of the said conspiracy accused Nos. 3 and 4 were in illegal possession of a wireless transmitter and other transmitting parts without a licence.

5. Whether accused Nos. 1 ,2 and 5 aided and abetted them in doing so.

6. Whether in pursuance of the said conspiracy accused Nos. 3 and 4 were without lawful authority or excuse in possession of home cut gramophone records containing prejudicial reports.

7. Whether those records are documents.

8. Whether accused Nos. 1,2 and 5 aided and abetted accused Nos. 3 and 4 in doing so.

9. Whether in pursuance of the said conspiracy the accused with the aid and abetment of each other without lawful authority or excuse committed prejudicial acts and spread prejudicial reports, by means of a wireless apparatus, such as were intended or were likely to cause the mischiefs described in the fifth clause of the charge.

My findings on these points are:-

No.1. In the affirmative.

Nos. 2 and 3. In the affirmative against accused Nos. 1,3 and 4 and in the negative against accused Nos. 2 and 5.

No.4. In the affirmative

No.5. In the affirmative against accused No.1 and in the negative against accused Nos. 2 and 5.

Nos 6 and 8. Do not survive in the view of the finding on point No.7.

No.7. In the negative.

And No.9. In the affirmative against accused Nos. 1 and 3 and in the negative against accused Nos. 2,4 and 5.

There is no doubt that soon after August 9, 1942, when several Congress leaders were arrested, a conspiracy did come into existence to establish a wireless transmitting apparatus for broadcasting programmes such as those contained in the records which were found in Parekh Wadi on November 12, 1942 when it was raided by the Police. I feel certain that in pursuance of the said conspiracy a transmitting apparatus was set up and was broadcasting such programmes regularly every day from 27th August 1942 till November 12, 1942, except on the 15th, 16th and 17th October 1942, when, according to Printer, the set was being strengthened. The matter that was broadcast was monitored by the Police reporters from October 9, 1942 to November 2, 1942. They have produced the original shorthand notes, their transcripts in long hand and the reports which they made to their superiors from day to day. The reporters have been examined for the prosecution and were not cross-examined. Very often the programmes could not be heard distinctly and the reporters had to content themselves with the substance of what they could make out. There is sufficient evidence to hold it proved that these programmes were broadcast from the transmitter which was found in Parekh Wadi when the Police raided it at about 9.5 p.m. on November 12, 1942. Mr. Tendulkar on behalf of accused Nos. 3 and 4 raised a doubt as to whether the programmes which were monitored by the Police reporters were really broadcast from the transmitter in Parekh Wadi. Inspector Kokje says that when the door of room No.106 was broken open it was 9.5 or 9.10 p.m. and the song 'Vande Mataram' was being played. The transmitter was actually working at that time and when the fuse was burnt the electric current was cut off just after the Police and Panchas entered the room. The Panch Dube says that before entering the room he heard what seemed to him as the tune of some stringed instrument. It is suggested for the prosecution that that must have been the sound emitted by the transmitter. On the other hand, Deputy Inspector Fergusson who was listening to the broadcast from the beginning that night says that he heard the broadcast on the same wave length as on the previous night and that it went off the air after the opening song 'Hindustan Hamara' was finished and the usual announcement was made in Hindi. This shows that the Radio Station went off the air at about 8.50 or so. From this it is argued that the transmitter in Parekh Wadi which went on till the end of the programme and was playing 'Vande Mataram', according to Inspector Kokje, could not have been the transmitter which broadcast the programme that was being heard by Dy. Inspector Fergusson. The learned Counsel for the prosecution explained this contradiction by suggesting that Inspector Fergusson must havemade some mistake. But even in cross- examination he repeated that on the night of the 12th the first song was played and when the Hindi announcements were being made the radio went off the air, and it is difficult to believe that he could have made any mistake. Unfortunately, when the detailed Panchanama of room No.106 in Parekh Wadi was made on November 13th, the description of the record on the gramophone motor connected to the transmitter was not given in the Panchanama; otherwise there would have been no room to doubt as to what record was being played when the Police entered the room. Inspector Kokje says that after the raid everything in the room was left untouched as it was and a watch was kept until he went there on the next day for a

Panchanama. On the next day, before going to the room a photograph was taken showing how the things were lying about in the room. If, as Inspector Kokje says, the fuse went off when the record was being played and nobody touched the record or the gramophone motor, the pick-up needle should have been found resting on the record at the time of the Panchanama on the next day, but the photograph (No.1 in Ex.Z-37) clearly shows that the pick-up needle was not on the record, but had been raised up by someone. There is nothing to show that the record was that of the song 'Vande Mataram'. It is also difficult to believe that if the broadcasting was going on when the Police reached the room, the Panch Dube should hear only the humming sound of a stringed instrument and Inspector Kokje should hear the song of 'Vande Mataram' being played. There was in the room a Philips radio receiving set which was intended for receiving the broadcast from the Station, and it is not unlikely that it had been tuned to it in order that those that were working the transmitter might see whether the broadcast was going on properly or not. In that case both the Panch and Inspector Kokje should have heard the broadcast clearly. It therefore appears that the fuse must have been gone off before Kokje broke open the door of the room and hence Dube did not hear that anything was being broadcast at the time. This fits in with the testimony of Deputy Inspector Fergusson which shows that the station went off the air at about 8.50 p.m. when the Hindi announcement was being made. When the electric current was cut off, the pick-up needle must have been raised from the record and the inmates of the room must have been waiting for someone, whom they must have sent, to fetch lights or another fuse. It was in that interval that Inspector Kokje raided the room. When the lights were brought, he saw that there was a gramophone record on the disc of the motor and, as the time was 9.5 p.m., he seems to have imagined that the record must have been of the song of 'Vande Mataram'. All doubts would have been set at rest if the Panchnama had noted down what that record was. But I would prefer to believe the evidence of Deputy Inspector Fergusson who was actually hearing the broadcast at that time. It does not, however, follow from this that the station which was being heard by Fergusson was different from the station located in Parekh Wadi.

It was next pointed out that the transmitting set at Parekh Wadi was fitted with a crystal having a frequency of 7075 k.c. The function of a crystal is to fix the frequency of a transmitter to a pin point and the frequency of 7075 corresponds to 42.40 metres, the formula being 300000 divided by the frequency in k.c. gives the wave length in metres. But as a matter of fact the monitoring reports show that the reporters always heard the broadcast on a wave length of 42.12 or 42.34 and never on 42.40. But there is no satisfactory evidence to show that the frequency of the crystal fitted on the transmitter in Parekh Wadi (C-10) was 7075. The inscription plate which is usually fixed on the crystal giving the specification has been removed and the frequency is written on the inner plate by some one in ink. It is not known by whom and when it was written. Inspector Kokje says that the frequency of the crystal C-10 was tested by Tanna and was found to be 7094 to 7096. This shows that the frequency written in ink on the crystal (C-10) as 7075 is not correct. The metre wave length which corresponds to frequency 7094 is 42.28 metres and Deputy Inspector Fergusson says that generally there is a margin of error up to 7 k.c. Allowing that margin, 7087 corresponds to wavelength 42.33 metres, which is close to the wave length on which the broadcast was actually heard by the Police reporters. It cannot, therefore, be said from the frequency written on the crystal, Ex.C-10, that the transmitter in Parekh Wadi was not broadcasting the programmes which were heard by the Police reporters.

Printer's evidence which is sufficiently borne out by other reliable evidence, shows that the transmitter in question was worked in the bungalow Sea View from August 26, 1942 to September 10, 1942. It was then shifted to Ratan Mahal* on September 25, 1942 and thence to Laxmi Bhuvan on October 4, 1942. From there it was taken to Parekh Wadi on October 15, 1942, and it carried on the broadcast from there till November 12, 1942. Deputy Inspector Fergusson says in paragraph 9 of his deposition that he used to hear the broadcast coming with the same strength at the same place for two or three days, and then it would become weaker, and that towards the end, that is to say before November 11, it came with the same strength for about five days. From this it is argued that the transmitter which was broadcasting the programmes that were monitored was shifted from one place to another only within two or three days and before the police raid it was working in the same place for only five days. This clearly contradicts Printer's version regarding the shifting of the transmitter from place to place. That transmitter was never shifted within two or three days from any place. But I do not attach much weight to Fergusson's evidence on this point. He was trying to locate the broadcasting station by moving about the City in his motor car with a receiving set in it and it is only his surmise that every two or three days the strength of the broadcasting used to become weaker. In fact he was unable to find out exactly where the broadcasting station was located and no inference can be drawn from the strength of the broadcast. It is significant that if that station was different from the one in Parekh Wadi, it would not have stopped working as soon as the set in Parekh Wadi was attached by the Police. Fergusson says that after November 12, the Congress Radio Station was not heard till the end of February. He says that when it started in February, it was announced that the radio had been off the air for three months. But that must certainly be a different transmitter and it was not working before the end of February. This clearly shows that the broadcast which was being monitored came from the Radio Station which was seized by the Police on November 12, 1942.

The presence of the records in that room is a convincing proof that the Congress Radio Station was located there. But it is argued that all the records which were attached at the Panchnama on November 13,1942 must not have been there when the Police raided the room. All the 120 records are described in detail in the Panchnama Ex Z-2. But unfortunately it is not stated in the Panchnama where the different records were lying. It appears from the evidence that the hat box was intended for keeping the records. Inspector Kokje says that some of the records were in the hat box and some in the suit case. Mr. Tendulkar points out that the contents of the hat box are given in detail in the Panchnama Ex.Z-2, but there is no reference to the records having been found there. The photograph, No.1 in Ex.Z-37, clearly shows that some records were lying on the floor, one record was on the gramophone motor and some records were lying near the hat box. Yet it is not stated in the Panchnama that there was any record on the gramophone motor. The total number of the records found is mentioned and the description of each is set out in detail. The Panch Dube says that there were 15 or 20 records, but he must be remembering only those records which he saw as soon as he entered the room and those were only the records lying on the ground and on the gramophone motor. Dube saw them only at night when no detailed Panchnama was intended to be drawn up. That was done on the next day and independent Panchas who were experts in radio engineering were kept present. Before entering the room photographs were taken and even then only a few records could be seen outside. It is inconceivable that some records should have been brought there from outside and incorporated in the Panchnama. I believe Inspector Kokje that there were some records in the hat box and in the suit case. It is unlikely that when the transmitter was to be worked all the records would be taken out and thrown about on the ground. It is significant that 35 of the records found there substantially tally with the monitoring reports. It was impossible for any one to cut such records in accordance with those reports as the reports could not be taken down word for word. Had these records been found elsewhere, it is unlikely that the Police would conceal the fact and plant those records in the room in Parekh Wadi. I feel no hesitation in holding that all the 120 records were found in that room.

Inspector Kokje got those records played and compared them with the monitoring notes. He has produced a statement, Ex.Z-13, showing that out of those 120 records, 35 tally with the monitoring reports. I verified this statement by having some of the records played in Court and compared with the corresponding monitoring notes. This shows that at least those 35 records were played into the Microphone and broadcast and the corresponding monitoring notes are substantially correct.

A cyclostyled compilation of those reports has been prepared for facility of reference and I have marked it as Ex.Z-42, only for the purpose of ready reference (the originals having been already placed on record). The passages which clearly amount to prejudicial reports as defined in rule 34 (7) of the Defence of India Rules are marked in blue pencil in that compilation, and in order to avoid quoting them in this judgement, I have appended to it a statement showing which of them were intended to or were likely to cause the mischief mentioned in the ten items of the fifth clause in the charge. (Vide Appendix to judgment). That they are prejudicial reports is so manifest that it is not disputed and it is not necessary to give any detailed reasons for holding them to be so.

The evident object of establishing the wireless telegraphy apparatus was to broadcast such prejudicial reports in the name of Congress Radio Station. The actual programmes to be broadcast would naturally be prepared from time to time and could not have been present before the minds of the conspirators from the beginning, but the very idea must have been conceived for the purpose of broadcasting such prejudicial matter. It is an offence to establish such an unauthorised transmitter without a licence and it is also an offence to broadcast such prejudicial reports. A conspiracy to do so would be a criminal conspiracy and all those who knowingly joined it at any stage would be responsible for everything done thereafter in pursuance of that conspiracy and in furtherance of its objects. It is common ground that Printer, his assistant Mirza and R.A. Mehta were in the conspiracy. R. A. Mehta says that he was at first unwilling, but was persuaded by Printer and actively helped in the working of the apparatus. Hence the finding on the first point must be recorded in the affirmative. But the real

question in dispute is whether any and which of the accused
are proved to have joined it.

The essence of the offence of criminal conspiracy, as
defined in section 120-A of the Indian Penal Code, is an
agreement between two or more persons to do or cause
to be done an illegal act or an illegal omission. But, as
observed by Jenkins C.J. in Barindra Kumar Ghose v.
Emperor, I.L.R. 37 Cal. 467 at p.507:

> 'Though to establish the charge of conspiracy there must
> be agreement, there need not be proof of direct meeting
> or combination, nor need the parties be brought into
> each other's presence; the agreement may be inferred
> from circumstances raising a presumption of a common
> concerted plan to carry out the unlawful design. So
> again it is not necessary that all should have joined in the
> scheme from the first: those who come in at a later stage
> are equally guilty, provided the agreement be proved.'

By reason of the secrecy of a criminal conspiracy, it is
often difficult, if not impossible, to obtain direct proof of
the alleged agreement, and in most cases, as observed by
Grose J. in R. v. Brisac, 4 East 164, affirmed by the House
of Lords in Mulcahy v. Reg. 3 H.L.306, the question
becomes a matter of inference 'deduced from acts of the
persons concerned done in pursuance of an apparent
criminal purpose in common between them.' In this case,
however, there is direct evidence of such an agreement in
the testimony of Printer who has given a consistent and
detailed story of the conspiracy from the beginning to
the end. But unfortunately he is not a witness on whose
word implicit reliance can be placed. Besides being an
accomplice, he is, on his own statement, a needy and

unscrupulous adventurer who does not care for honesty and has scant regard for truth. He admits that when he and Sharma were conducting the Bombay Technical Institute at Byculla 40 students lodged a complaint against him in Dadar Police Court for the offence of cheating. Many of them were compounded and one is still pending against him. When the war broke out, his licence for amateur transmitting was cancelled and he was required to deliver his transmitter to the Commissioner of Police or the Chief Engineer of Telegraphs. But he dismantled his transmitter and clandestinely retained the parts in his possession, although he admits that it was his duty to hand them over to the authorities. He on his own admission tried to cheat accused No.1 at least on two occasions by making false representations, once by fitting up his cracked crystal to the transmitter as a mere dummy and once by falsely representing to him that he had raised the strength of his wireless transmitter to 1,500 watts, although really he knew that he had not raised it to more than 100 watts. In fact Deputy Inspector Fergusson found that its strength was only 30 watts. He was in straitened circumstances and was all the while trying to screw out money and to defeat his creditors. There are several decrees passed by the Small Causes Court against him, some of them being for very small amounts. He had pledged all his articles for Rs.3,000 to one Malupchand Shantidas at the end of 1941 and they were all sold away by the pledgee in April 1942. Even the house which he occupies has been rented by him in the name of his assistant Mirza. He says that he has no other occupation except some business in chemicals, but even that business is carried on in the name of his assistant Mirza. He, however, claims that he is the proprietor of that business and it is conducted in Mirza's name in order to protect it from his creditors. Although he is the real owner of the business, he calls himself a mere manager. On March 10, 1942 he has made an affidavit to the effect that he is only a servant in that business. But now he says that he made a false statement on oath in order to defeat his creditors. He says that along with him there used to be a Parsi lady to speak into the microphone of the transmitter, but he tries to shield her and says that he does not remember her name. He is himself a Parsi and it is difficult to believe that a Parsi lady, who had joined him for the illegal purpose of broadcasting by means of an unauthorised transmitter, should be a stranger to him. Above all, shortly before the trial of this case commenced, a case was set up against him for an offence under rule 16(7) read with rule 121 of the Defence of India Rules and section 20 of the Indian Telegraph Act read with section 109 I.P.C. He appeared before the Chief Presidency Magistrate and that case has been adjourned to the 15th of this month. Although he says that he is not given any promise that if he gave evidence in favour of the prosecution in this case the case would be withdrawn, yet the institution of the prosecution only a few days before he entered the witness-box and the adjournment of its hearing until the decision of this case are bound to weigh upon him and affect the value of his evidence.

The evidence of such a witness, though it may appear cogent and plausible, requires to be scrutinised with the utmost care before it can be relied upon and as the evidence of an accomplice it requires corroboration in material particulars.

Besides Printer, several other witnesses for the prosecution were actively concerned in the conspiracy and the learned Counsel for the prosecution fairly and frankly conceded that Mirza, Killewalla, Bipin Inamdar, Jagannath, Shantilal, Jeychand and R.A. Mehta should be considered as accomplices. Hence the testimony of all these must be regarded as tainted evidence. A good many rulings were cited at the bar as regards the nature and extent of the corroboration which such evidence required before it can be acted upon. The law on the point may now be regarded as well settled.

On a consideration of section 133 and illustration (b) to section 114 of the Indian Evidence Act the Courts in this country have laid it down as a rule of prudence and practice, which practically amounts to a rule of law, that the evidence of an accomplice should not be acted upon unless it is corroborated as against the particular accused in material respects. It is not necessary to refer to all the cases cited. It will be sufficient to mention two recent decisions Emperor v. Allisab, 34 Bom. L.R. 1453 and Emperor v. Mataprasad Shivprasad, 45 Bom.L.R. 64, in both of which this Court, acting upon this rule, set aside convictions based on uncorroborated accomplice evidence. As regards the nature and extent of the corroboration required, Macleod C.J. has laid down in Emperor v. Bhimrao, 27 Bom.LR. 120, that in dealing with the evidence of an accomplice the Judge is not bound to rely on such statements only as are corroborated by other reliable evidence. 'Once a foundation is established for a belief that such a witness is speaking the truth because he is corroborated by true evidence on material points, the Judge is at liberty to come to a conclusion as to the truth or falsehood of other statements not corroborated.' There is, however, a limit to the application of this general rule. As observed by N.J. Wadia J. in Emperor v. Shankarshet Ramshet, I.L.R. 58 Bom. 40 at p.48, 'corroboration must not merely be such as to prove generally the truth of the approver's story but such as would connect the accused with the crime.'

In that case the learned Chief Justice has laid down four well recognised propositions viz. (1) that the evidence of an accomplice requires some independent corroboration as against each accused; (2) that though it may not be necessary that the evidence of an accomplice should be evidence which directly connects the accused with the offence, still there must be evidence that his story is true in so far as it relates to the accused, (3) that a mere probability of guilt is not any corroboration of the story of the accomplice and the mere fact that his story is a very probable one is no reason for dispensing with the rule that such evidence requires some independent corroboration, and (4) that a circumstance cannot furnish corroboration of the story of an accomplice against an individual accused if either it has no criminal significance apart from details of the accomplice's story which are not themselves proved by independent evidence or the circumstance is susceptible of an innocent explanation which the Court accepts as probable. Another point to be borne in mind in this connection is the rule laid down in Rex v. Baskerville, (1916) 2 K.B.658, viz. that if two or more accomplices are produced as witnesses, they are not deemed to corroborate each other, but the same rule is applied and the same confirmation is required as if they were but one. Following this ruling Sir Sidney Rowlatt, delivering the judgment of the privy Council in Mahadeo v. The King, 38 Bom.L.R. 1101, summed up the law in the following words: -

'It is well settled that evidence of an accessory must be corroborated in some material particular not only bearing upon the facts of the crime but upon the accused's implication in it, and further that evidence of one accomplice is not available as corroboration of another.'

It is, therefore, necessary to consider not only how far Printer's evidence is corroborated in material particulars but to see how far there is independent corroboration of that evidence which tends to show that his story relating to each of the accused is reliable.

That Printer is the mainstay of the conspiracy cannot be disputed. The wireless transmitter which was found in Parekh Wadi was built out of the parts which he had clandestinely retained after his licence was cancelled. He had close business relations with accused No.1 and R. A. Mehta and according to him they refused to finance him in his experiments any longer on the ground that the political situation in the country had become uncertain. It does not matter whether that was the reason given by accused No. 1 and R. A. Mehta or not, but the fact remains that he failed to get any further financial help from them and his experiments had to be stopped. It was in these circumstances that the idea of starting an unauthorised broadcasting station was mooted. According to him the idea was first conceived by accused No.1 and it was accused No.1 who asked him whether he could build a transmitter out of the parts which were with him. It is argued that accused No.1 could not possibly have been aware that Printer had clandestinely kept back any parts of his transmitter and therefore it is unlikely that he should approach Printer with the proposal for the building of a transmitter. It is immaterial who started the idea and it is more than probable that Printer himself wanted to make some use of the parts which were lying idle in his hands and made some money out of them. Accused No. 1 says that he never made any such proposal to Printer nor had he anything to do with the broadcasting. The full story of Printer regarding the help which he claims to have received from accused No.1 is virtually demolished by R. A. Mehta who admits that he was persuaded by Printer to join him and that much against his will he advanced sums to him for the rent of the rooms to which the transmitter was shifted from time to time, that he had taken the transmitter to his own house for some days and that he used to find out places for locating the transmitter. R. A. Mehta and several other witnesses who were concerned in the conspiracy refused to give any incriminating answers unless they were compelled to do so under section 132 of the Indian Evidence Act and thus made it sure that any statements that they might make would not be used in future against them. Being thus assured of his safety, Mehta did not hesitate to take all the blame on himself, possibly to screen the accused. Accused No.1 was his business partner and, therefore, he is an interested witness. I was not very well impressed by the way in which he gave the replies and I am not prepared to discard the whole of Printer's evidence merely because R. A. Mehta does not corroborate him as far as the accused are concerned. If Printer approached R. A. Mehta and succeeded in persuading him to join him in the criminal conspiracy, it is unlikely that he would not approach his partner, accused No.1.

It may be said to the credit of Printer that he has not tried to save his own skin and has unhesitatingly admitted the part played by him from the beginning to the end. Apart from his allegations regarding the complicity of the accused, the whole of his story rings true, and is sufficiently borne out. R. A. Mehta also was in the conspiracy almost from the beginning and he has admitted the part played by him, though he says that he did so reluctantly. Mirza, the assistant of Printer, bears out Printer's story where he is concerned. All these three witnesses are accomplices, but their story regarding the construction and the strengthening of the wireless transmitter and its removal from place to place is sufficiently borne out by other unimpeachable evidence. It was Printer himself who pointed out to the Police the room in Parekh Wadi where the transmitter was ultimately found, and there is no doubt that it was built out of the parts which had been secretly retained by Printer after the cancellation of his licence. He built the set with Mirza's help in his own house in Byculla. It is significant that a motor, Ex. D, and a valve, Ex. G, similar to those used in the transmitter were found in Printer's house when it was searched by the Police. R. A. Mehta says that when the construction of the set was complete, it started broadcasting from Printer's house on the wave - length of 41.78 metres about the end of August at about 7.45 p.m. (old standard time). It was then shifted to Sea View where it was set up by Printer and Mirza. R. A. Mehta bears this out. That the flat in Sea View was taken on hire by Printer and others on 26th August 1942 is proved by the evidence of the landlord, Ahmed Umerkhan (Ex. 6), and the watchman, Daraskhan, (Ex.5). It was hired in the bogus name of Keshvlal Chhaganlal for the alleged use of his uncle from Jamnagar. Printer was recognised by Darakhan at an identification parade held by the Police on November 28, 1942 (Ex.Z-25). Thereafter, on September 10, 1942, a flat on the third floor of Ratan Mahal was taken on hire by Printer, Mirza and R.A. Mehta from Kasturben Shroff (Ex.18). Killewala says that he had taken them to the landlady Kasturben and introduced them to

her. Printer says that it was Killewala who hired the flat for
them, and Killewala admits that although he did not hire
the flat, it was he who introduced them to the landlady.
After a fortnight the transmitting set was removed to
R. A. Mehta's residence in Ajit Villa on September 15, 1942.
R. A. Mehta himself admits this, and he was anxious that
it should not remain there for any length of time. So he
himself found out Laxmi Bhuwan on Sandhurst Road and
took the top floor on hire for a month, paying Rs. 120
as its rent. He gave his name as C. R. Thakore, and told
the landlord that the flat was wanted for his uncle who
was expected to arrive from Ahmedabad or some outside
place. This is borne out by Mr. Pandit (Ex.7) who was
the managing trustee of that building. He has produced
the counterfoil of the receipt (Ex. K), and identified
R. A. Mehta at the identification parade held on December
16,1942. The transmitting set was shifted there on 4th
October 1942, and when Printer wanted it to be shifted to
some other place, R. A. Mehta hired rooms Nos. 103 to
106 on the 5th floor of Parekh Wadi. R. A. Mehta says that
he took it on hire as it would not be let to a non-Hindu.
R. A. Mehta rented those rooms in the name of Mohanlal
R. Desai and he passed a receipt in that name (Ex.O). This
is proved by the rent collector, Ramsaran Dube (Ex.8) and
Fulchand (Ex.11). When the set was still there, Paradise
Bungalow was hired on 23-10-1942, as can be seen from
the bill (Ex. Z-27). It was taken in the name of S.B.Pandia
and its possession was taken on 3-11-1942. This is proved
by Badloo (Ex.48) But before the set was shifted there,
Printer pointed out Parekh Wadi to Inspector Kokje, and it
was raided on the night of November 12, 1942.

After the set was shifted to Laxmi Bhuvan, the idea of
increasing its strength was entertained, and the parts required

for that purpose were obtained. The original strength of
Printer's set when he purchased it from Dharap was 100
watts, but he had reduced it to 10 watts by means of a voltage
divider. Some more parts were required for strengthening
it, and they were procured, and the strength was increased,
ostensibly to 100 watts, but actually to 30 watts, according
to the evidence of Deputy Inspector Fergusson. For that
purpose it was announced on the radio that it would be
off the air for two or three days. Accordingly there were
no broadcasts on the 15th, 16th and 17th October 1942.
This bears out the story of Mirza and Printer that those days
were occupied in strengthening the set. As soon as the parts
were received, the dummy crystal which had been fixed by
Printer was removed and the crystal (Ex.C10) was fitted in
its place. This changed the wave-length from 41.78 to 42.12
metres. Fergusson says that on 13-10-1942 the broadcast
was received on 42.12 metres. Subsequently it was received
on 42.34 metres. This part of Printer's story is sufficiently
corroborated not only by the evidence of the accomplices,
Mirza and R. A. Mehta, but also by other independent
evidence to which I have already referred.

Thus, although the main history of the Congress
Radio Station from its commencement about the end of
August 1942 till its seizure on November 12, 1942, as
given by Printer, is substantially borne out in material
particulars, and may be accepted as true, it does not
follow that his statement about the complicity of the
accused is also true. As explained by Lord Abinger in
R. V. Farler (1837) 8 C. & P. 106, 'A man who has been
guilty of a crime himself will always be able to relate
the facts of the case, and if the confirmation be only on
the truth of that history, without identifying the persons,
that is really no corroboration at all. If a man were to

break open your house and put a knife to your throat and steal your property, it would be no corroboration that he had described how the person did put the knife to the throat and did steal the property. It would not at all tend to show that the party accused participated in it. The danger is that when a man is fixed and knows that his own guilt is detected, he will purchase immunity by accusing others . . . Hence the corroboration ought to consist in some circumstance that affects the identity of the persons accused.' For that purpose it is necessary to analyse the evidence against each of the accused and to see how far each of them is proved to have been concerned in the conspiracy and the other offences charged.

According to Printer, the idea of establishing the Congress Broadcasting Station originated with accused No.1, and it was accused No.1 who approached him with the proposal that he should build a wireless transmitting set out of the parts that were lying with him. It is argued that accused No.1 had no means to know that these parts had not been handed over by Printer to the proper authorities as required by law, and that it was not, therefore, likely that accused No. 1 should make the proposal to Printer. Printer says that he was making use of these parts to instruct his students, and that Mirza and several others knew that those parts had been secretly retained by him. There is no direct evidence that accused No.1 knew about these parts, but it matters little whether the proposal came from Printer himself or from accused No.1. Printer, who was in financially straitened circumstances, had obviously no use for the controlled parts which were lying idle on his hands, and he may have thought of inducing accused No.1 and R.A.Mehta to start a broadcasting station and pay him for the parts, which he was able to supply. In fact, he does say that he received Rs.2,000 or so for the parts from accused No.1. Several parts were missing and had to be purchased. An amplifier, a pick-up and a volume controller were purchased from Chicago Radio Company for Rs.599-8-0 on August 14, 1942, and a microphone was bought from that company on August 24, 1942 for Rs.250. Printer could certainly not afford to spend this amount of Rs.850 out of his own empty pocket. He would naturally seek monetary help from his earstwhile business financiers. It is admitted that accused No.1 and R.A.Mehta were financing Printer for his experiments in hydro-gas and calcium carbide. All that business had come to an end. The carbide account (Ex.Z3) shows that Printer was paid Rs.125 and Mirza Rs.25, recently. R. A. Mehta does admit that Printer approached him for money to pay the rent of the flats which were to be hired from time to time for setting up the transmitter, but he does not say that he had been approached for the amount required for the purchase of the parts from Chicago Radio Company. It, therefore, stands to reason that he may have approached his other financier, accused No.1. It is true that the cash memo for the amplifier (Ex. Z-4) was made in the name of Printer itself, although Printer says that it was made in his name by the vendor Deshpande as he was known to him, Deshpande says that he did not know Printer before. Mirza (Ex.3) says that he too had accompanied Printer and accused No.1 to Chicago Radio Co. when the amplifier was purchased. His explanation of his reason for going with Printer is that the amplifier had to be tested as to how it was working and although Printer knew about it, he thought that two heads were better than one. However, Mirza being an accomplice, his corroboration is not, by itself, sufficient. But the probability which I have already referred to inclines me to believe Printer's story on this point. But, by itself, it would not be sufficient to fasten complicity in the conspiracy on accused No.1. The amplifier was not a controlled part and could be purchased by any one in the market, and even if accused No.1 had gone with Printer to help him in the purchase of the amplifier and other uncontrolled parts and had even advanced a loan to him, it does not necessarily follow that he knew what the purpose of those parts was. But when it is taken into consideration with the subsequent purchase of a microphone a few days later, it would indicate that he must have been taking an active interest in the building of the wireless transmitting set. He did not personally go with Printer for the purchase of the microphone, but sent Killewalla with him. Of course, Printer had no money to buy the microphone, and he says that Killewalla had been asked by accused No.1 to pay for it. Unfortunately Killewalla (Ex.4) is not, for one reason or another, telling the whole truth. He says that when he had gone to the office of accused No.1, he asked him to go with Printer as he wanted to buy something. He does not admit that accused No.1 asked him to pay for what was to be purchased by Printer. When he and Printer went together to Chicago Radio Company in the car of accused No.1, Printer gave him a note containing details of the articles wanted by him. Printer then waited in the car outside, and Killewala went in, paid Rs.255 and bought the microphone. The story given by him as to why he paid for it is unnatural and cannot be believed. He says, 'When Printer and I got out of the office of accused No.1, Printer requested me to supply him with money to buy the thing. I immediately agreed. I took no writing from him for the loan advanced by me. Printer returned the money to me two or three days later.' He asserts that he himself had no money with him, but that he agreed to pay the amount required for purchasing the articles, and that he went with Printer to his sister's house and obtained the money from her. Printer must have been known to him to be a pauper. He was heavily in debt and many decrees had been passed against him. In these circumstances it is difficult to believe that Killewala would pay Printer Rs.250 at the mere asking without taking any document from him, especially when he himself had no money and had to borrow it from his sister. It is equally unlikely that he would allow Printer to remain outside in the car and go into the shop and buy the article himself. Printer's explanation that he did not like to go often into the Chicago Radio Company to buy such articles lest he might arouse a suspicion that a transmitter was being built by him, appears plausible. If Killewala innocently bought the microphone for Printer he would either have given his own name or Printer's name as the purchaser, but the cash memo shows that the purchase was made in the name of Messrs. Babubhai & Co., Laxmi Building. Fort, Bombay. No such company was in existence. It is significant that Babubhai is the name of accused No.1. Killewala does not even remember the exact amount he paid for the purchase of the microphone. If he had really borrowed the amount from his sister and it was returned to him by Printer, within two or three days, as he says, he would not have forgotten the amount. The cash memo (Ex.Z - 5) shows that the amount paid was really Rs.250, but Killewala says that he paid Rs.200 only. This also shows that the money had not been given out of his own pocket but that accused No.1 must have paid it into his hands as alleged by Printer.

When the construction of the set was completed, a demonstration was given by Printer in his house. Printer says that accused Nos. 1 and 3 and R.A.Mehta were then present, whereas R.A.Mehta says that he alone had gone to see the demonstration. It is argued that if the working of the set was to be tested as stated, accused Nos. 1 and 3 and R.A. Mehta would have been asked to listen to the broadcast from a receiving set, and would not have been taken to Printer's house to see the set, where they could not find out whether it was working properly or not. Printer says that he merely wanted to show the set to them in order to satisfy them that it had been completed and that it was working. At least R.A.Mehta admits that he went to see the demonstration in Printer's house. On this point again there is no independent corroboration of Printer's statement that accused Nos. 1 and 3 were amongst those who had gone to his house for the demonstration.

Printer wanted the set to be removed to some other place and accordingly accused No.1, R.A. Mehta, and himself were trying to find out some suitable place. Several places were seen and the flat in Sea View was fixed upon. For that purpose accused Nos. 1 and 3 and Printer had gone to Sea View and the flat was shown to them by the watchman Daraskhan (Ex.5). Daraskhan says that one Bania, one Parsi and one lady had come to the room on the top floor. He identified accused No.1 as the Bania, Printer as the Parsi, and accused No.3 as the lady. He remembers her because of the squint in her eye. He says that those three were going there at night at intervals of 4 or 5 days. They had taken some chairs, bedding, etc. and an aerial was put up and sometimes they used to visit the room at noon at 1 p.m. The landlord Ahmed Umerkhan (Ex.6) says that two men had been taken to him by Daraskhan as they wanted to have a flat. One of them gave his name as Keshavlal Chhaganlal and told him that his uncle was to come from Jamnagar. He says that he is unable to recognise that Keshavlal. He says that the two men who had come appeared to be Hindus, but Daraskhan is positive that one of them was a Parsi. Ahmed does not mention that a lady was with them. Possibly she may have been left behind. An identification parade was held by the police when accused No.1 and Printer were mixed up with other people and Daraskhan picked them out correctly and identified them as the persons who had taken the flat on hire. In his cross-examination, in reply to a leading question, he stated that accused No.1 was shown to him and that he was asked whether he would be able to identify him and he said that he would recognize him. The suggestion is that this identification parade was a mere farce and that accused No.1 had been separately shown to Daraskhan before he identified him. It is not so alleged by Ahmed Umerkhan, and the panchnama (Ex. Z- 25) clearly shows that accused No.1 and Printer were mixed up with 14 other persons of different communities and they were correctly identified. If a dishonest panchanama was to be made, Ahmed Umerkhan would also might have been made to identify them. Daraskhan is an independent witness and I see no reason to doubt his honesty. He used to see accused Nos. 1 and 3 and Printer frequently, even by day time and was, therefore, in a position to remember their features. In his statement, accused No.1 does not say that he was shown to Daraskhan before the identification parade was held, but frankly admits that he was identified by Daraskhan. But he says that he had gone to Sea view where Printer had called him, accused No.3 and Mirza, for an ice-cream party, towards the end of September. This story appears to have been put forward to explain why Daraskhan has identified him.

A wireless receiving set was required to test whether the transmitter was working properly or not and Printer says that that was supplied by accused No.1. When the room in Parekh Wadi was raided and the transmitter was seized, a Philips radio receiving set No.2983 was found. It is proved to have been purchased by Jamnadas from Precious Electric Co, and sold to B.S. Inamdar on 9-10-1942 and it was sold by B. S. Inamdar to one Maganlal T. Dalal living in Block A, Sonawala Building, Tardeo. A counterfoil of the bill and the guarantee forms have been produced, but none of these witnesses has made any reference to accused No.1. No man of the name M.T. Dalal could be traced by the police. It has not been proved who gave that bogus name. The conduct of B.S. Inamdar (Ex.10) appears to be suspicious and it is possible that he himself may have joined the conspiracy and supplied the Philips radio receiving set. Printer's statement that the radio receiving set was supplied is proved by the finding of the set in Parekh Wadi, but his allegation that it was supplied by accused No.1 is not borne out by any other evidence, and must, therefore, be left out of consideration.

Printer says that when the strengthening of the set was decided upon, accused No.1 promised to secure the necessary parts. He mentions one Dahyabhai Patel who took him with accused No.1 to Chicago Radio Company. He also refers to one Dr. Lohia from whom, he says, accused No.1 admitted to have received moneys to the extent of about Rs.10,000 to Rs.15,000. But on this point there is no independent corroboration. It is true that some parts were required for the strengthening the set, and that those parts were procured and the set was strengthened. It is similarly proved that the crystal (Ex.C10) was fixed in the transmitter in place of the dummy crystal originally used by Printer. Jagannath's evidence regarding all these parts does not help the prosecution. I shall refer to this again when dealing with the case of accused No.5. But so far as accused No.1 is concerned, Printer's story that he procured these parts stands uncorroborated.

It appears to be true that when the transmitter was being shifted from place to place accused No.I's car was used. Printer says that in order to give them the appearance of bona fide travellers he had purchased some kit. This is borne out by the fact that the kit was found in Parekh Wadi when it was raided by the police. But it is pointed out that the kit may have been bought to be used by Printer and even by R.A. Mehta. Mirza says that he and Printer alone shifted the set from one place to another and he does not bear out the story of Printer that accused No.1 also used to be with them on those days.

Printer says that accused No.1 introduced accused No.2 to him and the question of broadcasting from home cut records was discussed. Accused No.2 offered to supply the records. There is no evidence to corroborate the allegation of Printer that accused No.2 was introduced to him by accused No.1. Printer says that thereafter accused No.1 used to supply recorded programmes. Although there is no direct evidence to prove that he procured the records, yet, there is indirect but strong evidence to show that he was concerned in supplying the records for broadcasting.

Most of the records found in Parekh Wadi had on the labels captions written in ink or inscribed. It was suspected that they were written either by accused No.1 or accused No.2. Specimens of their handwriting were obtained in the presence of panchas and they were sent with the records to the handwriting expert attached to the C.I.D. , Poona. Mr. Gajjar, the handwriting expert, took magnified photographs of the specimen handwriting and the labels on the records (Ex.J-66 and J-74) and gave his opinion that the captions on them were in the handwriting of accused No.1. Ordinarily the opinion of an expert regarding the identity of the handwriting is not sufficient to prove conclusively that the document in dispute is in the handwriting of the suspect, but in this case there are so many peculiar features in the captions on the records and the specimen handwriting of accused No.1 that I feel no hesitation in holding that the captions were written by accused No.1. Mr. Gajjar (Ex.39) has given detailed reasons for his conclusions, and I find them to be convincing. In Ex.Z-21 Mr.Gajjar has placed the writings to be compared side by side. He has also produced the magnified photographs of the specimen handwriting and the writing on the labels. The most striking peculiarity is that accused No.1 being not well educated in English, his spelling is weak, and he has committed the same spelling mistakes in both of them. He has spelt 'cultivators' as 'cultivetors' and 'appeal' as 'apeal', both in the labels and in the specimen handwriting. Accused No.1 has stated in his written statement that when the specimen handwriting was taken in the presence of the panchas, Inspector Kokje dictated to him, and as he did not know the spelling of 'appeal' and 'cultivators' he asked him what the spelling was and wrote out the spelling of both those words according to his instructions. But Inspector Kokje says that both accused No.s 1 and 2 wrote to his dictation at the same time and no such spelling mistakes were committed by accused No.2 It is unlikely that Inspector Kokje would purposely give incorrect spelling to accused No.1 when dictating the passage. He was not concerned with the correctness of the spelling but with the handwriting, and it is improbable that accused No.1 would have asked the spelling of these words when the passage was being dictated to him. The letters 'c', 'a' , 'd' and 'f' have the same peculiarities in both. Particularly accused No.1's mode of writing 'f' is strikingly peculiar. Mr. Gajjar says that he has not come across similar peculiarity in the writing of 'f' by anyone else. It was pointed out that the initial 'S' in 'Starvation' written on the label is not similar to the initial 'S' appearing in several words in the specimen handwriting. There is some force in this contention, but there is a similar 's' in the word 'troops' appearing in the specimen handwriting; and although that 's 'is not the initial letter of the word, yet it is separated and appears to be written in the same way as the initial 'S' in 'Starvation' on the label. I have carefully compared the two writings and am satisfied that Mr. Gajjar's conclusion is correct and ought to be accepted. This brings the guilt home to accused No.1. If he was not concerned in the conspiracy, he had no reason to write the captions on the records which were actually broadcast. It is true that on record Ex J-66, relating to the air raid on Chitagong, it is written in the handwriting of accused No.1, that it was played on October 27, 1942, but the monitoring notes show that it was actually played on October 30. Possibly it may have been meant to be played on October 27, but for some reason or other it was actually played later. The other record (Ex. J-74), relating to 'Appeal to cultivators' was played on November 1, 1942, as shown by the monitoring reports. It is true that no typed programmes which are said to have been supplied by accused No.1 until the recorded programmes began to be broadcast has been found with him. They may have been destroyed or kept somewhere secretly. There is, however, no corroboration of Printer's statement that the typed programmes were supplied by accused No.1, but from the fact that the captions of at least some of the records were written by accused No.1, Printer's allegation that the records were supplied from time to time by accused No.1 can safely be believed. It must be pointed out that Gajjar has honestly stated that he could not identify the handwriting of accused No.2 on any of the records. The reason given by him is that the specimen writing of accused No2. was dissembled and could not, therefore, be used for comparison.

It was argued by Mr. Thacker that it was not proper for Inspector Kokje to compel accused Nos.1 and 2 to write out to his dictation in order to obtain specimens of his handwriting. In Emperor v. Ramrao Burde (1932) 34 B.L.R. 598, Wadia, J., says that a specimen signature made by an accused at the instance of a police officer while in custody of the police and in course of the investigation is admissible in evidence at the trial of the offence charged against the accused. It is true that he has observed that it would be generally desirable in the interests of the administration of justice in criminal trials that for the purpose of comparison the accused should be made to write or give his finger impression in Court under the direction of the Magistrate or Judge, and if the accused refuses to write or to give his finger impression in the Court then an adverse inference may be drawn against him. But in this case accused No.1 admits that the specimen handwriting sent to Mr. Gajjar is his and he has no complaint to make against the police.

In view of all this evidence it is probable that on certain other occasions referred to by Printer, accused No.1 may have been present, but as there is no independent corroboration to it, I need not refer to such occasions in detail. I must, however, refer to one other incident which, though not of much importance, is a circumstance which ought not to be lost sight of. It was intended that the transmitter should be shifted to Paradise Bungalow near Mahaluxmi Temple, that had been taken on hire by R.A. Mehta, but before the transmitter was actually shifted there, it was seized by the police. When Paradise Bungalow was searched several pieces of furniture and a table cloth were found, and that table cloth bears the letters 'B.M.K.' the initials of accused No.1. It is possible that others also may have the same initials, but it is a strange coincidence that in the room which was intended to be used for the transmitter there should be found a table cloth bearing the same initials. When the table cloth was shown to him and his attention was drawn to the initials, accused No.1 did not deny that the table cloth belonged to him. He said that he could not say whether it belonged to him, and that he did not remember whether he had a table cloth of that type. It is a very evasive reply and if he really had nothing to do with the table cloth, he could have immediately said that it was not his. It was argued that the police made no attempt to search his house and find out whether there was a similar table cloth in his house or whether there were other clothes in his house bearing the same initials. It is true that no other clothes belonging to accused No.1 bearing such initials have been produced by the prosecution, but this very coincidence is a circumstance which may be taken into consideration as a piece of evidence against accused No.1. Taking all these circumstances into consideration, I find that accused No.1 had joined in the conspiracy to establish, maintain and work a wireless transmitting apparatus for the purpose of broadcasting prejudicial reports.

Accused no.1 is thus proved to have been an active member of the conspiracy from the very beginning and it does not appear that he ever ceased to have anything to do with it. He is proved to have gone to hire the flat in Sea View and written captions on at least two records. The contents of the record (Ex.J-74) (Appeal to cultivators) was broadcast on November 1, 1942, as shown in the monitoring reports, that is to say, only about 11 days before the set was seized. He is, therefore responsible for everything that was done in pursuance of the conspiracy. There is no direct evidence to prove that he was in actual possession of the transmitter or that he actually spoke into the microphone, although Printer says that he often did. But Rule 121 of the Defence on India Rules provides that any person who attempts to contravene, or abets, or attempts to abet, or does any act preparatory to, a contravention of, any of the provisions of the rules or any order made thereunder shall be deemed to have contravened that provision, or order. There is no doubt that accused No.1 did certain acts preparatory to a contravention of the Defence on India Rules. He is, therefore, clearly guilty of the first, second, third and fifth counts in the charge.

As regards the fourth count, it is contended on behalf of the defence that gramophone records are not documents. Rule 39(1) (b) prohibits the possession of 'any document containing any prejudicial report' without lawful authority or excuse. Rule 3(1) provides that the General Clauses Act of 1897 shall apply to the interpretation of the Rules as it applies to the interpretation of Central Acts, and in Section 3 Clause 16, of the General Clauses Act, 1897, a document is defined as including 'any matter written, expressed or described upon any substance by means of letters, photographs or marks or by more than one of those means which is intended to be used or which may be used for the purpose of recording that matter.' The marks cut on a gramophone record do not convey any sense unless it is played on a machine. It is not to be read or seen, but heard. In fact it is a record of sounds with a view to their subsequent reproduction. According to Section 3 Clause 58, of the General Causes Act, 1897, 'expressions referring to 'writing' are to be construed as including references to printing, lithography, photography and other modes of representing or reproducing words in a visible form.' It is argued by the learned Counsel for the prosecution that this definition shows that it is only a 'writing' which has to be in a visible form, while in Clause 16, a document is defined as including matter not only 'written' but also matter 'expressed or described', and therefore it is not necessary that a document should contain a visible matter. Even if the matter can be made audible and understood thereby, the substance containing such matter would be included in the definition of a document. There is some force in this contention, but the Defence of India Rules themselves appear to have taken a different view and added an explanation to Rule 40 to the following effect: 'In this rule, 'document' includes gramophone records, sound tracks and any other articles on which sounds have been recorded with a view to their subsequent reproduction.' If a document, as defined in the General Clauses Act, 1897, includes a gramophone record, it was not necessary to add this explanation to Rule 40. If it was intended that the word document should carry the same meaning in all the previous rules also, then there was no propriety in expressly confining that definition of 'document' to Rule 40, as the explanation purports to do. There is no such explanation added to rule 39, with which we are concerned. Mr. Vimadalal pointed out that in section 131 of the Indian Penal Code, an explanation is added that the words 'officer', 'soldier' sailor' and 'airman' used in that section include any person subject to the Army, Navy,

Act[**] etc., and that although no such explanation appears
in the subsequent sections 132 to 138, the words 'officer',
'soldier, 'sailor', 'airman' in those sections would include
any person subject to the army, navy etc. and that in the
same manner the explanation to rule 40 of the Defence of
India Rules would apply to other rules in interpreting the
word 'document'. It is not necessary to consider whether
the explanation to section 132 of the Indian Penal Code
applies to the subsequent sections, but assuming that
it does, yet the meaning of the words 'officer, 'soldier',
'sailor', airman' is given in the earlier section, and the same
words may be taken to have been used in the same sense in
the subsequent sections. But the interpretation of the word
'document' given in rule 40 cannot be taken as applying
to that word used in the preceding rules. Otherwise the
explanation would have been added to rule 39 instead of
to rule 40. I, therefore, hold that the word 'document' used
in rule 39(1) (b) is not intended to include a gramophone
record. Hence the possession of the gramophone records
would not be in contravention of that rule. Accused No.1
cannot, therefore, be convicted of the offence in the fourth
clause of the charge. But I find him guilty of the offences in
the other four clauses.

Accused No.3 and 4 were caught red-handed when
they were in the room where the wireless transmitter had
been set up. I have already described in detail how on the
information given by Printer Inspector Kokje raided that
room, broke open its door and found the transmitter and
accused No.s 3 and 4. I have also referred to the discrepancy
in the statements of Inspector Kokje and Dy. Inspector
Fergusson, as to when the Congress Radio Station went
off the air, what record was being then played, etc. Printer
says that he heard the record of 'Vande Matram' being

played, but it is most probable that as Fergusson says, the station went off the air as soon as the first song 'Hindustan Hamara' was played and the announcement was being made in Hindi at about 8-50 p.m. or so, so that when Kokje and the panchas entered the room at about 9.5 p.m. it must have been dark. I have also held that it was this transmitter which was broadcasting the programmes that were monitored, and Deputy Inspector Fergusson heard the broadcast from this transmitting set. It was found to be in working order and accused No.3 has offered no explanation of her presence there. Accused No.4 says that he had gone there to keep company to accused No.3. and that within 5 minutes after he entered, the police arrived. He further admits that he himself had closed the door as instructed by accused No.3. He says that there was one other person already there, but he went away before he closed the door. It is highly improbable that if he was not in the conspiracy he would go with accused No.3 and remain there with her after the fuse was burnt and the current was cut off. There is ample evidence to prove that accused No.3 had joined the conspiracy almost from the beginning. She had accompanied Printer and accused No.1 to hire the flat in Sea View. She has been identified by Daraskhan as he saw her several times subsequently going to the flat both during day and at night. I have already discussed the evidence of Daraskhan at length and I believe it. It is suggested by Printer that she must have been typing the programmes on the typewriter in the Noble Chambers. He says that he had gone to the Noble Chambers when she was actually typing something and peeped into it, but as there is no corroboration to this story, it cannot be held proved. But there is sufficient corroboration to hold that she used to speak into the microphone of the transmitter frequently, before the recorded programmes began to be broadcast. He also says that he was present once when she spoke for the record when it was cut by accused No.2. Whether it was cut by accused No.2 or Printer or somebody else, there is sufficient corroboration that the matter was read out by accused No.3 when the record was cut. Printer stated that that record related to Chimur incident. There were three such records, and he was asked to point out which was the record he referred to. When the first record was played in Court, he said that that was not the record for which accused No.3 had read out the matter, and he gave the reason that it did not contain the words which he remembered to have been read out by accused No.3 when the record was cut in his presence. At the instance of the learned Counsel for accused No.3 he was asked to state the words which he remembered, and then he said that the words were '*mai garabhavati thee*'. When the second record, namely, the first side of exhibit J.61 was played, it was not found to contain these words. Then the other side of Ex.J.61 was played and it contained these words and he said that that was the record which was cut in his presence to the reading by accused No.3. This was an off-hand test which fully corroborated Printer's statement. It may be that the record was cut by anybody, but it is certain that it was cut in his presence, and in his cross-examination Printer has given an explanation as to why he particularly remembered those words. He says, 'I never heard the record, Ex.J.61 before it was played in Court. I had heard that when the typed script was read out by accused No.3 when the record was cut. I remember the expression 'I was pregnant'. It sounded strange in the mouth of accused No. 3 who was unmarried and I made a joke of it afterwards'. This is a strikingly reasonable explanation, and I believe that he must have been present when that record was cut and that accused No.3 must have read out the typed script for the record.

Accused No.s 3 and 4 were seen in the Noble Chambers when S.I. Pednekar went to arrest accused No.1 on November 12, 1942. Accused No.3 was sitting near a typewriter with some papers spread out on the table, but by the time Pednekar came out after arresting accused No.1, both accused Nos. 3 and 4 had disappeared. There is no evidence to show that this visit of accused Nos. 3 and 4 to Noble Chambers had anything to do with the conspiracy or broadcasting. Printer says that accused No.3 accompanied him also to Ratan Mahal when they went to hire it, but there is no corroboration of his statement. The landlady Kasturben says that all those who had come to take the flat on hire were men. Printer says that accused No.3 mostly read out the typed scripts for the records, but the monitoring notes show that out of 35, only 8 were in female voice. Mirza also says that he heard several female voices. Mirza swears that he recognised the voice of accused No.3 when he heard the broadcast, but he does not say that he ever recognised the voice of Printer, although Printer admits that he sometimes spoke into the microphone. Possibly it may be that at that time Mirza did not listen to the broadcasting and may not have noticed it. But Mirza and Printer are both accomplices, and, by itself, their evidence that they recognised the voice of accused No.3 cannot be accepted without corroboration. But Inspector Kokje, who heard the records being played says definitely that the record, Ex.J.44, is in the voice of accused No.3. He was asked as to whether he was familiar with her voice. He thought that the word 'familiar' was too strong and felt shy to admit that he was familiar with her

voice, but he asserted that he knew her voice and was able
to recognise it. From all this I am satisfied that accused
No.3 did read out the matter on some occasions for being
recorded and broadcast. The record, Ex.J-44, was played
on October 29,1942, and she was found in Parekh Wadi
on November 12, 1942.

If accused No.3 had gone there for any innocent
purpose in ignorance of what was going on, she could
have said so, but she deserves all the credit for refusing
to state a falsehood to save herself. However no adverse
inference need necessarily be drawn from her reticence.
As observed in Emperor V. Basangouda (1940), 43
Bom.L.R. 144, the accused is not bound to give any
explanation at all, and the fact that she does not open
her mouth cannot be used against her. The burden of
proof always lies on the prosecution and is not shifted
to the accused by her refusal to offer any explanation
of the circumstances appearing against her. But so far
as the possession of the wireless telegraph apparatus in
contravention of rule 16(2) of the Defence of India Rules
is concerned, sub-rule 8 provides that for the purposes of
that rule 'a Court may presume that a person possesses
wireless telegraphy apparatus if such apparatus is under
his ostensible charge or is located in any premises or place
over which he has effective control.' The circumstances
in which accused Nos. 3 and 4 were found in the room
where the transmitter was located do justify such a
presumption being raised against both of them. It is
pointed out that no key of the room was found in their
possession. But it appears from the statement of accused
No.4 himself that there was also a third person who must
have gone out when the lights were out, either for the
purpose of getting another light or another fuse. The key

may have been with him, and the absence of the key either with accused No.3 or accused No.4 does not lead to any conclusion. Both accused Nos. 3 and 4 must, therefore, be held to have been in possession of the transmitter in contravention of rule 16(5).

Accused No.3 is thus found to have joined the conspiracy from the beginning and to have continued taking active part in it, until the transmitter was seized by the police. She is, therefore, guilty of the offences in items Nos. 1, 2,3 and 5 of the charge. For the reasons already given, she cannot be convicted of the offence in item No.4.

As regards accused No. 4, there is no evidence about his participation in the conspiracy before he was found at the transmitting station on the night of November 12, 1942. Both Printer and Mirza say that they had seen him in the office of accused No. 1. Assuming that accused No. 4 had gone there occasionally it cannot be said that he had gone there for the purposes of conspiracy. He may have paid a casual visit for an innocent purpose. But it cannot be said that he was ignorant of the conspiracy when he went to Parekh Wadi on November 12, 1942. He must have known what was going on there and must have gone there for the purpose of taking part in the conspiracy, but he cannot be held responsible for all that had been done in pursuance of the conspiracy before he joined it. Mr. Vimadalal for the prosecution relied upon the wording of the illustration to section 10 of the Indian Evidence Act, and contended that when once an accused is proved to have joined the conspiracy, everything done by any conspirator would be relevant against him. That may be so for the purpose of proving the existence and the objects of the conspiracy, but that cannot fasten on him liability for anything done before he joined the conspiracy. This question was raised in O'Keefee v. Walsh, Irish Reports K. B. (1903), 681, and it was observed that a party to a conspiracy is not liable for the damage flowing from the conspiracy before the day of his joining it. But acts done in furtherance of the conspiracy prior to that date may be given in evidence against him for the purpose of showing the character of conspiracy which he joined. At page 702 Lord O'Brien, L.C.J., observed as follows:

> 'The true view, in my judgment, is rightly expressed in the head-note to the Queen (Shaw) v. Dwyer and Kelly (24 I.L.T.R. 111) that when the existence of a criminal conspiracy is proved, and it is shown that at a certain date the defendant joined the conspiracy, evidence of acts committed by the conspirators in pursuance of the conspiracy prior to that date is admissible as evidence against the defendant, not for the purpose of holding him criminally responsible for these acts, but for the purpose of showing the character of the conspiracy which he joined.'

Accused No. 4 cannot, therefore, be held guilty of the offences which were committed in pursuance of the conspiracy before he joined it. He must, therefore, be convicted only of the offences in the first, second and third items of the charge.

Accused No. 2 is not alleged to have been concerned in the possession, establishment or maintenance of the wireless transmitter in Parekh Wadi, Ex. C, but he is said to have joined the conspiracy at a later stage when it was decided to broadcast recorded programmes. He was introduced to him by accused No. 1 in Noble Chambers as a person who was interested in the work of broadcasting. Printer says that at that time Dr. Lohia and R. A. Mehta, and probably Mirza, were present. The idea of recording programmes was then thought of for the first time and accused No.2 is said to have offered to supply them with records of programmes from time to time, as the transmitter worked better with records. Printer says that he cannot say whence accused No.2 was going to supply the records. Dr. Lohia is not called to bear this out and R. A. Mehta and Mirza do not corroborate Printer's version. R. A. Mehta definitely says that he never saw any of the accused in connection with the broadcasting of programmes and Mirza says that he met accused No.2 only once in Noble Chambers and at that time no one else was present there. Thus Printer's statement that accused No.2 undertook to supply records stands uncorroborated. Printer says that recorded programmes began to be broadcast when the transmitter was in Laxmi Bhuwan, that is to say, after the 2nd or the 4th of October 1942. Deputy Inspector Fergusson says that he began to hear the broadcast from October 9, 1942 and for the first three days he did not notice whether records were played, but he is definite that from October 12, 1942, recorded programmes were broadcast. It thus appears that this interview must have taken place some time about the beginning of October, probably after October 4, 1942, if Printer is to be believed.

It is sought to be proved by the evidence of Jagannath Thakor, the radio mechanic in Chicago Radio Co., that accused No.2 was in possession of a recording machine. Jagannath says that he was once sent by accused No.5 to the house of accused No.2 to repair his recoding machine. He first said that that was in October 1942, but from his subsequent statements it appears that he has committed a mistake there. Accused No.2 lives with his brother Narottam

Bhau Jeweller in Bhaskar Bhuwan on Lamington Road.
Jagannath says that he went there, repaired the recording
machine and took a test by cutting a record of his own
voice. He says that he next met accused No.2 about 10 or
15 days thereafter when he had gone to his house to repair
a loudspeaking intercommunicating telephone machine in
the showroom on the ground floor of Bhasker Bhuwan.
In his cross-examination he says that about 10 or 15 days
after his second visit to Bhasker Bhuvan he had taken
accused No.2 to the Famous Cine Laboratory. The date
of their visit to the Famous Cine Laboratory is definitely
fixed. Majid (Ex.21), who is the chief technician in that
Laboratory, says that Jagannath and accused No.2 had
been there about the end of September, two or three days
before Gandhi Jayanti. Gandhi Jayanti fell on October 2,
1942, and therefore Jagannath's second visit to Bhasker
Bhuvan must have taken place about the 20th September,
and it was 10 or 15 days before that, that is to say, about
the 5th or the 10th of September 1942 Jagannath must
have repaired the recording machine as alleged by him. But
as I have already pointed out, accused No.2 is said to have
agreed to supply recorded programmes in the beginning of
October 1942. Hence when he got his machine repaired
he had no idea that he would have to cut records for the
Congress Radio Station. Thus the only use which the
prosecution can make of the evidence of Jagannath on this
point is to show that accused No.2 was in possession of a
record cutting machine. But Jagannath also is admittedly an
accomplice and there is no corroboration to his statement
that accused No.2 had a record cutting machine.

Printer says that he once saw accused No.2 cutting
a record in his presence in a bungalow near French
Bridge. He says that one night accused No.1 picked him

up at Byculla and drove him in his car to a bungalow in Lamington Road, evidently Bhasker Bhuvan, that he was made to wait in the car when accused No.1 went upstairs and after a long time returned saying that accused No.2 had shifted to another place, that they then drove to the bungalow near French Bridge where accused No.2 received them, that Mirza and accused No. 3 were also with them, that Jagannath was also present there, that in their presence accused No.2 took out a record cutting machine from a box or a suitcase, took the test of the voice of accused No.3 and recorded something which was read out by accused No.3 from a manuscript. He has now identified that record as Ex.J-61 relating to the Chimur incident. I have already dealt with the identification of that record by Printer when it was played in Court and I have come to the conclusion that the record must have been cut either by Printer himself or by some one else in his presence. That record was broadcast on October 28,1942, and presumably must have been cut a few days before that. It is therefore clear that programmes were being recorded every day long before this record was cut. If so it is difficult to understand why accused No.1 should take all the trouble of taking Printer and Mirza all the way from Byculla to be present to witness the cutting of the record by accused No.2. It is also strange that accused No.1 did not know where accused No.2 was going to cut the record. He first took the party to Bhasker Bhuvan where accused No.2 usually resides. This shows that there was no pre-arrangement and it was only after accused No.1 went to Bhasker Bhuvan that he learnt that accused No. 2 had gone somewhere. It is strange that accused No.2 should have been waiting for the arrival of accused No.1 and his colleagues till late at night and that Jagannath also should have been present to welcome the party. This shows the improbability of Printer's story on this point. That bungalow has not been identified and no one from that bungalow has been called to give evidence. Jagannath (Ex.19) positively asserts that he never saw any record being cut in his presence. Mirza also does not support Printer about this incident. Jagannath says that he has not even seen accused Nos. 1 and 3 until he met them in the lock-up and he had not gone to any bungalow near French Bridge. Printer says that he does not know whence the record cutting machine had been obtained by accused No.1. He saw on it the name plate of Chicago Radio Co. But Jagannath is certain that the record cutting machine which he had repaired for accused No.2 in Bhasker Bhuvan had no such name on it and that it had not been supplied by the Chicago radio Co. Chicage Radio Co. dealt in similar machines, but that machine had no name on it. Thus the story of Printer that accused No.2 cut the record Ex.J-61 in his presence in a bungalow near French bridge is uncorroborated.

It is suggested that accused No.2 was concerned in the cutting of another record, namely, Ex.J(10 ")4. On one side of that record is cut the song 'Hindustan Hamara' which was sung by Master Krishna at the A.I.C.C. Session on August 7 and 8, 1942, and on the other side are cut two speeches made at that session. Chicago Radio Co. had supplied loudspeakers to the A.I.C.C. for that session and had also arranged to take a film of the proceedings of the session. The sound recording truck had been hired from the Famous Cine Laboratory and the sound film was taken by Majid (Ex.21). After the Session was over the exposed film was taken to the Famous Cine Laboratory for being developed and edited. Those reels were kept in 22 tins after they were developed, but they were never edited. Majid

says that two or three days before Gandhi Jayanti, accused
No.5, the partner of Chicago Radio Co., sent him a word
that somebody from his firm would go that night for editing
that film. Jagannath says that accused No.5 asked him to
go to Famous Cine Laboratory and see how the film of the
A.I.C.C. had come out, that on his way he met accused No.2
who asked him where he was going, that he told him that
he was going to see the A.I.C.C. film, that accused No.2
expressed his wish to see it, that both of them then went
to the residence of accused No.2 and took their meals, that
they then went in the car of accused No.2 to the Famous
Cine Laboratory, that Majid showed the film to them, and
that they examined the film till midnight and thereafter
saw the picture *Soonbai* which was being screened, and
returned home at about 3 a.m. He says that no records
were cut at that time and that he did not see any record
cutting machine there. There is no doubt that the record
Ex.J(10 ") 4 must have been cut from the film taken by the
Famous Cine Laboratory. Master Krishna says that he has
never given any record of the song 'Hindustan Hamara'
sung by him and when the record was played in Court he
recognized it as the song sung by him at the A.I.C.C. Session.
It was suggested that any one living in a house adjacent to
the pandal of the A.I.C.C. meeting could cut a record from
the loudspeaker. But in that case the background noise also
would have appeared in the record, but there is no such
noise in Ex.J(10 ")4. I visited the Famous Cine Laboratory,
saw the editing room and also had the films exhibited.
I have no hesitation in holding that Ex.J(10 ")4 has been
cut from the corresponding films in that Laboratory. But
this is not sufficient to prove the connection of accused
No.2 with the cutting of that record. Jagannath says that
no record was cut at the time and Majid does not say that

there was any record cutting machine in that room, nor was one taken with them by accused No.2 and Jagannath. If accused No.5 wanted to see the film, he could have got it exhibited in the theatre in his own shop. If it had to be edited that also could have been done in his shop which then possessed an editing table. Moreover Jagannath says that he was not asked to edit the film, but merely to see whether the picture had come out properly. In fact the film has not yet been edited and the sound record film has not been synchronized with the picture film. Majid does say that next morning he saw some scrapings lying on the ground in the editing room and he is of opinion that they may be scrapings of the film. They were black and were of celluloid, and it is suggested that these must be scrapings from the blank record which had come out when it was cut. The scrapings were swept away and Majid says that he could not arrive at any conclusion from those scrapings. Accused No.2 admits that he had gone with Jagannath to see the film that night, but denies that any record was cut. Thus all that this evidence goes to prove is that the record Ex.J(10 ")4 must have been cut from the film in the possession of the Famous Cine Laboratory and that even according to the prosecution witness Jagannath no such record was cut on the night on which accused No.2 and he had gone to inspect the film. Majid says that the films had not been handed over to any one else before that night, nor after that night until they were produced before the police. From this it is sought to be concluded that the only occasion when such a record could be cut was on the night when accused No.2 and Jagannath visited the editing room of the Laboratory. But Majid admits that the films are kept in the department shelves and anybody can take them, that the shelves are not locked and that the technicians have often to handle them for testing them or correcting them under instructions. If so it is possible that even Jagannath may have gone at some other time and cut the record Ex.J(10 ")4. It was sought to be proved by the evidence of Jagannath Joshi (Ex.34) that Jagannath Thakor had been supplied with some blank records at the instance of accused No.5. Jagannath Joshi says that he left the service of Chicago Radio Co. in September 1942 and a week before that 12 pieces of blank records were given to Jagannath Thakor. That must have been somewhere about the 22nd or 23rd of September 1942, and, as I have already pointed out , accused No.2 had not then even met Printer and had not offered to supply recorded programmes. Whatever Jagannath may have done before the alleged offer was made by accused No.2 cannot connect No.2 with the conspiracy.

It was argued that Jagannath had met accused No.2 only twice before and it is not likely that accused No.2 should have acted so familiarily towards him as to take him to his bungalow to dine with him and then take him to the Famous Cine Laboratory in his own car. That only shows the curiosity of accused No. 2 to see and listen to the films of the proceedings of the A.I.C.C., but it does not follow that he had then the sinister idea of cutting a record. Jagannath does not say that any record cutting machine was then taken with them in the car. The scrapings found in the editing room next morning do not necessarily show that they were scrapings of the record, but they may have been scrapings of some other film which might have been edited in the editing room. Majid says that they looked like scrapings of a film. However suspicious the conduct of accused No.2 may have been, the evidence is too filmsy and insufficient to justify the conclusion that the record

Ex.J(10 ")4 was cut that night and that accused No.2 was concerned in it.

Jagannath Joshi says that accused No.2 had been to the godown of Chicago Radio Co. twice or thrice, but no materials were ever supplied to him. He also says that Jagannath Thakor told him that the blank records were required for the Congress Radio. This only suggests that even before accused No.2 is said to have joined the conspiracy Jagannath was concerned in preparing records for the Congress Radio, and as, according to Printer, accused No.1 always used to supply the records, it is more than probable that he used to get them from Jagannath. It is significant that although most of the records have captions written or inscribed on them, none of them is proved to be in the handwriting of accused No.2.

There is one other incident by which accused No.2 is sought to be connected with the conspiracy. Jagannath Thakor says that in October 1942 accused No.5 asked him to help accused No.2 in solving some difficulties. He accordingly went to the house of accused No.2 and was taken by him in his car to a bungalow in Banganga. There he saw some transmitting parts and accused No.2 said that he wanted to test and study the different parts and learn how to operate upon them. The parts were not complete and an amplifier was wanting. Jagannath remained with accused No.2 for about two hours explaining the various parts and then went away. He did not come to know why accused No.2 had the transmitting parts in that bungalow or why he wanted to study them. There is absolutely no corroboration to this story of Jagannath. Printer, who was in the conspiracy from the beginning and was practically acting as the radio technician for the transmitter, knew nothing about this set. He says that he learnt from Jagannath that another transmitter had been built and that the test would be taken shortly, but that must not be the transmitting parts which Jagannath claims to have seen at Banganga. It is in evidence that a different transmitting set was produced by Jaichand Sheth from Khandke Building and possibly he may have been referring to it. I have already ruled out the evidence regarding that set as irrelevant. (Ex.60). It is also pointed out that on October 18 it was announced on the Congress Radio that the English programmes would be broadcast on 39 metres wave length. But Fergusson says that it was never heard on that wave length. This does show that those who were in charge of the Congress Radio Station were referring to a completed transmitting set expected to be working on 39 metres wave length. That could certainly not be the transmitting parts said to have been seen by Jagannath in the Banganga bungalow. Nothing is known as to what happened to those parts. Trikumdas (Ex.36) is examined to show that some two or three gentlemen not known to him took a flat in a bungalow on the Banganga Road about the end of September 1942 on a rent of Rs. 60 per month in the name of Babulal Bhagwandas. Those tenants used to sleep in that bungalow sometimes, but he is certain that they were not any of the accused before the Court. The flat was vacated after a month, although three months' rent had been paid in advance. It is not clear whether it was the same bungalow that is referred to by Jagannath. Assuming that it was the same, still Trikumdas does not say that accused No.2 had anything to do with that bungalow or had ever been there. In the absence of any evidence to support the story of Jagannath, it is not safe to hold that accused No.2 was building a transmitting set in that bungalow or that that set had anything to do with the conspiracy in question. If really any such set was being built in pursuance of the conspiracy, Printer would not have remained aloof and accused No.2 would not have sought the help of Jagannath for building it. Printer is an expert radio technician and he could have easily built the other set also, if the necessary parts were supplied to him. But Printer was kept entirely in the dark regarding the construction of that set. This shows that if any such set was really built in the Banganga bungalow it was not in pursuance of this conspiracy.

This is all the evidence against accused No.2. If he had joined the conspiracy it is strange that Printer never asked for any monetary help from him for the purpose of carrying out its objects. As I have already said, Printer had really started the conspiracy, in order to make money out of the parts which were lying on his hands. But he never seems to have touched the pockets of accused No.2 and therefore I am not satisfied that accused No.2 had at any time joined that conspiracy. Moreover it is not alleged that accused No.2 ever took part in the hiring of the flats for the location of the Congress Radio Station, nor was he ever present in any of the flats at any time. It must therefore be held that he is not proved to have committed any of the offences charged against him.

A good deal of evidence adduced against accused No.5 has now to be left out of consideration under the order passed by me at Ex.60. It was sought to be proved that a wireless transmitter was built for the Congress Radio with the parts knowingly and clandestinely supplied by him. That set was produced by Jaichand Sheth and, as I pointed out in Ex.60, it had nothing to do with the conspiracy with which we are concerned in this case. The only evidence which remains for connecting accused No.5 with this conspiracy is that he supplied some parts for strengthening Printer's transmitter, that he supplied a home recording machine and blank records and that he purposely gave instructions to Jagannath to go to the Famous Cine Laboratory. The last three points have been sufficiently dealt with already, but I will briefly deal with the evidence regarding the home recording machine and the blank records.

It appears from Ex.Y-12 that one Hiralal Saraf of Deoghar ordered out a Chicago Home Recorder from Chicago Radio Co. on August 22, 1942. Shamrao Urankar (Ex.42), who is the order clerk in that company, found that there was only one home recorder in stock and that it was out of order. He therefore sent it to the mechanic for repairs and when he got it back repaired, he wrote a letter to Hiralal to send some advance. He had packed the home recorder and kept it separate, along with some blank records and three needles wrapped in a brown paper as Hiralal wanted to have them also. After a couple of days accused No.5 took away the packet of blank records and needles from his table. Thereafter the home recorder was also sent to the show room to be shown to another customer. That customer was Mr. Hill and the correspondence Ex.Y-13 shows that the recorder was sold to him on November 11, 1942. On the cash memo prepared for Hiralal, Ex.Y-12, a note is made that the home recorder was sold to Mr. Hill by accused No.5. This cannot be disputed, but it is suggested that during the interval the home recorder was available for being used for the purpose of cutting records for the Congress Radio. This is only a surmise which has no foundation in the evidence. It is suggested that this home recorder was sent to accused No.2 for that purpose, then the one which Jagannath claims to have repaired in accused No.2's house must be different since that recorder was not the one meant for Hiralal. From the mere fact that there was a home recorder in Chicago Radio Co. available for temporary use it cannot be inferred that it must have been sent to some one for being used for cutting records for the congress radio.

It is also pointed out that some blank records and three cutting needles found their way into the house of Mr. Aildas Thakor, the advocate for accused No.5, and that they must have been purposely secreted there. Lakha, the Court Clerk of Chicago Radio Co. has explained the circumstance under which he left the packet of those records and needles in the house of Mr. Thakor by mistake. There whould be no point in accused No.5 making an attempt to conceal those records. Those blank records show that they bear the name of Chicago Radio Co., whereas the records found in Parekh Wadi were R.C.A. records. Chicago Radio Co. does not deal in R.C.A. blank records and even if the blank records bearing the name of the company were found in the shop, they could not be connected with the R.C.A. records which were found in Parekh Wadi. Accused No.5 had no reason to be afraid of the records made by his company.

I have already referred to the alleged instructions given by accused No.5 to Jagannath to go to the Famous Cine Laboratory to see how the film of the A.I.C.C. meeting had come out. Jagannath says that he had been sent merely for that purpose, while Majid says that a word was sent to him that some one from the company would go to edit the film. Accused No.5 says that he never gave any such instructions to Jagannath and Majid's evidence does not show that instructions were given by accused No.5. Jagannath himself may have phoned to Majid if he was in the conspiracy. Thus this circumstance does not connect accused No.5 with the conspiracy.

Printer has vividly described how accused No.5 was prevailed upon to supply the necessary parts for strengthening his transmitter. When it was decided that the power of the transmitter should be raised from 10 watts to 100 watts, accused No.1 took upon himself the burden of securing the necessary parts which were not ordinarily available in the market. Accused No.1 then took Printer to Dahyabhai Patel at the Oriental Insurance Co. and the situation was explained to Dahyabhai Patel. They all then went together to Chicago Radio Co. where Dahyabhai was greeted by accused No.5 and had some private talk with him. Printer was waiting outside and could not hear their talk. When he went in, accused No.5 said that he would put them into touch with the right man and called Jagannath Thakor. Dahyabhai Patel then left. Printer had a list of the parts required for strengthening the transmitter. Jagannath saw the list and said that all the parts were not available but were expected shortly and that he would give delivery within a few days. He then had some talk with accused No.5 and said that the parts would be kept ready at 1 p.m. the next day. The next day accused No.1 went to Jagannath, but the parts were not delivered to him, as he was told that the name of Chicago Radio Co. appearing on those parts had to be removed. After some days accused No.1 rang up and told Printer that he had received the parts. He was shown a box containing the parts which included six crystals. The specification plates had been removed from them and the frequency on them was written in ink. With those parts Printer increased the power of the transmitter to 100 watts. On this point there is only the evidence of Printer, Mirza and Jagannath, all of

whom are accomplices. There is no satisfactory evidence
to show that the other parts required by Printer came
from accused No.5, and stress is laid upon the crystal
used in the transmitter Ex.C. That crystal Ex.C-10 has its
specification plate removed and the frequency of 7075 is
written on the inner plate in ink. An attempt is made to
prove that Chicago Radio Co. did possess a Bliley crystal
of the type B.5, having the frequency 7075, that it was
not sold to anyone and that it has not been accounted
for. From this it is sought to be inferred that it must have
been given to Printer for being fitted up in the transmitter
Ex.C. I have already referred to the fact that the old crystal
which Printer possessed was out of order and he had fitted
it up as a dummy to deceive accused No. 1. He therefore
changed it before increasing the power of the transmitter
and changed the wave length from 41.78 to 42.34 metres.
As most of the evidence in this connection has a bearing
on the transmitter produced from the Khandke Building,
I will try to avoid as much as possible discussing it in
detail except where it is necessary. I may state at once that
after going through the evidence I find that at least three
crystals in the stock of Chicago Radio Co. have not been
satisfactorily accounted for. Raman (Ex.33), who acts as
the Secretary to Mr. V.G. Motwane, the brother of accused
No 5, and looks to the imports of articles from foreign
countries, has prepared a statement Ex. Y-6 showing the
number of crystals received and disposed of. In September
1941, after the Government Notification, a list of
controlled parts in stock was prepared (Z-32). It was sent
to the Commissioner of Police along with the original of
the letter Ex.Y-4. In Ex.Z-32 158 crystals are mentioned.
On September 7, 1942, the godown clerk Shantilal
prepared a list of the crystals in the godown for being sent

to the Burma Posts and Telegraphs for their information. In that list (Ex.Z-13) the frequencies of all the crystals in stock were mentioned. After taking into consideration 30 crystals subsequently received and 16 found in excess in the godown, it is shown in Ex.Y-6 that there ought to be 65 crystals in stock. Of those 65, 60 were taken by the Police from the Lucknow branch of the company and the remaining five are shown in Ex.Y-6 as three of type HF/2 and two of type B/5 and they have been produced in Court. But I find on comparing the frequencies of the three of type HF/2 with the frequencies of the crystals of that type in stock mentioned in the list sent to Burma Posts and Telegraphs (Ex.Z-13) that the three produced in Court were never in the company's stock. There is a good deal of force in the contention of the prosecution that these three must have been obtained from somewhere else and produced to make up the five which ought to be in stock. It is argued from this that three crystals have gone away somewhere and not accounted for. On the other hand, Ex.Z-13 shows that there was in stock a crystal of B/5 type having the frequency 7075 k.c. and it does not appear from the record that that crystal was sold to any customer. It follows that since the crystal Ex.C10 bears frequency 7075 k.c. it must be the same which was in the stock of Chicago Radio Co. when Ex.Z13 was prepared. This argument appears plausible on the face of it and I need not refer to the other documents leading to that conclusion. But this is not sufficient to prove that accused No.5 gave that crystal for the use of the transmitter Ex.C. Moreover there is one other flaw in this reasoning which is almost fatal to this contention. There is no evidence to prove that the crystal Ex.C10 is a Bliley crystal of type B/5 and that its frequency is 7075 k.c. Its specification plate having been removed, somebody must have written 7075 on the inner plate. But that is obviously incorrect. When the new crystal was fitted up, it was announced from the Congress Radio Station that it was broadcasting on 42.34 metres wavelength. This wave length in metres did not appear on the crystal and Printer, who is an expert technician, must have calculated it from the frequency appearing on the crystal. The frequency corresponding to 42.34 metres is 7086, whereas the frequency 7075 expressed in kilocycles corresponds to 42.40 metres. If the frequency had been already written on the crystal as 7075 when Printer fitted it on Ex.C, the Congress radio would have announced that it was broadcasting on 42.40 metres wavelength. It may be inferred from this that at that time the figure written on the crystal was 7086 and not 7075. It is also admitted by Inspector Kokje that he got this crystal tested by Tanna and its frequency was found to be 7094 or 7096. In either case it is not proved that its frequency ever was 7075. It is not proved who wrote that figure on the crystal or when it was written, but it is certain that it is inaccurate. If so, it cannot be said that it was the same crystal which was described in Ex.Z13 as the crystal of type B/5 with the frequency of 7075 k.c. It follows therefore that accused No.5 cannot be said to have sent that crystal for being fitted up on the transmitter Ex.C. It is in evidence that there were some crystals with the set in Khandke Building and the crystals unaccounted for may have gone there.

A good deal of stress was laid upon the note Ex. UU prepared by Shantilal showing that after September 7, 1942, six crystals were supplied from the godown in accordance with the instructions of accused No.5 and one of those crystals is mentioned to have been of the type B/5 with the frequency 7075 k.c. Shantilal did not know to whom it had been supplied and therefore he has put in a mark of interrogation in Ex.UU against the six crystals. This note appears in a file which was attached from the Chicago Radio Co. in the presence of Panchas and was signed by both the Panchas at the time of the Panchnama. The genuineness of this document is challenged by the defence and it is pointed out that it is an unusual document which would not ordinarily appear in that file. It is formally proved by the evidence of Shantilal and as it consists of other crystals also I refrain from expressing any opinion about its genuineness, as I find it unnecessary. We are concerned with the crystal which was fitted on Ex.C and although its frequency is written in ink on its plate as 7075, I have pointed out that its frequency is different and the description is not correct. Hence even if a crystal of that frequency was given away to some unknown person by accused No.5 as shown in Ex.UU, it was not given for being used for the Congress radio transmitter, Ex. C. Ex. UU is therefore irrelevant for the purpose of the present trial.

The only other circumstance pointed out against accused No.5 is his conduct in sending away all the crystals and blank records to the Lucknow branch of the company with Rupani. The correspondence relating to the circumstances under which Rupani was called here and all the crystals were taken away by him has been produced. It shows that there was an order for as many as 56 transmitters for the Military and as all the controlled parts were kept in the head office here, it was necessary to send the crystals to Lucknow with Rupani. There was no propriety in concealing the existence of those crystals. They had been already notified to the Police Commissioner and an account had to be regularly kept. All those crystals were seized by the Police and the fact that they were sent to Lucknow under these circumstances does not indicate that accused No.5 had a guilty conscience. This is all the evidence on which the prosecution relies for connecting accused No.5 with the conspiracy.

Dahyabhai Patel, who is said to have been introduced by accused No.1 to accused No.5, has not been called and it is not shown what influence he has on him. Printer's testimony on that point is not corroborated by any other evidence and cannot therefore, be accepted. Hence on the evidence as it stands it is not proved that accused No. 5 had joined this conspiracy or did anything in furtherance of carrying out its objects. He must therefore, be acquitted of all the charges.

Thus out of the five accused only accused Nos. 1,3 and 4 are found to have been concerned in the conspiracy to establish, maintain and work an unauthorised wireless transmitter. That in itself is a serious offence, but to use it for broadcasting prejudicial reports intended or likely to spread disaffection and hamper war efforts is, to say the least, grossly heinous and deserves a deterrent sentence. Accused No.1 took a leading part not only by financing the project but also by taking an active part at every stage, and I see no reason why he should not be given the maximum sentence of imprisonment under rules 16(7) and 38(5) of the Defence of India Rules. Accused No.3 seems to be equally guilty. She was playing the second fiddle and has not stooped to put forward a false defence to escape conviction. She will, therefore, be dealt with more leniently. Accused No.4 had apparently joined the conspiracy recently, and before he could take a more active part in carrying out its objects, everything was exposed and the transmitter was seized. The offence of criminal conspiracy is by itself separately punishable under section 120B I.P.C., even though the offences which had formed the object of the conspiracy were not committed at all. In the present case, however, the offences which constituted the object of the conspiracy were actually and in fact carried out. A separate sentence for the offence under section 120B I.P.C. is, therefore, not called for (Harsha Nath Chatterjee v. Emperor, I.L.R. 42 Cal. 1153 and Punjab Singh v. The Crown, I.L.R. 15 Lah 84). The sentences for the offences under the different counts in the charge will, therefore, be ordered to run concurrently.

It is unfortunate that men like Printer, Mirza and R.A. Mehta, who played a very prominent part in the conspiracy and actively carried out its objects in various ways, had to be examined as witnesses for the prosecution instead of being placed in the dock to be tried along with the accused. Many of the witnesses, who came after Printer and Mirza, seemed to have a soft corner for the accused, and from the outline of the evidence which Mr. Vimadalal, the learned Counsel for the prosecution, in opening the case, said that he was going to lead, it appears that they were not prepared to state what he expected from them. Yet unruffled by the discomfiture which this must have caused, he made the best of the materials available and conducted the case with conspicuous fairness and equanimity, conceding every point that his witnesses had rendered untenable and giving every facility asked for by the defence.

Before concluding, I must record my appreciation of the intelligent investigation of the case by Inspector Kokje and acknowledge the help which I received from the learned Counsels on both the sides throughout this protracted trial.

I convict accused No.1 Vithaldas Madhavji Khakar
alias Babubhai (a) under section 120-B I.P.C., (b) rule
16(7) read with rule 16(3) and 121 of the Defence of India
Rules along with section 20 of the Indian Telegraph Act,
1885, (c) rule 16(7) read with rule 16(5) and rule 121 of
the Defence of India Rules and (d) rule 38(5) read with rule
38(1)(a) and (c) and rule 121 of the Defence of India Rules,
and sentence him to undergo rigorous imprisonment for
a period of five years for each of the four offences, the
sentences to run concurrently. He is acquitted of the charge
under rule 39(6) read with rule 39(1)(b) and rule 121 of
the Defence of India Rules.

I convict accused No.3 Usha Mehta (a) under section
120-B I.P.C,(b) rule 16(7) read with rule 16(3) and rule
121 of the Defence of India Rules along with section 20
of the Indian Telegraph Act, 1885, (c) rule 16(7) read
with rule 16(5) of the Defence of India Rules and (d) rule
38(5) read with rule 38(1) (a) and (c) and rule 121 of
the Defence of India Rules and sentence her to undergo
rigorous imprisonment for a period of four years for each
of the four offences, the sentences to run concurrently. She
is acquitted of the charge under rule 39(6) read with rule
39(1)(b) and rule 121 of the Defence of India Rules.

I convict accused No. 4 Chandrakant Babubhai Jhaveri
(a) under section 120-B I.P.C., (b) rule 16(7) read with rule
16(3) and rule 121 of the Defence of India Rules along
with section 20 of the Indian Telegraph Act, 1885, and
(c) rule 16(7) read with rule 16(5) of the Defence of India
Rules and sentence him to undergo rigorous imprisonment
for a period of one year for each of the three offences,
the sentences to run concurrently. He is acquitted of the
remaining two charges.

Accused No.2 Vithaldas Kanthadbhai Jhaveri and accused No. 5 Nanak G. Motwane are acquitted of all the charges and discharged.

14-5-1943

Sd. N.S. Lokur
SPECIAL JUDGE

Certified to be a true copy this 26th day of May 1943.
Clerk of the Crown
This 26th day of May 1943.

Note: The text of the judgment is reproduced as per the original document.

[1]   Usha Mehta Congress Radio Papers, Mani Bhavan Gandhi Sangrahalaya, Mumbai
*   (and then to Ajit Villa)
     It seems that these words are inadvertently left out in the typed copy.
**   There seems to be a typographical error. This might be Air/Airforce.

Appendix II

Ushaben's Reminiscences

Childhood

Ushaben talked about her childhood with childlike innocence. Born on 25 March 1920 in the village of Saras in the Surat district of Gujarat, to Hariprasad Mehta and Mahimangauri, she was the youngest child and the only daughter. She had three elder brothers: Dhruv, Janak and Chandrakant. Since Hariprasad Mehta was in the government judicial service, he was frequently transferred. Hence, Ushaben studied at various schools in the districts of Kheda and Bharuch (both in Gujarat) and finally, Mumbai.

Ushaben remembered her first meeting with Gandhiji around 1926 or so. At that time her father was stationed in the district of Kheda. While her family, especially her mother, grandmother and aunt, were happy visiting holy places like Dakor, Bahucharaji and Khedbrahma, little Ushaben had set her heart on visiting Gandhi Ashram near the Sabarmati River. Initially her father was reluctant since he was in the government service, but he finally gave in and the family paid a visit to the ashram.

Little Ushaben was happy, and time failed to diminish her first impression of Bapu: 'We were moving around, and there was Gandhiji in front of us! He patted me lightly on my cheek and asked, "What will you do?" My answer was "I shall stay in the ashram." He was amused and quipped, "You are too young for that. Have you taken permission from your father?" Before I could respond, Lalu kaka said, as an elder of the family, in

Ushaben on her release from jail

English, "Bapu, if you are prepared to accept her, we do not mind." Bapu had immediately retorted, "Oh brother, you are Hindi, I am Hindi. You speak Gujarati, I speak Gujarati. Then why should we talk in English? I stayed in South Africa for years, but I have not forgotten my mother tongue." A button in my frock was not properly closed. Turning to me he said, "Look here, this would not do in the ashram. If you want to live in the ashram, you will have to do physical work, and remain organized and clean, and should look after all small things and details. You will have to observe the ashram discipline and cleanliness."' Little Ushaben nodded her head with rapt attention and learnt her first lessons of self-reliance and love for her mother tongue.

By that time Gandhi was at the centre stage of Indian politics. The Simon Commission, which visited India in 1928, had been trying to discuss the constitutional reforms with the leaders of the nation, and to understand the prevailing mood of the people, the members travelled to various places. The nation was gripped by a storm of opposition against the Commission. The atmosphere was charged with the slogans like 'Simon Commission, go back!', 'Inquilab Zindabad!' and 'Vande Mataram!'. Young Ushaben remembered shouting such slogans and joining *prabhat pheri*s with her friends.

Acceptance of Khadi at a Young Age

Local leaders had organized a camp on Gandhian principles at Olpad in Surat district. Young Ushaben and her cousin Sukanya were allowed to go to this camp. Ushaben had worn a frock of foreign fabric, and Gandhiji naturally did not approve of it. He said, 'If you want to stay in the camp, you will have to forgo such cloth. Our battle is for Swaraj. You know that Swaraj–Swadeshi–Swabhasha (self-rule, indigenous goods and the mother tongue) is our three-pronged slogan.' These words had a deep impact on young Ushaben and she decided to wear khadi for life. Gandhi advised these two young girls to serve the nation and not get married and they were ready to accept this too. However, the aunt who accompanied these girls protested: 'How can these young girls make a solemn promise not to get married? They do not even know the meaning of the term "marriage".' Gandhi accepted this argument and advised the girls, 'If you decide to get married on growing up, go ahead. But find a groom who does not demand dowry and who helps you in serving the nation.' Ushaben, however, never thought of marriage and remained unmarried.

Having accepted khadi, she wore it happily and gracefully. Her mother's desire to make her only daughter (Ushaben) wear fancy clothes and accessories thus remained unfulfilled. However, she was very happy and proud of having Ushaben as her daughter and being known as Ushaben's mother.

Ushaben and her friends learnt the lessons of patriotism and service to the nation at this camp. Mithuben Petit, Raihana Tyabji, Hitendrabhai and Pramodbhai were among the speakers to address the young participants. The participants were exposed to new ideas about national rejuvenation and would mull over them. The morning started with flag hoisting coupled with the song 'Vijayi Vishwa Tiranga Pyara, Jhanda Uncha Rahe Hamara'. This was followed by a morning procession wherein the participants would walk through the streets, singing songs of communal unity like 'Yagna Ame Mandyo Re Tan Man Shuddhi Karawa' and 'Hindu Muslim Parsi Bano Ekta Ni Arasi'. Prayers would be held in the mornings and evenings. Mithuben would play the *manjira* while Raihanaben would sing. Bhajans would be sung even while picketing the liquor shops. All this had a deep impact on Ushaben's mind; these ideas germinated and grew stronger over the years and her love for bhajans and nationalist songs increased with the passage of time.

There would be regular spinning classes at the camp. Once, when all the women and girls were spinning and singing 'Takli Takli Takli Raje', Ushaben found that she couldn't spin a long thread. Observing her, Gandhi advised, 'Do not fear or falter. Keep your mind steady and focused.

The thread will not break and will be of good quality.' It was a lesson on steady minds as propagated in the Gita.

Ushaben remembers an important incident in this context, which conveyed the power of satyagraha to bring about a change of heart. In the area there was a liquor shop owned by a Parsi. People going into the shop would see the women picketing outside; some would go back and some would go in and some would go to the extent of abusing them. But the courageous picketers would not give up. Once when a person came to buy liquor at the shop, Mithuben lay prostrate on the ground. Ushaben and the other girls followed her. Mithuben told the man quietly, 'Brother, if you decide not to give up your habit of drinking, it is okay. Now you will have to muster gallantry to cross over these tender girls.' The man obviously was struck with the seriousness of the situation. He not only gave up drinking, but also started wearing khadi and participating in the satyagraha movement.

The Manjarsena

Ushaben remembers the days of 1930–31 as a time of great fervour. 'People were thrilled with Gandhiji's ideas and work. They were ready to implement his techniques with all dedication and enthusiasm. It appeared to them as if the struggle was between Ram and Ravan, between good and evil. Naturally, Ram's army would have monkeys; Gandhiji's soldiers were children jumping and shrieking hoop-hoop like monkeys. When we saw boys getting organized as the Vanarsena (army of monkeys), we girls thought why not a Manjarsena (army of cats)?'

And the girls did organize a Manjarsena. Once they walked in a procession with national flags in their hands and the patriotic song 'Nahi Namashe, Nahi Namashe, Nishan Bhumi Bharat Nu' on their lips. A troop of policemen ordered them to lay down the national flag and disperse, but the girls were firm in their resolve to proceed. They said, 'Bapu has given the command that the flag cannot be put down.' Whereupon the policemen started hitting the girls with lathis (rods), but the girls braved the attack. A volunteer named Sarala fainted and fell on the ground holding the flag in her hand. The disheartened girls appealed to the local leaders to find a way out. When nothing came up, they devised a plan of their own.

Dr Chandulal Desai was the group's favourite leader who was known as 'Chhote Sardar' because of his leadership qualities. The girls requested his colleagues to open the khadi shops. They picked up materials in colours of white, green and saffron, and immediately it appeared as if tailoring shops had opened up on the road! Women and girls were busy stitching saffron blouses, green petticoats and white scarfs (odhni). When the girls marched the next morning, everybody noticed that that they did not carry flags in their hands, but had become living flags to combat the blows of the police. Their hearts were filled with love for the motherland, and the words they uttered were challenges to the police: 'Chalao Lathi, Chalao Danda, Jhuk Na Sakega Apna Jhanda!' The girls were triumphant.

Dr Chandulal Desai (Chandu mama for Ushaben) described this incident to Gandhi. Ushaben was also there. She remembers Gandhi smiling and saying, 'These cats have given the lessons of non-violence and fearlessness to the nation and the world. I am proud of them.' Turning to Ushaben he had said, 'Convey Bapu's thanks to all the girls who were with you.'

Gandhi was very particular about the details. In this case also he asked, 'Was any khadi material left?' Neither Ushaben nor Chandu mama, excited as they were with their adventure, had noticed. Gandhi drew their attention to their mistake. 'Every pie/paisa of the khadi-bhandar has to be accounted for. They are not the shops owned by individuals. How can you forget that?' Chandu mama and Ushaben realized their mistake and agreed to correct it. Experiences of the Manjarsena left an indelible imprint of discipline and collective strength on the mind of young Ushaben. She fondly remembered women leaders of that time like Mridulaben (daughter of Dinkar Desai) and Pushpaben Desai who showered affection on these girls.

Salt Satyagraha

After the Dandi March, the tidal wave of the Salt Satyagraha had swept the country and entered every home. Ushaben and her brothers used to go to their maternal grandmother's home during the summer holidays. When the children reached her home, they did not find their grandmother waiting to receive them. Instead they found her in the backyard, putting salted water in a pan to boil on a stove; she was breaking the law by preparing salt! She told the children, 'Sweets and snacks are already prepared for you. But you will not get them immediately. First go and sell packets of salt prepared by me, and shake the very foundations of the British empire!'

Her father was initially concerned about Ushaben's nationalist involvement, but after he retired and moved to Bombay, she found more opportunities to be involved in nationalistic activities.

'As children, our work was to distribute bulletins, make salt from the Chowpatty water and sell it in small packets. We used to visit our relatives in jail who were undergoing a lot of hardship.'

Ushaben's family had shifted to Mumbai in 1932 after her father retired. Some active camps (*chhavanis*) had been organized in Mumbai consequent to the Salt Satyagraha. Young schoolgoing girls, including Ushaben, were enthusiastic participants in the camps set up at the Rashtriya Shala in Vile Parle. Maniben Nanavati had a major role in guiding these camps.

Gandhi had emphasized that when satyagraha was not practised, the activities of the constructive work would have to be followed with enthusiasm and devotion. Accordingly, Ushaben and her friends like Hasu Modi and Sarla Munim used to go to the Harijan bastis (homes of the people called untouchables) to propagate khadi and to organize classes for the children. Perinben Captain had taken up the work of propagating the national language. This activity had also attracted Ushaben, and her love for Hindi extended throughout her life.

Ushaben often remembered her friend Kisantai's experience in the context of Gandhi's ways of working. Kisantai, like Ushaben, wanted to live in Gandhi's ashram from an early age. When she expressed her desire to him, he was reading a long letter. He just took out a pin from the letter and placed it in Kisantai's hand, and started talking about other issues. Kasturba had already welcomed her very affectionately. After staying in the ashram for a fortnight, Kisantai went to Gandhi and expressed her resolve to stay there. He said, 'This means that Bapu has passed your examination. Now let me examine you.' She immediately got a paper and a pen and was ready for the examination. Bapu said, 'There is no reading or writing in my test. However, there is a small issue. When you came to me the first day, I had given you a pin. Please return it to me.'

Kisantai was awestruck! She had forgotten that he had given her a pin! Thus, she learnt the first lesson of the stay in the ashram. She learnt a lot from Kasturba too and stayed in the ashram for a long time. Kisantai had narrated her experience to Ushaben, who tried her utmost to imbibe this lesson.

Years in Wilson College

Ushaben chose to study at Wilson College because she did not want to go to a government college. Wilson College had a number of nationalists on its rolls, as the Scottish members of the staff did not discourage the students' nationalist aspirations. Wilson College nurtured Ushaben intellectually and emotionally. She was proud of her Alma Mater and its nationalist students and teachers.[1] Here she found affectionate friends and excellent teachers.[2] Remembering her teachers she said, 'Professor Wadia was one of the senior-most members of the staff. He taught us subjects as varied as Logic and Philosophy, Politics and Economics, Biology and even French. Professor Velankar and Professor Choksi could keep us spellbound by reciting verses and passages from poets and playwrights like Kalidasa and Bhavabhuti, Wordsworth and Shakespeare. Some of the laboratories were always open because teachers like Dr Taylor used to conduct experiments till late in the night. Our teachers taught us to think independently and to live by ideals. I remember once when we were attending Professor Wadia's class, a public meeting was being addressed by the leaders of the Congress at Chowpatty.

(Wilson College is opposite Chowpatty beach.) Professor Wadia explained to us how dissent becomes a duty when the government is tyrannical. He told us, 'You know about the life of Lord Jesus Christ and how he dreamt of uniting the world through the bond of love. His mission has been made more clearly manifest in the life and work of Gandhi. So, today, you should be not in your classroom but in the public meeting at Chowpatty where Gandhi's followers are trying to rouse the people to contribute their might to achieve freedom for the country and establish a new world based on fellowship and friendship.' Professor Wadia and Dr Mclean had established the 'Inter-religious Students' Fellowship' that met once a week to discuss the current issues and to read together passages from texts like the Bible, Gita, writings of Tagore, Swami Vivekananda and saints from various religions.

'Yusuf Meherally, a dynamic leader of the Congress, had established the Youth League that met regularly at its office near the College. Members met there and discussed the main principles of different political ideologies like liberalism, socialism and communism. They were also encouraged to take up constructive activities recommended by Gandhiji. Aloo Dastur, Manek Gandhi, R.J. Shah, Gulab Shroff and others took us juniors along with them to these meetings. Inspired by these meetings, some of us joined the Congress Volunteer Corps. Two of my friends, Hasu Modi and Sarla Munim, were very active in the Sevika Dal and took regular training there. I too used to go for the training but not as regularly as Hasu and Sarla. This gave us a good opportunity to come into contact with many leaders and we thought of taking up some constructive activities.

'We adopted a Harijan locality at Walpakhadi in Mazgaon and started classes for young children, sewing classes for women and literacy classes for men. The Kavadia brothers, Namjoshi and Jyotsna Thakor were actively involved with this work. Usha Setalvad had started such an experiment in the village Tara near Juhu. We were helped by our teachers like Dr Hivale. The Harijan Sevak Sangh and local Congress leaders like Jinabhai Joshi, Kajrolkar and Sopariwala gave us the necessary help and guidance.

'Some of us, including Suman Khandwala and I, were interested in learning and propagating Hindi, our national language, for fostering unity in the country. This was advocated by Gandhiji. So we joined the Hindi classes. The textbooks prescribed for the examinations and the atmosphere in the classes instilled in us a sense of intense patriotism. The nationalist fervour we had imbibed in the college was strengthened by our reading of the history and revolutions in other countries as also by the literary works of Maithili Sharan Gupt, Dinkar and Subhadra Kumari in the classes.

'Some of the students in this class—especially Babubhai, Inamdar, Suman, Rasika (both Wilsonians) and I—attended the historic session of the AICC at the Gowalia Tank Maidan on 7 and 8 August 1942. We heard the speeches of Gandhiji, Nehru, Sardar Patel, Maulana Azad and others with rapt attention and resolved to contribute our humble might to the struggle of freedom by becoming our own leaders and deciding upon a programme that would carry the message of defiance of the unjust government and its evil laws. And we thought of starting the underground radio.'

Arrest and Imprisonment

In Ushaben's words, 'I was taken to the lock-up at Crawford Market after my arrest for operating the Congress Radio.

My cellmate was an old lady who was using the room as her dining-cum-bedroom and toilet. She was fast asleep. The cell was very dirty and I could not get even a wink of sleep though I was badly in need of some rest.

'I realized that the lock-up period was perhaps the most trying time in the life of a prisoner. During the day one had to face the policemen, and at night the only possible activity could be either to kill the bugs or to kill time. Again it was humanly impossible to sleep in a cell full of filth, dirt and nauseating smells.

'My father, who had retired as a judge, was keen that I complete my studies. He happened to know Mohanlal Desai, chief of the CID, and requested him to shift me to a cleaner place. Desai had a soft corner for political prisoners. And so the next day I was taken to the Arthur Road Prison and lodged in a dingy solitary cell. I spent nearly six months in that cell during which time I was not allowed to meet anyone, not even my mother. What was worse, I was not even allowed to read books. It was only when Mrs McKenzie, the official jail visitor and wife of the principal of my college (Wilson College), certified that I was not of a questionable character that books, mainly from the Wilson College library, were sent to me. The jailor had initially pleaded his inability to allow books as there were strict orders from the authorities against giving out books. But Mrs McKenzie had said, "What nonsense! I can understand you not allowing her to read seditious literature, but how about giving her books on religion, philosophy, ethics and others? You make a special case for her. I shall send books from our college library and you will give them to her." Reading was like oxygen for me in the solitary cell of the prison. It was here that I began studying for my PhD degree, which I obtained ten years later. I shall always remain grateful to Mrs McKenzie.

'Almost every day, my colleagues—Vithalbhai, Babubhai, Chandrakantbhai, who were in the male ward—and I were taken to the CID office for questioning. All sorts of methods, from persuasion to coercion, were used to extract information from us. In the beginning, my interrogators tried to tempt me by saying that they would send me to one of the best universities in England or the US to complete my studies. When this did not work, they threatened that they would stop my father's pension, harass my mother and even administer electric shocks on me. However I was unaffected. The freedom of the motherland was of utmost importance.

'An experience that boosted my morale was the recitation of a song by a prisoner from the male ward opposite mine. It was the song that Bhagat Singh had sung before he was sent to the gallows and went on something like this: "It is not my going to the gallows but separation from Mother India that pains me most."

'The police had got many a missing clue from Printer and had arrested Vithalbhai the day after my arrest and Nanak Motwane of the Chicago Radio Company later. Along with them Jagannath Thakor of the Chicago Radio Company was also arrested and harassed by the police.'

In this context, Ushaben remembered her mother with great affection: 'When word spread about these terror tactics, a rumour was floated that I might buckle and tender an apology. My mother was terribly distressed when she heard this. She rushed to the jailor and begged with folded hands for a brief audience with me. He refused permission but finally agreed to let her send to me a home-cooked lunch. The tacit understanding was that the contents of the tiffin box would be given to the jailor's children before it reached me. I was very excited as it was the first time in three or months that I was getting a chance to eat home food. But on opening the tiffin box what did I find? Squeezed in between the chapattis was a small chit written by my mother which said, "I have heard that you are thinking of coming out of jail by tendering an apology. I am deeply pained and want to tell you that in case you do this, you will find the doors of our house closed for you." I was proud of my mother as I was of my Motherland.' Ushaben again recounted this to me nostalgically, barely a few weeks before she passed away on 10 August 2000.

In Yervada Jail

Ushaben further remembered, 'I was taken to the Yervada jail in Pune after the judgment. I had a very warm and almost a rousing reception from about 250 prisoners including Safia Khan, Kisantai Ghumatkar, Ava Havewala and Maniben Patel from Bombay; Prematai Kantak, Anutai Limaye, Mrinalini Desai and Savitriben Madan from Pune; Kamala Ashtaputre from Dhule; Susheela Kuber from Satara and others from different places of Maharashtra. Not knowing how a welcome should be organized in jail, they had stealthily plucked a few flowers from the jail garden and had tied them up in hand yarn; they also managed to prepare chikkis out of the groundnuts and jaggery they got in their daily rations and sang songs like "Hum Marange Ladte Ladte Ladaai Na Marane Wali". In addition they raised slogans including "Vande Mataram" and "Up Up the National Flag; Down Down the Union

Jack" for hours. This grand reception helped me a great deal in settling down and following the jail routine.

'I was asked to be in the same barrack where Safiaben, Kisantai and Satyabhamabai Borkar stayed. The matron of the jail gave me a mattress, plate and glass but did not provide other essential things due to the shortage of such articles. I accepted them but Safiaben and Kisantai opposed this strongly and insisted on my getting things like a jug, a spoon and a mug. From my childhood I was impressed with Safiaben's work and affectionate nature. I had seen her working at the Bombay Congress session at Abdul Gaffar Nagar in 1934 and at the AICC session at Mumbai in August 1942.

'Our day began with morning prayers, which were led by Prematai Kantak. During the day, those of us who were sentenced to rigorous imprisonment had to do the work allotted to them, including gardening, grinding corn, attending to patients in the dispensary, stitching jail uniforms and knitting socks and sweaters for the soldiers. Some of us used to help the warden with the office work. Safiaben, who had mastered the art of knitting, never got tired of teaching knitting to us young girls. She taught us so well that today some girls who had learnt knitting from her have established their own business. Tarabai from Pune gave lessons in nursing to those interested. Prisoners from Gujarat taught embroidery also to the warden. Kaveriben Divecha and Urmilaben Mehta were also there. Talking to all of them was interesting and often educative.

'Maniben Patel also organized a spinning class and saw to it that as many prisoners as possible did regular spinning over and above their jail work. She was very happy with me and Sumati as we were very regular in her spinning class. Maniben looked stern but was affectionate at heart.

She would often put oil in my hair and make two neat plaits. At night she would even check if we were covered with a blanket. During the evening prayers, rendering of devotional songs by Prematai, Sumati, Avaben, Susheela and others proved to be very soothing. I liked to join in the prayers and bhajans. I used to go to Gandhiji's prayers at Rungta House after my release.

'We young students were interested more in studying revolutionary tactics adopted in other countries and getting whatever information we could about the struggle from those who came to visit their relatives in jail. We also held discussions and started study circles with a view to understand and evaluate Gandhian, socialist and communist ideologies. Kamalabai Ashtaputre, Mrinalini Desai and Anutai Limaye were the ones to organize intellectual activities. I was especially interested in this activity. We used to have sharp discussions between persons of different ideologies like Gandhian or socialist. Safiaben would often mediate between different groups.

'Taking an evening walk was a favourite hobby of many prisoners, including Maniben Patel, Premaben, Khurshidben Naoroji and Purnima Banerjee who had joined us much later after almost all the other prisoners were released. We used to walk and talk. Listening to Maniben narrating stories about Sardar Patel, Khurshidben about her grandfather Dadabhai Naoroji, the Grand Old Man of India, or Purnimaben telling us all about her rebel sister Aruna Asaf Ali who revelled in defying all traditions—all this was education for us.

'We were very excited to receive Purnimadidi, a well-known revolutionary and an underground worker in jail. She soon entered our hearts with her affectionate nature and her love for books. Once Sukanya, Leela and

I were discussing our favourite colours and other things.
Sukanya said that she liked green, Leela liked red. I said
that I liked poets like Makhanlal Chaturvedi, Subhadra
Kumari, Maithili Sharan Gupt and Sumitranandan
Pant. But at that time I enjoyed reading Harivansh Rai
Bachchan. After Purnimadidi was released from the jail,
she sent us gifts—a sari of green colour for Sukanya, a red
sari for Leela and a complete set of Bachchan's poems for
me. We were so touched.

'Yusuf Meherally used to send books to us political
prisoners. I went to see him and thanked him after my
release. He looked at me and said, "You are the first
political prisoner to return the books!"

'Some of us, especially the younger ones, were keen on
organizing some morale-boosting programmes. We would,
therefore, try to prevent the warden from taking her
rounds by locking her up in the office room, especially on
the ninth of every month when we would try to organize
the flag-hoisting ceremony. Once, young Kusum climbed
to the top of the women's jail and hoisted the national flag.
On coming down, she went to the warden and said, "It is
I who has hoisted the flag. You may punish me. But I hope
you also will join us in saluting the flag and sing the song
'Jhanda Uncha Rahe Hamara'."

'According to the jail rules, all the prisoners were
locked up from 7 p.m. to 8 a.m. All of us resented this very
much. So one day we thought of protesting against it by
refusing to be locked in. That day all of us, including senior
inmates, sat down on the lawn of the ward refusing to be
locked up at the appointed time. The warden and even
some other inmates tried their level best to persuade us to
go in but we did not budge. Ultimately, at about midnight,
all the prisoners were forcibly carried to their barracks.

'During this interval of about six hours, Kamalabai and Savitriben thought of an indigenous plan to fool the jail authorities. Once they came to me and said, "Usha, come in." I refused. They said that they wanted to discuss a plan with me. I consented. All three of us went to our barracks. They opened a big shelf given to us for keeping milk and medicines, took out the middle piece, emptied the shelf and asked me to get into it. (Ushaben was slightly built.) I obeyed. Then they said, "You will sit here and come out only when we come back and ask you to do so." Then they shut the door of the shelf and went out. I sat there till the end. In between they would come to the barrack under one pretext or the other, open the door of the shelf for a few minutes so that I may not feel suffocated and give the latest news from outside in hushed tones.

'At the end, after all the prisoners were forcibly put in their barracks, a count was taken first by the assistant warden, then by the warden, at last followed by the jailor. All of them were shocked to find that one prisoner was missing. They counted and recounted and yet could not solve the mystery. Ultimately, being at their wits' end, they alerted all the police stations in the city instructing them to be on a lookout for the escaped prisoner, rang the alarm bell in our jail and informed the jail superintendent about what had happened. He came fretting and fuming and began the count himself. During this period of commotion and utter confusion, my two colleagues and conspirators Kamalabai and Savitriben who had kept my bed ready near the shelf just opened the door and beckoned me to slowly slip into it, which I did. All three of us then pretended to be fast asleep. The superintendent entered our barrack with his whole platoon and took the count; on realizing how all of them had been fooled, he took all the officers including the jailor and the warden to task saying, "The count is absolutely right. I know you were inefficient but did not know that you did not even know elementary arithmetic which a student of the primary class is supposed to know. Some very serious action will have to be taken against all of you." All of us were triumphant and began lustily cheering the superintendent. All of them left in a huff.

'Next day, early morning, the warden sent for me as soon as she came to the office. All the prisoners gathered near the gate, some advising me to strongly protest against my punishment, others said I must keep quiet and the senior ones advised me to admit my guilt. Some began to offer prayers and came to the gate with rosaries in their hands. In a very angry tone the warden said, "Miss Mehta, I want to punish you." I replied, "As per Gandhiji's orders I am prepared for any punishment you inflict on me. But please let me know what rules of the jail manual I have flouted." She became furious and asked me, "What do you mean?" I replied, "I was in the barrack quietly sleeping in my bed when others were defying your rules." I said that it was not I but she who should be punished for harassing a completely law-abiding prisoner. Not knowing what to do, she said, "You can go."

'I went in and was cheered; the atmosphere was rent with slogans like "Inquilab Zindabad", "Vande Mataram", and "Mahatma Gandhi ki Jai". A meeting to celebrate our success was called, as not only was I not punished, but also the rules were relaxed and the time for locking us up was changed from 7 p.m. to 9 p.m. Everyone was in a mood to celebrate the occasion and promised to present me with a mini-shelf on my marriage whenever it took place. I thanked them and said, "It is extremely nice of you to make such a fine goodwill gesture. I do not know whether

I would be getting married or not, but if I do and even if
the gift comes to me from dear friends like you, I will not
accept it because a cage is a cage even if it is a golden cage."

'Our standard diet was half-baked bajra rotis and
vegetable of bhopla (pumpkin). In the morning we used
to get groundnuts and jaggery. It was a favourite pastime
for almost all the prisoners to prepare chikkis out of these
ingredients. Gradually my health started to deteriorate. In
the beginning neither the jail authorities nor I bothered
about it. On feeling weak I went to the jail doctor who
said that I was suffering from some mysterious disease and
he had no cure for it.

'My brother, Chandrakantbhai, was also arrested for
participating in the freedom movement. He was kept in
the Byculla jail, thereafter in the Arthur and Nasik jails;
he was transferred to Yervada jail three months after his
request (the intention was to be near to me). Sardar Patel
and Shankarrao Deo were also in Yervada jail.

'As my health started deteriorating, Maniben got
concerned and informed Chandrakantbhai, who in turn
informed Sardar Vallabhbhai Patel. He took the jail
doctor and superintendent to task for not giving me the
proper treatment and asked them to see that my case was
thoroughly investigated.

'Within a week, I was brought to Bombay and admitted
to J.J. Hospital, where I was given hormone treatment
instead of being treated for the real trouble—intestinal
disorder. I felt weaker when brought back to Yervada jail.
Again Sardar intervened and told the authorities, "You
must release her and if you cannot do so, then at least
give her some milk and a supplementary diet." He used
to inquire after me almost daily. Once, the superintendent
said, "Your Usha is hale and hearty. Unnecessarily you

people are creating fuss about her." Sardar Saheb retorted, "I did not know this. But if it is really so, can we ask Usha and your wife to exchange places?" From that day I began getting the right drugs and extra milk.

'Gradually, prisoners started getting released because their sentences were over. As far as the detenues, the government decided not to detain them any longer. Ultimately, out of 250 prisoners only two of us, Leela Patil who was arrested in a bomb case and I, were left. We missed our colleagues but were quite reconciled to our plight. After a few days Leelatai complained of stomach trouble and was taken to the Sassoon Hospital. She was to return the same day but she did not return. I was worried and kept on asking the warden about her condition. She would only say, "Do not worry, everything is all right." Two days later I was informed by Janabai, one of the gossipmongers from the criminal ward, that Leelatai had escaped and I was the only political prisoner left in the jail. Thus, I was in isolation. In Bombay, in the beginning of my sentence, the cell was a very small and dingy one meant only for one prisoner; after the escape of Leelatai I was all alone in a big barrack meant for forty prisoners. Earlier also I was in solitary confinement for six months.'

Release and Welcome

Ushaben continued further, 'The Congress governments were installed in the provinces in March 1946. Soon thereafter, the warden came to me saying "You are released." I could not believe it, but it was true. The first order Morarji Desai had passed as the minister for home and revenue in Bombay was that of my release. I packed up my things and within minutes I was made to board a

Bombay-bound train from Poona. The news of my release spread. I was warmly welcomed by people at all the main stations. At Dadar there was a big crowd, with the socialist leaders in the forefront. The train stopped for quite a long time. A large number of people got into my compartment and accompanied me to Victoria Terminus. They sang and danced, blew bugles and beat drums. At V.T. Station, apart from my mother, father and all members of my family and all the front-rank leaders of the Congress, my old colleagues and their relatives and a huge crowd were present to accord a hearty welcome to me. I found it difficult even to alight from the train. I was overwhelmed by the tumultuous welcome though I knew it that these men, women and children, students and leaders and doctors, people from all classes, communities and localities of the city had thronged V.T. not to honour Usha Mehta of the prestigious Congress Radio group as an individual but as a representative of all those who had participated in the struggle and suffered for the sake of the Motherland.

'As I was thinking about this and thanking the Lord for showering His grace on me, an old man with shaking hands came near me and put a small silver idol of Lord Krishna in my hands. I gave it to my mother who was a great devotee of Lord Krishna, her dear Ranchhodji as he is popularly known and worshipped in Gujarat. She asked me, "Who gave you this?" I said, "This old man, who is hardly able to walk." Looking around I did not find him. He was either pushed out by the surging crowd or he disappeared on his own. While I was trying to solve this riddle, my mother said, "My Ranchhodrai came to bless you. We are unfortunate; we could not have His darshan. We are fortunate we got His blessings. Let us bow down to Him and pray that India becomes free soon."'

* * *

Life Sketch

During her jail term, Ushaben had calmly channelized her intellectual inclination to reading serious texts that led ultimately to her completion of her PhD after she was released from jail. Her thesis was: *The Social and Political Thought of Mahatma Gandhi* (School of Economics and Sociology, University of Bombay, 1951). In independent India she chose the path of Gandhi's constructive work for a better India. Many advised her to enter the political arena; offers came her way at that time and continued almost till the end. But she preferred the field of education. In her words, 'I felt that after Independence, the main task was to build India out of Gandhi's dreams. I thought I could contribute to this by going into the field of education, by inculcating sound values in the students.' She had decided to join the profession of teaching, the work she liked and continued till the end, the work of instilling values in the minds of the young, making the young generation explore the avenues of knowledge and sharpening their inquisitiveness and research. She made the grades from research assistant, lecturer, reader to professor and head of department of civics and politics of the University of Bombay (now the University of Mumbai). She remained there, with all her involvement in public life, till her retirement. Her students remember her as the committed teacher who took a deep interest in their lives. This devoted teacher taught numerous batches of students, guided them for their PhDs and helped them imbibe the abiding values of liberal education. She continued writing on her research and perception of politics. She wrote for scholarly journals as well as for magazines and newspapers. She was often invited to public discussions, meetings, seminars and conferences at various places and platforms. She had also received the Fulbright Fellowship to go to US for academic work.

Gandhi, Sri Aurobindo, Vivekananda, Radhakrishnan, Tagore and T.H. Green were her favourite authors. She was fond of literature, though her involvement in public life did not leave much time for reading. She liked writers like Zaverchand Meghani, Karsandas Manek (in Gujarati) and Subhadra Kumari Chauhan, Dinkar and Maithili Sharan Gupt (in Hindi).

Interestingly, she was the adviser to the foreign students enrolled in the University of Bombay. For a little less than a decade she was the warden of the International Students' Hostel of the University of Bombay. She handled the tough challenge of maintaining amicable relations among students from different cultures in her serene Gandhian way.

She served on a number of bodies, both national and state, with distinction, including the University Grants Commission, the Union Public Service Commission and many Gandhian organizations. She was conferred the Padma Vibhushan (the second highest civilian honour of India) in 1998 and was also a recipient earlier of the Tamra Patra (plaque of honour) as a freedom fighter.

She was awarded an LLD (Hon.) by the University of Mumbai and D.Litt (Hon.) by the Shreemati Nathibai Damodar Thackersey (SNDT) Women's University, Mumbai. One of her major achievements was that she introduced Gandhi to schools and colleges by initiating the Annual Gandhi Competitions at Gandhi Smarak Nidhi, Mumbai, and Mani Bhavan Gandhi Sangrahalaya. The number of participants, from 80 or so in the beginning, expanded to 7,000–8,000 during her own lifetime. After her retirement, she devoted herself entirely to both these organizations in Mumbai (Gandhi Smarak Nidhi, Mumbai, and Mani Bhavan Gandhi Sangrahalaya).

Ever since she was young, she had been very sensitive to women's causes/issues. Her admiration for women who participated in the freedom struggle was natural, and equally natural was her support to the contemporary women's movement. She worked actively in organizing and participating in debates and discussions pertaining to women's issues.

Her spirited nature and her passion for freedom of speech and expression made her active during the Emergency in India. She was very busy with meetings and forums, expressing her views fearlessly. Her work with the People's Union for Civil Liberties was commendable. Yogesh Kamdar remembered her involvement in some cases that were concerned with the violation of human rights. According to him, two such important matters were: (i) the arrest and transportation to Punjab of Professor Dalip Singh, vice principal of G.N. Khalsa College, Mumbai, in connection with the assassination of Prime Minister Indira Gandhi; and (ii) the arrest and inhuman treatment meted out to the scientist Captain Dr B.K. Subba Rao on charges of being a spy. In both these sensitive matters, Ushaben unhesitatingly became one of the petitioners to seek justice for them. Both Professor Dalip Singh and Captain Dr B.K. Subba Rao were exonerated by the courts.[3]

Ushaben is fondly remembered for her human values, her unswerving faith in Gandhian and democratic norms and her devotion to the nation.

Notes

Most of the information above is obtained through personal communication of the author with Ushaben.

1. Dr Aloo Dastur, a close friend and colleague of Ushaben for decades, remembered her years in the Wilson College. She has narrated that in the past the authorities were convinced that teaching the Constitutional History of England and Indian Economics would put wrong and dangerous ideas into young Indian minds. So, when a resolution was to be moved in the University Senate for introducing the two subjects, the government decided to oppose it. The principal of Elphinstone College, an Englishman, called a young teacher, Pestonji Ardeshir Wadia, and conveyed to him the order of the government. Wadia, who had just started cutting his teeth as a lecturer, blandly replied that he was a government servant in the college but he was elected to the senate by the registered graduates. As such he had to respect the wishes of his constituency and second the resolution. As was to be expected, he lost his job. The principal of Wilson College, Dr Mackichan, came to know this and invited Wadia to Wilson College. Wadia went and continued at Wilson College for forty years to the delight of his colleagues and students.

   Dr Dastur recalled that the Salt Satyagraha of 1930 again brought Wilson College to the fore. The Chowpatty foreshore was one of the main battlefields for manufacturing salt from the seawater. When the police batons and lathis were in full swing, the satyagrahis found the Wilson College grounds a place of shelter. Dr John McKenzie was firm in his resolve that his jurisdiction prevailed over the college building and the police would not be allowed to enter it. Their duty and functions lay on the other side of the iron railing. In other ways too, Dr McKenzie unobtrusively helped students. The college was open to the students who had participated in the freedom struggle. Admission was never denied to them, not even when they had been jailed. Prominent politicians like B.G. Kher, Morarji Desai, S.A. Dange and Ashok Mehta were Wilsonians. (Dr Aloo Dastur, 'A Salute to Wilson College', *The Wilsonian* Vol. 90, 1997–98).

2. Personal communication of the author with Ushaben; also Usha Mehta, 'My Alma Mater', *The Wilsonian* Vol. 90, 1997–98.

3. I thank Yogesh Kamdar for sharing this information. He was a co-petitioner with Ushaben in both these cases.

References

CHAPTER 1

1. Satyagraha Begins! Abdul S. Parekh, H.Z. Gilani, Secretaries. Bombay Students' Union, ExpressP. Press, Bombay-3. File 1020 (5) C 1, 1940–41. (All files used in this book are Home Department (Special), from Maharashtra State Archives, Mumbai.) The poster displays students' determination to participate in the movement and announces the students' meeting on 3 December urging them to buy a flag with Jawaharlal Nehru's words.

2. Personal communication of the author with Ushaben.

3. In addition, about 200 students from the schools in the Fort area marched in procession from Esplanade Maidan to Chowpatty where they took the Independence Pledge. Smaller processions were also organized by students in other parts of the city to sell the small button flags that they had prepared. In fact, Congress workers spent the entire day going around the city, selling these flags. The main procession, however, was organized by the BPCC and started from the Esplanade Maidan in the evening. There were about 3,000 persons when it began, but by the

time it reached Chowpatty going along Kalbadevi Road, Bhuleshwar, C.P. Tank, Vithalbhai Patel and Sandhurst Road, it had swelled to 10,000. The participants carried banners with words proclaiming 'Independence Day', 'People's Voice Means Constituent Assembly', and 'Freedom, Peace and Progress'. Bombay City S.B. (I), 27 January 1942, Part I Vol. 15, police reports.

4. The pledge was also read in Marathi by Dr D.D. Sathaye, in Gujarati by Bhavanji Arjun Khimji, in Urdu by Abedally Jafferbhai and in English by Joachim Alva. Bombay Provincial Congress Committee, Bombay City S.B. (I), 27 January 1942, Part I Vol. 15, police reports.

5. A meeting of 500 workers, presided over by Munshi Mohiuddin, was held at Kamgar Maidan under the auspices of the Girni Kamgar Union (Red Flag). Bombay City S.B. (I), 27 January 1942, Part I Vol. 15, police reports.

6. 624, Sir R. Lumley (Bombay) to the Marquess of Linlithgow, (Extract), MSS, EUR, F. 125/56, Bombay, 24–27 August 1942, in, Nicholas Mansergh, ed., E.W.R. Lumby asst. ed., *Constitutional Relations between Britain and India: The Transfer of Power, 1942–7*, Vol. II, 30 April–21 September 1942, Her Majesty's Stationery Office, London, 1971, p. 804.

7. Shankarrao Deo, speaking in Marathi at this meeting, said that the Congress was demanding complete independence because it realized that a slave nation could not render assistance to others in safeguarding democracy. He appealed to the people to respond wholeheartedly to the call of the nation. B.G. Kher emphasized that the visit of Sir Cripps had left behind nothing but bitterness and hatred. He appealed to the people to respond to the nation's call. About 5,000 persons, including Dr T.R. Naravane, S.K. Patil, R.A. Khedgikar, Rajaram Khandray, G.G. Mehta, Ambaram Tullockchand, Ashok Mehta, P.K. Sawant, Dr D.D. Sathaye, G.P. Hutheesingh, Shantabai Vengaskar,

Jinabhai P. Joshi, Pratap Singh and Keshav Laxman Borkar, attended. Bombay City. S.B. (I), 27 July 1942, No. 5352/H/3036 dated 27 July 1942, Advance copy forwarded to the Secretary to the Government of Bombay, Home Department (Special), Bombay, from Commissioner of Police, File 1110 (1) 1942.

8. The meeting, presided over by Ashok Mehta, was attended by about 500 students, including some women. An ardent appeal was made to the students to renounce their studies and join the struggle by 1 August. Bombay City. S.B. (I), 29 July 1942, No. 5391/H/3221 dated 29 July 1942. Advance copy forwarded to the Secretary to the Government of Bombay, Home Department (Special), Bombay, from Commissioner of Police, File 1110 (1) 1942.

9. A small group of influential local leaders, including S.K. Patil, B.N. Mehisheri, Bhawanji Arjun Khimji, Purshottam Trikamdas, V.R. Tulla, Shantabai Vengaskar, P.K. Kurne, N.L. Upadhyaya, S.L. Silam, Ratilal Gandhi and Manecklal Vakharia, participated in this meeting. P.K. Kurne and N.L. Upadhyaya however walked out as they wanted the resolution to be postponed. A Board of Control for the Congress Dal, consisting of Nagindas T. Master, S.K. Patil, Ishwarbhai Patel, Dr T.R. Naravne and Safia Khan, was appointed, and interestingly an amount of Rs 1,000 was sanctioned to pay for the uniforms of the Dal volunteers. Bombay City. S.B. (I), 28 July 1942. Advance copy to the Secretary to the Government of Bombay, Home Department (Special), Bombay, from Commissioner of Police, File 1110 (1) 1942.

10. Bombay City. S.B. (I), 30 July 1942, No. 5463/H/3035 dated 30 July 1942. Advance copy forwarded to the Secretary to the Government of Bombay, Home Department (Special), Bombay, from Commissioner of Police, File 1110 (1) 1942.

11. It is further reported in the official note that a few communists tried to disturb the meeting by shouting

slogans, but were silenced by the Congress volunteers. After the meeting they had a scuffle with the volunteers. Bombay City. S.B. (I), 30 July 1942, No. 5509/H/3036 dated 31 July 1942. Advance copy forwarded to the Secretary to the Government of Bombay, Home Department (Special), Bombay, from Commissioner of Police, File 1110 (1) 1942.

12. The meeting was presided over by Nagindas T. Master. Many prominent leaders and citizens, including Mangaldas Pakwasa, Soonderdas Murarji, Bhawanishankar Oza, B.N. Maheshwari, S.K. Patil, I.S. Patel, P.K. Sawant, Manibhai Jaimal Sheth, Manecklal Vakharia, V.R. Tulla, Devji Ratansey, S.G. Songaonkar and Baburao Gholap, were present there. Bombay City. S.B. (I), 3 August 1942, No. 5584/H/3036 dated 3 August 1942. Advance copy forwarded to the Secretary to the Government of Bombay, Home Department (Special), Bombay, From Commissioner of Police, File 1110 (1) 1942.

13. 624, Sir R. Lumley (Bombay) to the Marquess of Linlithgow, (Extract), MSS, EUR, F.125/56, Bombay 24–27 August 1942, in, Nicholas Mansergh, ed., E.W.R. Lumby asst. ed., *Constitutional Relations between Britain and India: The Transfer of Power, 1942–7*, Vol. II, p. 806.

14. A public meeting, presided over by Prof. D.R. Gharpure, was held at Ghorupdeo Maidan, Reay Road on 3 August. About 300 persons attended. Bombay City, S.B. (I), 4 August 1942, File 1110 (1) 1942. On 4 August, at the meeting at Sewree, B.G. Kher described events leading to the Wardha resolution and urged the audience to support the movement, while Shankarrao Deo deprecated the propaganda of the communists and royalists. Later, that same night, Shankarrao Deo addressed another meeting of about 200 students, organized by the North Bombay Students' Union at Vanmali Hall, Dadar. It was presided over by Raja Kulkarni. Students were advised not to be led astray by the advice of other interested parties but to act

as ballast in the ship which the Congress desired to steer in the stormy sea towards the goal of freedom. Bombay City, S.B. (I), 5 August 1942, File 1110 (1) 1942.

15. B.T. Randive and S.S. Chowdankar also spoke about their Party's attitude to the Congress' new initiative. Bombay City, S.B. (I), 4 August 1942, File 1110 (1)1942. In March 1942, Prabhakar Sanzgiri, joint secretary of the All India Students' Union, had issued leaflets entitled 'Forward to Freedom', which expressed the communist views. According to them, only a national government that enjoyed the people's confidence could organize a successful resistance to the invaders, and that an armed population and supporting the army was the only way to defeat the fascists. It also mentioned that the ban on the Communist Party, which had extended unconditional support to the war, must be removed. Bombay City S.B. (I), 27 March 1942, Part I Vol. 15, police reports.

16. Leaders like Nagindas T. Master, Jinabhai P. Joshi, S.K. Patil, Bhawanji Arjun Khimji, Ishwarbhai Patel, B.G. Kher, Yusuf J. Meherally, Vallabhbhai J. Patel, Maniben Patel, Ashok Mehta, S.L. Silam, P.K. Sawant, S.G. Songaonkar, Safia Khan, T.R. Naravne, Shivaji Dongre, J.C. Maitra, B.N. Maheshri, Shantabai Vengaskar, Mridula Sarabhai and Keshav Laxman Borkar were there to greet him. Bombay City. S.B. (I), 3 August 1942, No. 5583/H/3001 dated 3 August 1942, Advance copy forwarded to the Secretary to the Government of Bombay, Home Department (Special), Bombay, From Commissioner of Police, File 1110 (1) 1942.

17. Bombay City, S.B. (I), 4 August 1942, No. 5623/M/4009 dated 4 August 1942, Advance copy forwarded to the Secretary to the Government of Bombay, Home Department (Special), Bombay, From Commissioner of Police, File 1110 (1) 1942.

18. Members of the Working Committee—Vallabhbhai Patel, Jawaharlal Nehru, Dr Pattabhi Sitaramayya, Sarojini

Naidu, Shankarrao Deo, Dr Prafulla Chandra Ghosh, Dr Syed Mahmud, Asaf Ali and Govind Vallabh Pant—all attended the meeting. Bombay City, S.B. (I), 5 August 1942, File 1110 (1) 1942.

19. Bombay City, S.B. (I), 6 August 1942, File 1110 (1) 1942.

20. Rumours had been floating throughout the night of 6 August that nearly 2,000 warrants had been issued, and that the AICC members were being rounded up. There was an unusual rush of people towards Birla House on that evening, as nearly a thousand persons flocked there between 6 p.m. and 7 p.m. to have a darshan of Gandhi. The Congress Socialist Party met at the residence of Purshottam Trikamdas. Kamaladevi Chattopadhyaya presided over the meeting, where Acharya Narendra Deo, Y.J. Meherally, Ashok Mehta, Achyut Patwardhan and other leading socialists pledged their full support to Gandhi's movement. Bombay City, S.B. (I), 7 August 1942, File 1110 (1) 1942.

21. Leaders like Govind Vallabh Pant, Krishna Hutheesingh, S.K. Patil, Ashok Mehta, Saad Ali, L.K. Oak and K.N. Joglekar were present at this meeting presided over by Nagindas T. Master. Bombay City, S.B. (I), 6 August 1942, File 1110 (1) 1942.

22. Ashok Mehta presided over and addressed this meeting, referring to the war situation and the hardships suffered by the workers. He expressed hope that the workers would support the non-violent movement that the Congress was launching. Achyut Patwardhan and Acharya Narendra Deo supported his plea, exhorting the audience to join the movement. Appeals for the people's support were the main issue at another meeting presided over by S.L. Silam, held in Telugu Wadi, Kamatipura, on the same evening. Shankarrao Deo went further by assuring his audience that the movement would succeed if all the workers in the mills, factories and even government services refused to go to

work. Bombay City, S.B. (I), 7 August 1942, File 1110 (1) 1942.

23. To the students, Students' Action Committee, Bombay, 5 August 1942; Bombay City, S.B. (I), 6 August 1942, File 1110 (1) 1942.

24. Bombay City, S.B. (I), 8 August 1942, File 1110 (1) 1942. The list of leaders included J.B. Kriplani, Sarojini Naidu, Asaf Ali, Kamaladevi Chattopadhyaya, Hansa Mehta, Dr Ram Manohar Lohia, Dr Pattabhi Sitaramayya, Shankarrao Deo, Govind Vallabh Pant, Harikrishna Mehtab, Acharya Narendra Deo, Achyut Patwardhan, Maniben Patel, Yusuf Meherally, S.K. Patil, Morarji Desai, B.G. Kher, Ashok Mehta, Dr D.D. Sathaye, Safia Khan, Lilavati Munshi, Mangaldas Pakwasa, Dr Jivrraj Mehta, Miraben, Salebhoy Abdul Kadar, Jaishri Raiji, Anusuyabai Deshmukh, Sucheta Kriplani, Surji Vallabhdas, Krishna Hutheesingh, T. Prakasham, Bhawanji Arjun Khimji, Nagindas T. Master, Mrudula Sarabhai, D.G. Tendulkar, Suhasini Jambhekar, Nargis Batliwalla, Khwaja Ahmad Abbas, Miss Anil De'Silva, Indira Gandhi, Pheroz Gandhi and Sardar Prithvi Singh. Bombay City, S.B. (I), 8 August 1942, File 1110 (1) 1942.

25. *Bombay Chronicle*, 7 August 1942.

26. Bombay City, S.B. (I), 8 August 1942, File 1110 (1) 1942.

27. Gandhi's speech at the AICC on 7 August 1942. *The Hitavada* 9-8-1942; *Bombay Chronicle* 8-8-1942, CWMG 76 (1 April 1942–17 December 1942), The Publications Division, Ministry of Information and Broadcasting, Government of India, New Delhi, 1979, p. 379.

28. Gandhi's speech at the AICC on 7 August 1942. *The Hitavada* 9-8-1942; *Bombay Chronicle* 8-8-1942, CWMG 76, p. 380.

29. File 1110 (1) 1942.

30. Gandhi's speech at the AICC on 8th August 1942. *Mahatma Vol. VI*, pp. 154–64, CWMG 76, p. 392.

31. Gandhi's speech at the AICC on 8th August 1942. Courtesy Nehru Memorial Museum and Library, CWMG 76, p. 399.

32. Gandhi's speech at the AICC on 8th August 1942. *Mahatma Vol. VI*, pp. 154–64, CWMG 76, p. 394.

33. Gandhi's speech at the AICC on 8th August 1942. *Mahatma Vol. VI*, pp. 154–64, CWMG 76, pp. 391–92.

34. Gandhi's speech at the AICC on 8th August 1942. Courtesy Nehru Memorial Museum and Library, CWMG 76, p. 400.

35. Sadiq Ali, 'Gandhi and Nehru Threatened to Resign from the Congress!' *Bhavan's Journal*, Congress centenary issue, Vol. 32, No. 10, 16–31 December 1985, p. 144.

36. File 1110 (1) 1942.

37. Khwaja Ahmad Abbas, *Let India Fight For Freedom*, Sound Magazine, (Publication Department), Bombay, 1943, p. 30.

38. No. 174, Bombay, 24 August 1942, report for the week ending 15-8-1942, From G.W. McElhinny, The District Magistrate, Bombay Suburban District, File 1110 (6) A(2) 1942.

39. Sanjiv P. Desai, ed., *Calendar of the Quit India Movement in the Bombay Presidency*, Department of Archives, Government of Maharashtra, Bombay, 1985, p. 1.

40. Such incidents included looting of a government sugar shop at Bhuleshwar, the cutting of telephone wires near Byculla, Saitan Chowki, Kingsway and Bhoiwada, and the burning of seven police chowkies and one BEST chowki at King's Circle. Most of the schools and colleges were closed. Cloth markets, Jhaveri Bazar, Dana Bunder and many shops in Girgaum, Bhuleshwar, Kalbadevi, Dadar and Matunga were closed. The police opened fire on 26 occasions, killing 16 and injuring 57. Sanjiv P. Desai, ed., *Calendar of the Quit India Movement in the Bombay Presidency*, pp. 3–4.

41. During the days from 9 to 14 August 1942, many street lamps were broken in Bandra, Danda, Santacruz, Vile Parle, Kurla, Ghatkopar and Chembur, and some telephone and telegraph wires were cut in Santacruz, Vile Parle, Versova, Andheri, Kurla and Bhandup areas. Two police sentry boxes at Kandivali and Khar and a Prohibition Chowki at Versova were badly damaged. Two cabins of Bandra Bus Company at Bandra and Danda were burnt. Some post boxes at Khar, Vile Parle, Santacruz, Andheri, Kurla and Ghatkopar were either damaged or found missing. On 10, 11 and 13 August, some boys indulged in uprooting road signs, bus stop posts and trees, thereby blocking roads at Khar, Santacruz, Vile Parle and Ghatkopar. Some groups of students had to be dispersed by the police at Santacruz, Andheri, Ghatkopar and Malad. Schools were closed during the disturbances. A complete hartal was observed by shopkeepers on 9 August. No. 174, Bombay, 24 August 1942, Bombay Suburban District, Report for the week ending 15-8-1942, G.W. McElhinny, The District Magistrate, Bombay Suburban District, File 1110 (6) A(2) 1942.

In the morning on 11 August, buses of the Bandra Bus Company were held up at Khar by the students. In Santacruz a procession of the students of Anandilal Podar School was stopped at 11.30 a.m. and dispersed with a mild lathi charge; 30 students were apprehended. 26 boys and girls were also apprehended as they were found picketing near the Ghatkopar Post Office; 24 of them were prosecuted. No. 174, 15 August 1942, Daily reports-11-8-1942, To, The Secretary to Government, Home Department (Special), From, The District Magistrate, Bombay Suburban District, File 1110 (6) A(2) 1942.

On 12 August 1942, a few students managed to enter the Secretariat building from the rear door near the Elphinstone College and left by the front gate. After removing two or three notice boards from the building, they proceeded to the Oval maidan where they removed benches and put them in the centre of the road near the University Building and the High Court. Then they went towards Churchgate. About 500 students gathered at the junction of Churchgate street and Queen's Road and 30 of them went to the Asiatic (Society) building to induce office clerks to strike. The police dispersed them and a large number of students ran into Churchgate station, boarded a suburban train, intending to travel without tickets. No. 5829/A/320, Office of the Commissioner of Police, Special Branch I, CID, Bombay, 13 August 1942. To, The Secretary to the Government of Bombay, Home Department, Bombay. Subject: Mass Movement and Disturbances. Part II Vol. 15, police reports.

42. 662, The Marquess of Linlithgow to Mr Churchill (via India Office) Telegram, MSS, EUR F. 125/158, 31 August 1942, in, Nicholas Mansergh, ed., E.M.R. Lumby asst. ed., *Constitutional Relations between Britain and India: The Transfer of Power, 1942–7*, Vol. II, p. 853.

43. Personal communication of the author with Ushaben.

44. Vithaldas (alias Babubhai) Madhavji Khakar was a Gujarati, then about 20 years old, and a native of district Una in Junagad state. He studied up to fourth English standard in Bombay, and in 1929 gave up his education and went to his father's tile business. Then he had some business connection with Printer. Thereafter he opened a firm of commission agents. He had not previously come to notice for his Congress activities.

History sheets of the persons connected with the enterprise. Report on the Congress Radio Case by the Commissioner of Police, Bombay, No. 1419 dated 26-1-1943 from Commissioner of Police, Bombay, to the Additional Secretary to the Government of Bombay, Home Department (Special), Bombay, File 1110 (31) 1942–43.

45. Nariman Adarbad Printer, a Parsi, was about 40 years of
     age. He was a matriculate from the Punjab University and
     was a member of the Society of Great Britain in Radio
     Engineering. He was in the service of the Singer Sewing
     Company in Lahore in 1922 and came to Bombay in 1928,
     and in 1931 he started working as the principal of Bombay
     Technical Institute at Byculla (also called Technical Institute
     of India, Ltd, Head Office Delhi), conducted by S.D.
     Sharma. The institute was recognized by the government
     for training students in radio and electrical engineering.
     In 1933 he became the owner of the institute. His ways
     of working were not free from faults. Forty students had
     lodged complaints against him and Sharma under Section
     420, IPC., in Dadar Police Court. There were also several
     decrees in Small Cause Court against him and some for
     very small amounts. Eager to expand his avenues he had
     gone to England, but did not succeed in getting a television
     apparatus for India, and returned in 1938. He had taken
     five students, including Rustom Cowasji Mirza (Mirza)
     with him at the expense of the Institute. After he returned,
     he affiliated the Institute with Khalsa College. However, in
     1940 he parted ways with Khalsa College.
     He had secured a licence for amateur transmitting in 1938.
     It entitled him to transmit and receive messages by wireless
     'only for the purpose of testing'. He had also purchased
     a transmitter. His amateur transmitting license was
     cancelled when war broke out in 1939 and the authorities
     wanted him to produce the transmitting apparatus.
     Instead, he dismantled the transmitter and claimed that he
     had avoided producing the parts as they were needed 'for
     giving training to the students'. These parts remained in his
     possession and were taken to Byculla where he lived.
     In March 1942, he closed down the Institute for want of
     students, and admitted that from 1940 to 1942 he had
     incurred heavy losses of between Rs 30,000 and Rs 40,000

and a huge debt of nearly Rs 60,000. What is significant is that he had pledged all his articles (except the parts of his transmitter) to Malupchand Shantidas for Rs 3,000 at about the end of 1940. By 1943, his only business was in chemicals, and that too was conducted under the name of Mirza to protect him from his creditors.
Deposition of Nariman Adarbad Printer for the prosecution concluded on 20-4-1943.

46. History sheets of the persons connected with the enterprise, Report on the Congress Radio Case by the Commissioner of Police, Bombay, No. 1419 dated 26-1-1943 from Commissioner of Police, Bombay, to the Additional Secretary to the Government of Bombay, Home Department (Special), Bombay. File 1110 (31) 1942–43.

47. Deposition of Nariman Adarbad Printer for the prosecution concluded on 20-4-1943.
Ravindra A. Mehta knew Babubhai since 1935. He was running a cloth shop in Girgaum, and Mehta was his customer. Then he became his partner in the sole selling agency of Kerogas manufactured by Printer.
Deposition of Ravindra Ajitrai Mehta for the prosecution concluded on 20-4-1943.

48. Deposition of Nariman Adarbad Printer for the prosecution concluded on 20-4-1943.
According to Ravindra A. Mehta his business connection with Babubhai ended in July 1942, and did not know what Babubhai did thereafter. Deposition of Ravindra Ajitrai Mehta for the prosecution concluded on 20-4-1943.
Babubhai had purchased some zinc scraps for the manufacture of zinc chloride. The zinc scraps were delivered to Printer's place for his experiments. Printer had given a hundi for Rs 6,000 or Rs 7,000 to Babubhai and R.A. Mehta. It was dishonoured, but Printer said that he had an understanding with them on that point. There was no pressing demand from them and their relations

continued to be cordial. Deposition of Nariman Adarbad Printer for the prosecution concluded on 20-4-1943.

49. Deposition of Nariman Adarbad Printer for the prosecution concluded on 20-4-1943.

50. Vithaldas Kanthadbhai Jhaveri was a Gujarati, about 28 years old, and a native of Bhavnagar state. He had been educated up to the Matriculation standard. He was a partner in the well-known Bombay firm of jewellers, Messrs Narottamdas Bhau of Lamington Road. The partnership was dissolved by his uncle on account of the increasing part the accused was taking in unlawful Congress activities. The accused was an ardent Congressman and was convicted in the last civil disobedience movement in Bombay.

History sheets of the persons connected with the enterprise, Report on the Congress Radio Case by the Commissioner of Police, Bombay, No. 1419, dated 26-1-1943 from Commissioner of Police, Bombay, to the Additional Secretary to the Government of Bombay, Home Department (Special), Bombay. File 1110 (31) 1942–43.

50. Deposition of Nariman Adarbad Printer for the prosecution concluded on 20-4-1943.

Ramchandra Mohanlal Killewala taught languages: Hindustani, Gujarati, Marathi and English. Generally, he gave private tuitions. In 1942 he was a tutor for Hindi classes that were held on Sundays at R.M. School, near Royal Opera House, for some time. Babubhai was his pupil there. Usha Mehta also was attending these classes. Killewala knew Printer and Mirza as they used to go to Babubhai's office, where Killewala used to go sometimes to give Hindi lessons to Babubhai. Deposition of Ramchandra Mohanlal Killewala for the prosecution concluded on 9-4-1943.

51. Judgment as in Appendix I. According to R.A. Mehta, a few days after the AICC session, Printer went to R.A. Mehta's home, Ajit Villa, and gave him the idea of starting the

radio. Mehta showed no interest in such illegal activities. But Printer persisted, and Mehta gave him Rs 200. About a fortnight after it, Mehta gave Printer another sum of Rs 200 for the same purpose. Some days later again he gave Printer Rs 250. Deposition of Ravindra Ajitrai Mehta for the prosecution concluded on 20-4-1943.

52. Deposition of Nariman Adarbad Printer for the prosecution concluded on 20-4-1943.
    Mirza was a radio technician, educated in Bombay Technical Institute and also in England. He had gone with Printer to England in 1937 with five other students. He had worked with Printer in his institute. Deposition of Rustom Cowasji Mirza for the prosecution concluded on 26-4-1943.

53. Deposition of Nariman Adarbad Printer for the prosecution concluded on 20-4-1943.

54. The house he lived, 13 Victoria 3 Cross Lane in Byculla, was rented in Mirza's name. The institute was on the ground floor and Printer lived on the first floor of the same building.
    Deposition of Nariman Adarbad Printer for the prosecution concluded on 20-4-1943.

55. Printer said that Babubhai, Vithalbhai and R.A. Mehta were then present. Deposition of Nariman Adarbad Printer for the prosecution concluded on 20-4-1943. But according to the judge, on this point there is no independent corroboration of Printer's statement that Babubhai and Ushaben were amongst those who had gone to this house for the demonstration. Judgment as in Appendix I.

56. Deposition of Ravindra Ajitrai Mehta for the prosecution concluded on 20-4-1943.

57. Deposition of Nariman Adarbad Printer for the prosecution concluded on 20-4-1943.

58. Depositions of the witnesses for prosecution, Case No. 7 of 1943 in the Court of the Special Judge appointed under Section 4 of the Special Criminal Court Ordinance, 1942, and the Judgment as in Appendix I. All the depositions of witnesses for the prosecution, and the statements and

examinations of the accused before the Special Judge in this book have been taken from the Usha Mehta Congress Radio papers, Mani Bhavan Gandhi Sangrahalaya, Mumbai.

59. It means 599 rupees, 8 annas and 0 paisa. This is as per the system of coinage prevalent before the decimalization of the currency in 1957. A rupee was divided into anna and paisa. 1 rupee was equal to 16 annas and 1 anna was 4 paisa.

60. Deposition of Nariman Adarbad Printer for the prosecution concluded on 20-4-1943. Date and amount are as in the Judgment as in Appendix I. However, it is interesting to note that later Deshpande said that he did not remember who had come for the articles mentioned in the bill and he entered in the bill the name that was given to him by the purchaser. Deposition of Vishvanath D. Deshpande for the prosecution on 27-4-1943.

61. Deposition of Nariman Adarbad Printer for the prosecution concluded on 20-4-1943. Date is as in the Judgment as in Appendix I.

62. Deposition of Ramchandra Mohanlal Killewala for the prosecution concluded on 9-4-1943. According to Killewala both Printer and he went to the sister's house.

63. Deposition of Nariman Adarbad Printer for the prosecution concluded on 20-4-1943.

64. Judgment as in Appendix I.

65. G.C. Awasthy, *Broadcasting in India* (Bombay: Allied Publishers Private Limited, 1965), p. 1.

66. Partha Sarathi Gupta, 'Radio and the Raj', in Sabyasachi Bhattacharya (ed.), *Power, Politics and the People: Studies in British Imperialism and Indian Nationalism* (London: Anthem Press, 2002), p. 469.

CHAPTER 2

1. Deposition of Nariman Adarbad Printer for the prosecution concluded on 20-4-1943.

2.   Deposition of Ahmed Umarkhan for the prosecution
     concluded on 27-4-1943. Ahmed Umarkhan did not
     mention that a lady was with them. Possibly she might
     have been left behind. Judgment as in Appendix I.

3.   Deposition of Daraskhan Ambaskhan for the prosecution
     concluded on 26-4-1943. However, Babubhai said later
     in his evidence that he had gone to Sea View where
     Printer had called him, Ushaben and Mirza for an ice
     cream party towards the end of September. According to
     the judge, this story appeared to have been put forward
     to explain why Daraskhan had identified him. Judgment
     as in Appendix I.

4.   Deposition of Nariman Adarbad Printer for the prosecution
     concluded on 20-4-1943.
     According to Printer, Babubhai had paid some money for
     the parts of the apparatus supplied by him. The main parts
     of the apparatus were power pack, complete oscillator and
     final unit, an amplifier purchased from Chicago Radio
     Company and gramophone motor and pick-up. The
     pick-up was not in good order so another one had to be
     bought from Chicago Radio Company and fitted. His old
     transmitter had two 866 junior valves (Taylor) and one
     was a spare. The oscillator valve was 646. In the final stage
     he had two Radio-trone R.C.A. 807. All these valves were
     already with him. As the crystal had been fractured by the
     students, he used the system of self-oscillation (electron-
     coupled oscillator). He had the crystal holder and used it
     as a dummy. He did not tell Babubhai that the crystal was
     not working.

5.   Deposition of Nariman Adarbad Printer for the prosecution
     concluded on 20-4-1943.

6.   Judgment as in Appendix I.

7.   Report on the Congress Radio Case by the Commissioner
     of Police, Bombay, No. 1419, dated 26-1-1943, from
     Commissioner of Police, Bombay, to the Additional

Secretary to the Government of Bombay, Home Department
(Special), Bombay. File 1110 (31) 1942–43.

8. No. 6499/A/320, Office of the Commissioner of Police,
    Special Branch I, CID, Bombay, 7 September 1942.
    To, Secretary to the Government of Bombay, Home
    Department, Bombay. Subject: Congress Mass Movement,
    1942 Part II Vol. 15, police reports.

9. Bombay Congress Bulletin, Vo. I, No. 37, 21 September
    1942, Bombay, Vol. I, No. 39, 23 September 1942, 1942
    Part II Vol. 15, police reports.

10. Deposition of Nariman Adarbad Printer for the prosecution
    concluded on 20-4-1943. The name of this Parsi lady was
    not revealed till the end; she was Kamal Wood nee Coomie
    Dastur. Zenobia E. Shroff, 'Professor Kamal Wood: The
    Voice of Nationalism', in Nawaz B. Mody, ed., *Enduring
    Legacy: Parsis of the Twentieth Century Vol. II* (Mumbai:
    Nawaz B. Mody, 2005), pp. 650–55.

    R.A. Mehta in his evidence said that he did not know who
    rented the building. Deposition of Ravindra Ajitrai Mehta
    for the prosecution concluded on 20-4-1943.

11. Deposition of Ramchandra Mohanlal Killewala for the
    prosecution concluded on 9-4-1943.

12. Deposition of Kasturbai Hansraj Shroff for the prosecution
    concluded on 12-4-1943.

13. Personal communication of the author with Ushaben.

14. There were incidents of displaying the defiant mood
    among the students—the students of the Elphinstone
    College protesting against the suspension of a student
    by the Principal on 27 August (Sanjiv P. Desai, *Calendar
    of the Quit India Movement in the Bombay Presidency*,
    Department of Archives, Government of Maharashtra,
    Bombay, 1985, p. 42) and hoisting the Congress flag on the
    college building on 16 September (p. 69); some students of
    the Wilson College standing at the entrance picketing and
    obstructing other students from going to the college on 4

September (No. 6482/A/320, Office of the Commissioner of Police, Special Branch I, Bombay, 5 September 1942. To, The Secretary to the Government of Bombay, Home Department, Bombay. Subject: Congress Mass Movement, Part II Vol. 15, police reports); and about 300 girls in the north of the city attempting to prevent students from attending school on 7 September (Desai, *Calendar of the Quit India Movement*, p. 55).

15. 'To Wilsonians', Bombay, September 1942, Part II Vol. 15, police reports.

16. September 1942, Part II Vol. 15, police reports.

17. August 1942, Part II Vol. 15, police reports.

18. Personal communication of the author with Ushaben.

19. Deposition of Ravindra Ajitrai Mehta for the prosecution concluded on 20-4-1943.

20. Deposition of Nariman Adarbad Printer for the prosecution concluded on 20-4-1943.

21. Deposition of Ravindra Ajitrai Mehta for the prosecution concluded on 20-4-1943.
    The judgment as in Appendix I mentions Rs 120 as the rent.

22. Deposition of Siddheshwar Vishnu Pandit for the prosecution concluded on 27-4-1943. Incidentally Ushaben's father H.N. Mehta was a tenant in the same building staying on the first floor. Ushaben continued living there till she passed away in 2000.

23. Personal communication of the author with Ushaben.

24. Deposition of Nariman Adarbad Printer for the prosecution concluded on 20-4-1943. However, as mentioned in the judgment, there was no evidence to corroborate the allegation of Printer that Vithalbhai was introduced to him by Babubhai. Although there was no direct evidence to prove that Babubhai procured the records, yet, there was indirect but strong evidence to show that he was involved in supplying the records for broadcasting. Judgment as in Appendix I.

25. Personal communication of the author with Ushaben.

26. Deposition of Nariman Adarbad Printer for the prosecution
     concluded on 20-4-1943.

     Jagannath Raghunath Thakor had studied at King George
     English School at Dadar up to matriculation and had been
     with Chicago Radio Company in service since 1933. At
     first he worked as an apprentice in the radio line, then
     as a radio repairer, and from 1942 as a radio mechanic
     in Chicago Radio Company; he worked under Nanak
     Motwane's orders. Deposition of Jagannath Raghunath
     Thakor for the prosecution concluded on 27-4-1943.

27. Deposition of Nariman Adarbad Printer for the prosecution
     concluded on 20-4-1943.

28. Deposition of Jagannath Raghunath Thakor for the
     prosecution concluded on 27-4-1943.

     Nanak Motwane was a Sindhi Hindu aged about 40
     years and hailing from Barkhana, Sind. He was a wireless
     expert and one of the directors of the Chicago Radio &
     Telephone Co. Ltd, Bombay's largest wireless dealers.
     The other directors were his brother V.G. Motwane and
     his father Gainchand. This family also owned the Eastern
     Electric & Engineering Co. Both these firms had their
     premises on 129 Mahatma Gandhi Road, Bombay. The
     Chicago Radio & Telephone Co. Ltd also had branches at
     Lucknow, Lahore, New Delhi and Calcutta. The accused
     held 'decided pro-Congress views'. In addition to the
     part played by him in the Congress Radio enterprise, he
     arranged for the sound filming of the leaders' speeches at
     the AICC session in August 1942 and later transposed the
     speeches from the film to gramophone discs which were
     used in the Congress Radio broadcasts. Both the films and
     records had been seized by the police.

     History sheets of the persons connected with the
     enterprise. Report on the Congress Radio Case by the
     Commissioner of Police, Bombay, No. 1419 dated

26-1-1943 from Commissioner of Police, Bombay, to the Additional Secretary to the Government of Bombay, Home Department (Special), Bombay, File 1110 (31) 1942–43.

29. Personal communication of the author with Ushaben.

30. Deposition of Nariman Adarbad Printer for the prosecution concluded on 20-4-1943. Dahyabhai Patel was Sardar Vallabhbhai Patel's son, a freedom fighter himself, and later a member of the Rajya Sabha; he was working for an insurance company.

31. Deposition of Nariman Adarbad Printer for the prosecution concluded on 20-4-1943.

32. Deposition of Nariman Adarbad Printer for the prosecution concluded on 20-4-1943.

33. Judgment as in Appendix I.

34. Deposition of Nariman Adarbad Printer for the prosecution concluded on 20-4-1943.

35. Judgment as in Appendix I.

36. Deposition of Nariman Adarbad Printer for the prosecution concluded on 20-4-1943.

37. Deposition of Jamnadas Ratansi for the prosecution concluded on 12-4-1943.

38. Deposition of Bipin Chandra Shantilal Inamdar for the prosecution concluded on 12-4-1943.

39. Judgment as in Appendix I.

40. Deposition of Nariman Adarbad Printer for the prosecution concluded on 20-4-1943.

41. Judgment as in Appendix I.

42. Deposition of Jagannath Raghunath Thakor for the prosecution concluded on 27-4-1943.

43. Deposition of Jagannath Raghunath Thakor for the prosecution concluded on 27-4-1943.

44. Deposition of Jagannath Raghunath Thakor for the prosecution concluded on 27-4-1943.

45. Deposition of Nariman Adarbad Printer for the prosecution concluded on 20-4-1943.

46. Deposition of Ravindra Ajitrai Mehta for the prosecution concluded on 20-4-1943.
47. Deposition of Ramsaran Jagdish Dube for the prosecution concluded on 27-4-1943.
48. Deposition of Fulchand Jethabhai for the prosecution concluded on 12-4-1943.
49. Deposition of Nariman Adarbad Printer for the prosecution concluded on 20-4-1943.
50. Judgment as in Appendix I.
51. Personal communication of the author with Ushaben.
52. Deposition of Ravindra Ajitrai Mehta for the prosecution concluded on 20-4-1943.
53. Judgment as in Appendix I.
54. Deposition of Badlu Ramchandran for the prosecution concluded on 19-4-1943.
55. No. 7204/A-320 from the Office of the Commissioner of Police, Special Branch I, Bombay, 29 September 1942. To, The Secretary to the Government of Bombay, Home Department, Special Branch, Bombay. File 1110 (6) A(1)I 1942.
    Programme for Gandhi Week:
    • 2 October: Complete hartal
    • 3 October: Tricolour Day. Women would go about in groups of three—one wearing a white sari, one green and the third a saffron-coloured one. The object was to avoid being arrested, which would happen if they carried a Congress flag.
    • 4 October: Do or Die Day. There would be *prabhat pheri*s (morning processions) in all Wards and spinning.
    • 5 October: Quit India Day
    • 6 October: Azad Day
    • 7 October: Flag Day, flag salutations in all Wards
    • 8 October: Complete hartal; at 5 p.m. general prayers in all the Wards
    • 9 October: The programme would depend on the public's response during the week.

56. File 1110 (6) A(1)I 1942.

57. Such instances included: breaking out of a serious fire at the Mazagaon Police Court resulting in complete gutting of the building and causing the damage of about Rs 1.5 lakh, 3 October (Sanjiv P. Desai, ed., *Calendar of the Quit India Movement in the Bombay Presidency*, p. 95); breaking out of fire in the Cotton Godown of the Mayer Sassoon Mill due to some hidden chemicals, 4 November (p. 139); occurrence of two bomb explosions occurred in the Shell Shop of Messrs Richardson and Cruddas, 8 November (p. 144); and a small explosion occurred in a cupboard of Elphinstone college, 11 November (p. 148).

58. Usha Mehta was a Gujarati, aged about 22 years, and a native of Surat district. She had passed B.A. examination in 1939, LL.B. in 1941, and was studying for M.A. She had also passed the 'Kovid Examination' in Hindi. She was 'the lieutenant of Vithaldas Khakar throughout all the stages of the Congress Radio enterprise'. She made several of the records used in the broadcasts, repeating speeches written by Ram Manohar Lohia. She also operated the transmitter and did the necessary announcements through this microphone. She was 'obviously an ardent Congress woman but not come to notice before in this connection'.

Chandrakant Babubhai Jhaveri, aged 23 years, was known to Printer as he used to be present at Babubhai's office. He was, prior to his arrest, assisting his father in a jewellery business. According to the history sheet prepared by the police, he 'played an insignificant role in the enterprise' and appeared to have been drawn into it by virtue of his prior association with Usha Mehta and Vithaldas Khakar.

History sheets of the persons connected with the enterprise. Report on the Congress Radio Case by the Commissioner of Police, Bombay, No. 1419, dated

26-1-1943, from Commissioner of Police, Bombay, to the Additional Secretary to the Government of Bombay, Home Department (Special), Bombay. File 1110 (31) 1942–43.

CHAPTER 3

1. Deposition of Ganesh Keshav Kokje for the prosecution concluded on 28-4-1943.

2. Deposition of Manuel Morrison Fergusson for the prosecution concluded on 27-4-1943.

3. Deposition of Ganesh Keshav Kokje for the prosecution concluded on 28-4-1943.

4. Deposition of Ganesh Keshav Kokje for the prosecution concluded on 28-4-1943.

5. Deposition of Jagannath Raghunath Thakor for the prosecution concluded on 27-4-1943.
    Jagannath Raghunath Thakor worked under the orders of Motwane. Jagannath Joshi and Shantilal Kadakia, godown keepers between August and November 1942, also worked under Motwane's orders. In August, September and October 1942, Jagannath Thakor's duties were to repair the amplifiers, etc. and the construction of some parts. Deposition of Jagannath Raghunath Thakor for the prosecution concluded on 27-4-1943.

6. Deposition of Jagannath Raghunath Thakor for the prosecution concluded on 27-4-1943.
    According to Majid Karim Kazi, the chief technician in the Famous Cine Laboratories, who was in charge of the Famous Cine sound truck at the AICC meeting, there was also another truck taking sound film. He did not know whose it was. Deposition of Majid Karim Kazi for the prosecution concluded on 27-4-1943.

7. Deposition of Jagannath Raghunath Thakor for the prosecution concluded on 27-4-1943.

Krishnaji Ganesh Phulumbrikar, known as Master Krishna, said that he had given a record of 'Vande Mataram' for Odeon Company, but had not given any record of 'Hindustan Hamara'. He was present at the AICC meeting on 7 and 8 August and had sung the songs 'Hindustan Hamara' and 'Vande Mataram'. He was asked to sing them but was not given any time limit. After listening to the record before the Court at slow speed, he said that it was his voice. There was an abrupt ending of the song in the record that he heard, but at the AICC meeting he had sung the song ('Hindustan Hamara') to the end 'Malum Kya Kisi Ko Dard-e-Nihan Hamara'. Deposition of Krishnaji Ganesh Phulumbrikar for the prosecution on 16-4-1943.

8. Deposition of Jagannath Raghunath Thakor for the prosecution concluded on 27-4-1943.

9. Judgment as in Appendix I.

10. Deposition of Jagannath Raghunath Thakor for the prosecution concluded on 27-4-1943.
    Jagannath was arrested on the night of 11 November, and was in custody till 12 or 14 January. He had sent a sick note to Chicago Radio Company that he would be unable to attend office after he was arrested. On 14 January 1943 he resigned from the services of Chicago Radio Company and started his own business. Mansukhlal Nihalchand Shah was the financing partner and he was the working partner. Their firm was called 'Radio Combine'. Mansukhlal and he had become friendly when they both were in the lock-up. Jagannath knew him before as he was in charge of the Lamington Road branch of Chicago Radio Company. Deposition of Jagannath Raghunath Thakor for the prosecution concluded on 27-4-1943.

11. Deposition of Majid Karim Kazi for the prosecution concluded on 27-4-1943.

12. Deposition of Majid Karim Kazi for the prosecution concluded on 27-4-1943.

13. Deposition of Abdul Karim Rashid Kazi for the prosecution concluded on 29-4-1943.

14. Deposition of Ganesh Keshav Kokje for the prosecution concluded on 28-4-1943.

15. Deposition of Jayachand Tarachand Sheth for the prosecution concluded on 19-4-1943.

16. Deposition of Ganesh Keshav Kokje for the prosecution concluded on 28-4-1943.
    Report on the Congress Radio Case by the Commissioner of Police, Bombay, No. 1419 dated 26-1-1943 from Commissioner of Police, Bombay, to the Additional Secretary to the Government of Bombay, Home Department (Special), Bombay. File 1110 (31) 1942–43.
    The report stated that following the seizure of the Congress Broadcasting Station, further enquiries revealed that yet another transmitter had been constructed by Jagannath at the insistence of his employer N.G. Motwane and Vithalbhai Jhaveri from the parts supplied entirely by the Chicago Radio & Telephone Co. Ltd. When completed, this set was to be used in place of Transmitter No. 2, as it was a great deal more powerful than the latter. This set was finally located on 19-11-1942 in a room in Khandke Building, Walkeshwar Road, where it was being assembled. According to the police report, this was transmitter No. 3 and its description was given as: An improvised transmitting set, complete with two amplifiers, power-packs, one microphone, and an electrically driven gramophone pick-up, the set having an output of about 400 Watts. Spare parts seized included a large number of valves, three crystals, coils, insulators, etc.
    The total value of the wireless equipment seized by the police in these three cases (of the seized transmitters) was estimated at between Rs 7,000 and Rs 10,000.

17. Deposition of Ganesh Keshav Kokje for the prosecution concluded on 28-4-1943.

18. Deposition of Jamnadas Devkaran Chandriani for the prosecution concluded on 20-4-1943.
19. Deposition of Jayachand Tarachand Sheth for the prosecution concluded on 19-4-1943.
20. Judgment as in Appendix I.
21. Deposition of Ganesh Keshav Kokje for the prosecution concluded on 28-4-1943.

    Report on the Congress Radio Case by the Commissioner of Police, Bombay, No. 1419 dated 26-1-1943 from Commissioner of Police, Bombay, to the Additional Secretary to the Government of Bombay, Home Department (Special), Bombay. File 1110 (31) 1942–43.

    According to it, this was transmitter No. 1 and its description was given as: An improvised transmitting set fitted with seven valves, amplifier, power-pack, transformer, and having an output of about 50 Watts. The accessories included a microphone.

    On 30 November 1942, Kokje made a report that Manukumar Madhavji and Madhavji Sunderji should be discharged. The set found was confiscated and handed over to the military. No further proceedings were taken in that behalf. Deposition of Ganesh Keshav Kokje for the prosecution concluded on 28-4-1943.
22. Deposition of Ganesh Keshav Kokje for the prosecution concluded on 28-4-1943.
23. Deposition of Ganesh Keshav Kokje for the prosecution concluded on 28-4-1943.
24. Deposition of Nariman Adarbad Printer for the prosecution concluded on 20-4-1943.
25. Deposition of Ganesh Keshav Kokje for the prosecution concluded on 28-4-1943.

    The four hired rooms had separate doors leading into the gallery and also had interconnecting doors. The door of the gallery was mostly closed. It was locked from inside at the time of the transmission and someone was kept outside to watch. The door of each of the rooms also used to be closed at that time. Nobody lived in those rooms when the transmission was not going on. When nobody was there, it used to be locked from outside. Deposition of Nariman Adarbad Printer for the prosecution concluded on 20-4-1943.

26. Deposition of Ganesh Keshav Kokje for the prosecution concluded on 28-4-1943.

Report on the Congress Radio Case by the Commissioner of Police, Bombay, No. 1419 dated 26-1-1943 from Commissioner of Police, Bombay, to the Additional Secretary to the Government of Bombay, Home Department (Special), Bombay. File 1110 (31) 1942–43.

According to the report, the transmitter of Congress Broadcasting Station was Transmitter No. 2. Following the seizure of Transmitter No. 1 and the arrest of some persons, further inquiries, combined with assistance received from the military and naval authorities, led to the location and seizure of the Congress Radio at Parekh Wadi while it was actually in operation. Usha Mehta and Chandrakant B. Jhaveri were found attending to the operation of the set. Around this time Jagannath Raghunath Thakor, N.A. Printer, Babubhai, Vithalbhai Jhaveri and Nanak G. Motwane were also arrested.

From enquiries made with these persons, it was ascertained that Transmitter No. 2 had been constructed by N.A. Printer partly from equipment which was already in his possession and partly from articles supplied by the Chicago Radio and Telephone Co. Ltd, Bombay. Babubhai and Vithalbhai were closely connected with these activities. Babubhai was the chief organizer of the Congress Radio broadcasts and it was he who commissioned Printer to construct this set, arranging for the supply of certain parts from the Chicago Radio and Telephone Co. Ltd. It was he who also arranged the Congress Radio programmes after the records had been made at the residence of Vithalbhai (on a portable record maker which the latter is alleged to have obtained from the Chicago Radio and Telephone Co. Ltd). It was he who arranged for the installation of the set at different places: first at Sea View, Chowpatty, then at Ratan Mahal, Walkeshwar Road, later at Ajit Villa, Laburnum Road, Laxmi Building, Sandhurst Road, and finally at Parekh Wadi, Girgaum Back Road, where it was located and seized. It was suspected that this accused received funds for these activities from Ram Manohar Lohia, the Congress socialist leader, who directed the general scheme from 'underground'. Vithalbhai was mainly concerned with the recording of the songs and speeches, etc. on blank discs which were purchased in the local market. He was also instrumental in arranging for the construction of Transmitter No. 3. Jagannath Raghunath Thakor was commissioned by his employer to maintain Transmitter No. 2 in working order, to assist in the 'cutting' of the gramophone records and finally to construct Transmitter No. 3.

Description of Transmitter No. 2 was given as: An improvised transmitting set having an output of about 50 Watts, complete with amplifier, power-pack, one microphone and an electrically driven gramophone pick-up. Found also at the Congress Radio Station were a small receiving set, and 120 gramophone records which were being used for the broadcasts.

27. Deposition of Ganesh Keshav Kokje for the prosecution concluded on 28-4-1943.

28. Deposition of Manuel Morrison Fergusson for the prosecution concluded on 27-4-1943.

29. Deposition of Ganesh Keshav Kokje for the prosecution concluded on 28-4-1943.

30. Judgment as in Appendix I.

31. Personal communication of the author with Ushaben.

32. Judgment as in Appendix I.
33. Usha Mehta Congress Radio Papers, Mani Bhavan Gandhi Sangrahalaya.
34. Judgment as in Appendix I.
35. Judgment as in Appendix I.
36. Judgment as in Appendix I. The Judge observed that the essence of criminal conspiracy, as defined in Section 120-A of the IPC, is an agreement between two or more persons to do or cause to be done an illegal act or an illegal omission. He cited the observations by Jenkins C.J. in Barindra Kumar Ghose v. Emperor, I.L.R. 37 Cal. 467 at p. 507; Grose J. in R. v. Brisac, 4 East 164, affirmed by the House of Lords in Mulcahy v. Reg. 3 H.L. 306.
37. *Times of India*, 15 May 1943. Usha Mehta Congress Radio Papers, Mani Bhavan Gandhi Sangrahalaya, Mumbai.
38. Judgment as in Appendix I.
39. Judgment as in Appendix I.
40. Judgment as in Appendix I.
41. Judgment as in Appendix I.
42. Judgment as in Appendix I.
    Abdul Karim Kazi, manager of Famous Cine Laboratories, had also tested crystals. Metre wavelength corresponding to frequency 7094 kc was 42.28; and 7087 kc corresponded to wave length 42.33 metres. Frequency of 7101 kc corresponded to wave length 42.24 metres. The formula is: 3,00,000 kilocycles divided by the frequency in kc = the wavelength in metres. However, he said that it was not possible to accurately test the frequency of a crystal, there always remains a margin of error. Deposition of Abdul Karim Rashid Kazi for the prosecution concluded on 29-4-1943.
43. Judgment as in Appendix I.
44. Judgment. as in Appendix I.
45. Judgment as in Appendix I.

46. Judgment as in Appendix I.

47. Judgment as in Appendix I.

48. Judgment as in Appendix I.

49. Lohia's statement, Intelligence Bureau, Home, New Delhi to Special Branch, Bombay, 21 October 1944, CP File No. 1581/B/I, cited in, K.K. Chaudhari, *Quit India Revolution: The Ethos of Its Central Direction* (Mumbai: Popular Prakashan, 1996), p. 248.

50. Broadcast on the Congress Radio, 9 November morning and 10 November night 1942.

CHAPTER 4

1. Personal communication of the author with Ushaben.

2. Statement and examination of Vithaldas (Babubhai) Madhavji Khakar concluded on 29-4-1943.

3. Judgment as in Appendix I.

4. Deposition of Ganesh Keshav Kokje for the prosecution concluded on 28-4-1943.

5. Deposition of Thakurdas Jekisondas Gajjar for the prosecution concluded on 28-4-1943.

6. Judgment as in Appendix I.

7. Deposition of Ganesh Keshav Kokje for the prosecution concluded on 28-4-1943.

8. Judgment as in Appendix I.

9. Judgment as in Appendix I.

10. Judgment as in Appendix I.

11. Judgment as in Appendix I.

12. Judgment as in Appendix I.

13. Judgment as in Appendix I.

14. Statement and examination of Vithaldas Kanthadbhai Jhaveri concluded on 29-4-1943.

15. Deposition of Nariman Adarbad Printer for the prosecution concluded on 20-4-1943.

16. Judgment as in Appendix I.

17. Personal communication of the author with Ushaben.

18. Judgment as in Appendix I.

19. Statement and examination of Usha Hariprasad Mehta concluded on 29-4-1943.

20. Judgment as in Appendix I.

21. Deposition of Nariman Adarbad Printer for the prosecution concluded on 20-4-1943.

22. Judgment as in Appendix I.

23. Personal communication of the author with Ushaben.

24. Judgment as in Appendix I.

25. Judgment as in Appendix I.

26. Judgment as in Appendix I.

27. Judgment as in Appendix I.

28. Judgment as in Appendix I.

29. Statement and examination of Chandrakant Babubhai Jhaveri concluded on 29-4-1943.

30. Judgment as in Appendix I.

31. Deposition of Ganesh Keshav Kokje for the prosecution concluded on 28-4-1943.

32. Judgment as in Appendix I.

33. Deposition of Manuel Morrison Fergusson for the prosecution concluded on 27-4-1943.

34. Deposition of Dinanath Krishnarao Pednekar for the prosecution concluded on 27-4-1943.

35. Statement and examination of Nanak Gainchand Motwane concluded on 29-4-1943, and the written statement submitted by him on 29-4-1943.
Purshottam Chhotalal Subhedar said that he was the sound recording engineer of Jupiter Studio. In August 1942 he was working in the Bombay Studio, Goregaon. He was engaged by Motwane to record the speeches at the AICC meeting on 7 and 8 August 1942. Subhedar was to take the sound-truck of the Bombay Studio there. Motwane gave him the raw film. There was also the truck of Famous Cine Laboratory. It was at a distance of 20 feet from Subhedar's

truck. After the exposure of the films, he delivered the films to Motwane; Subhedar did not wash or develop them and did not know what happened to them. He exposed about 3,000 feet and had recorded sound only.
Deposition of Purshottam Chhotalal Subhedar for the prosecution concluded on 29-4-1943.

36. Statement and examination of Nanak Gainchand Motwane concluded on 29-4-1943, and the written statement submitted by him on 29-4-1943.

37. Statement and examination of Nanak Gainchand Motwane concluded on 29-4-1943, and the written statement submitted by him on 29-4-1943.

38. Statement and examination of Nanak Gainchand Motwane concluded on 29-4-1943, and the written statement submitted by him on 29-4-1943.

39. Judgment as in Appendix I.
40. Judgment as in Appendix I.
41. Judgment as in Appendix I.
42. Judgment as in Appendix I.
43. Judgment as in Appendix I.
44. Judgment as in Appendix I.
The frequency corresponding to 42.34 metres was 7086, whereas the frequency 7075 expressed in kc corresponded to 42.40 metres. If the frequency were 7075 as written on the crystal when Printer fitted it, the Congress Radio would have announced that it was broadcasting on 42.40 metres wavelength. Judgment as in Appendix I.
45. Judgment as in Appendix I.
46. Judgment as in Appendix I.
47. Judgment as in Appendix I.
48. Judgment as in Appendix I.
49. Judgment as in Appendix I.
50. Judgment as in Appendix I.
51. Judgment as in Appendix I.
52. Judgment as in Appendix I.

53. Judgment as in Appendix I

54. Judgment as in Appendix I.
The judge took note of the cases of Emperor v. Allisab, 34 Bom. L.R. 1453 and Emperor v. Mataprasad Shivprasad 45 Bom. L.R. 64; and observations of Macleod C.J. in Emperor v. Bhimrao, 27 Bom. L.R. 120, and N.J. Wadia J. in Emperor v. Shankarshet Ramshet I.L.R. 58 Bom. 40 at p. 48. He also referred to Rex v. Baskerville, (1916) 2 K.B. 658, and Sir Sidney Rowlatt delivering the judgment of the Privy Council in Mahadeo v. The King, 38 Bom. L.R. 1101. At another point regarding Printer's statement about the complicity of the accused, the judge referred to the views of Lord Abinger in R.V. Farler (1837) 8 C. & P. 106. Judgment as in Appendix I.

55. Judgment as in Appendix I.

56. Judgment as in Appendix I.

57. Judgment as in Appendix I.

58. Judgment as in Appendix I.

59. Deposition of Mahomed Ashroff Fiz Ahmed Choudhary for the prosecution concluded on 12-4-1943; Deposition of Raymond Ben Raymond for the prosecution concluded on 12-4-1943; Deposition of Hansraj Sardarchand Ghaia for the prosecution concluded on 12-4-1943; Deposition of Bhagsing Sardar Hajara Singh for the prosecution concluded on 12-4-1943; Deposition of Harischandra Shrivastav for the prosecution concluded on 12-4-1943; Deposition of Rama Harittar Iyer for the prosecution concluded on 14-4-1943.

60. Judgment as in Appendix I.
There was a news item soon after the judgment of the Congress Radio case about the 'Bombay Legal Defence Committee'. This committee was formed to provide facilities for the legal defence of the persons in the city and the province of Bombay who faced grave charges in cases consequent to the disturbances on the arrest

of the Congress leaders on 9 August 1942. Haridas
Madhavdas (Chairman, Indian Merchants' Chamber) was
its chairman, and Chimanlal Shah and Vithalbhai Jhaveri
were joint secretaries. Members included Jayshree Raiji,
M.C. Setalvad, J.C. Setalvad, K.R.P. Shroff, Shantikumar
Morarji, Trikamdas Dwarkadas, P.A. Wadia, R.A.
Jagirdar, Motichand G. Kapadia, Vaikunth L. Mehta,
C.N. Kanuga, K.F. Nariman, S.A. Brelvi, Vithaldas D.
Govindji, Chhotalal P. Mehta, Jaisukhlal K. Mehta, S.R.
Tendolkar, H.R. Pardivala, Kamalnayan Bajaj, Pratap
Dialdas, Vasant Mashruvala, M.J. Gordhandas, V.R.
Upadhyaya and M.M. Jape. The office of the committee
was at the Examiners' Press Building, Dalal Street, Fort,
Bombay. *Bombay Chronicle*, 3 August 1943. Details of the
working of this committee, however, could not be found.
61. Personal communication of the author with Ushaben.

CHAPTER 5

Note: Copies of the transcripts of the broadcasts for
most of the days during the Congress Radio's functioning
are found in Usha Mehta Congress Radio Papers, Mani
Bhavan Gandhi Sangrahalaya, Mumbai. All the transcripts
of the broadcasts referred to in this chapter are from Usha
Mehta Congress Radio Papers, Mani Bhavan Gandhi
Sangrahalaya, Mumbai. The copies of the transcripts of
the broadcasts from 9 October to 2 November prepared by
Police Wireless Monitoring Report (for 'Illegal Congress
Radio' Station) are available in these papers and also in
File 1110 (31) 1 1942.

1. The authorities had issued a circular dated 17 July 1942,
signed by Sir Frederick Puckle, Secretary to the Government
of India, Department of Information and Broadcasting, to
chief secretaries of all provincial governments (and chief
commissioners, Delhi, Ajmer-Merwara, Baluchistan and

Coorg) to mobilize public opinion against the Congress
Resolution. This happened to fall into the hands of Gandhi
who gave it a wide circulation in Bombay with a prefatory
note. *See:* Pattabhi Sitaramayya, *History of the Indian
National Congress Vol. II 1935–1947* (Bombay: Padma
Publications, 1947), pp. 359–60. Further, the British
government tightened its control over the press—even in
the matter of selection and presentation of factual news
relating to the disturbances. The press was warned that
"The editor of any newspaper who supports or encourages
the mass movement . . . or who opposes the measures taken
by government to avert or suppress that movement, will
be guilty of an offence against the law. Moreover, it is also
undeniable that the publication of factual news, both by the
selection of events reported and by the manner in which
they are displayed, can do even more to advertise, and thus
support, the movement than editorial comment thereon."
Further, what was published had to be 'derived only from
recognized and responsible sources'. *See:* 'India Unreconciled'
(A documented history of Indian political events from
the crisis of August 1942 to February 1944), *Hindustan
Times*, New Delhi, first edition 1943, second edition 1944,
pp. 135–36. There were individual supporters of the
government who were allowed to broadcast. For example,
in a broadcast on the Bombay station of All India Radio on
30 July 1942, Rustom Masani urged the AICC not to accept
the Working Committee's decision and see whether it cannot
still suggest ways and means of Congress cooperation with
the government. *Bombay Chronicle*, 31 July 1942.

2. Francis G. Hutchins, *Spontaneous Revolution: The Quit
    India Movement* (Delhi: Manohar Book Service, 1971),
    pp. 214–15.

3. Paul R. Greenough, 'Political Mobilization and the
    Underground Literature of the Quit India Movement,
    1942–44', *Social Scientist* 27, no. 7/8 (Jul–Aug 1999): 12.

One of the first papers to be closed down was Gandhi's *Harijan*; the police seized every copy of the fiery issue of 16 August, and only one other issue appeared a week later. For Gandhi's own estimate of the place of *Harijan* in national life, see the article 'If *Harijan* Is Suppressed', *Harijan*, 19 July 1942, in *The Collected Works of Mahatma Gandhi* Vol. 76 (1 April 1942–17 December 1942), The Publications Division, Ministry of Information and Broadcasting, Government of India, New Delhi, 1979, pp. 288–89. Gandhi in his speech on 8 August 1942 had asked the journalists to snap the chains that bounded them. His advice to them was to give up writing under the prevailing restrictions and to tell Sir Frederick Puckle not to expect a command performance from them and to refuse to publish his press notes that were full of untruth. Gandhi's speech at the AICC meeting on 8 August 1942, *Mahatma* Vol. VI, pp.154–64, in *The Collected Works of Mahatma Gandhi* Vol. 76, pp. 392–93.

4. *August 9*, 25th Anniversary, All India Congress Committee, New Delhi, 1967. pp. 19-21.

5. For details see K.K. Chaudhari, *Quit India Revolution: The Ethos of Its Central Direction* (Mumbai: Popular Prakashan, 1996), pp. 100–132.

6. Greenough, 'Political Mobilization', p. 12.

7. In addition to simple censorship of the nationalist press, the governments of both India and Britain waged a steady campaign against the British-owned and edited *Statesman* in India, against the *London Times* and against the American wire services to persuade them to report news of the Quit India movement with a pro-government slant; this campaign was successful only in the case of the *Statesman*. Greenough, 'Political Mobilization', p. 43.

8. Speech made in the Indian Legislative Assembly by K.C. Neogy on 17 September 1942. *India Ravaged* (Being an account of atrocities committed, under the British

aegis, over the whole subcontinent of India in the latter part of 1942), January 1943, p. 127. The government published a special booklet *Congress Responsibility for the Disturbances: 1942–43* (Published with the authority), Manager of Publications, Delhi, 1943, to present its case against the Congress and Gandhi. It was issued in February 1943 when Gandhi had undertaken his fast and his health was deteriorating.

9.   C.K. Narayanswami, 'The Underground Press: Journalists' Honeymoon with Death', *Bombay Chronicle*, 9 August 1942. It highlights the dramatic adventure of the publication of the Congress Bulletin. When the police located and raided the place where it was being produced, those engaged in the work converted a moving automobile into a 'printing shed', and all that the police found were a dilapidated typewriter and ink-soiled foolscap papers. While the police was raiding the place, the bulletin was actually being duplicated in the car.

10. 138, Mr Amery to the Marquess of Linlithgow, MSS. EUR.F. 125/11, India Office, 3 November 1942, in, Nicholas Mansergh, ed., E.W.R. Lumby asst. ed., *Constitutional Relations between Britain and India, The Transfer of Power, 1942–7* Vol. III, 21 September 1942–12 June 1943, Her Majesty's Stationery Office, London, 1971, p. 197.

It is interesting to note that during the Second World War, radio stations from countries like Germany and Japan were active in broadcasting. Subhash Chandra Bose and other Indians made regular broadcasts from the Azad Hind Radio. People were becoming aware of the importance of the radio as a means of getting news. As observed by Melissa Lauren Dinsman, the World War II had become 'a radio war'. Most people experienced the war through sound in the comfort of their living rooms. In the US alone, one or more radios were found in 90 per cent of homes during World War II, and listening in accounted for three to four hours each day. Melissa Lauren Dinsman, *Radio at War: Literature, Propaganda, and the Emergence of New Modernist Networks during World War II*, Ph.D. dissertation (Notre Dame, IN: University of Notre Dame, Indiana, 2013), p. 10.

11. *Bombay Chronicle*, 10 August 1942.

12. *Bombay Chronicle*, 11 August 1942.

13. Personal communication of the author with Ushaben.

14. Home Department (Special) No. 3021 Date- 6-10-1942. File 1110 (31) II 1942.

15. Home Department (Special) No. 3158 Date- 9-10-1942. File 1110 (31) II 1942.

16. Very bad reception of the Congress Radio on 10 and 11 October but very clear reception on 12 October on 42.34 metres, Home Department (Special) No. 3322 Date: 13-10-1942. File 1110 (31) II 1942.; very bad reception on 42.34 metres but good reception after switching to 39 metres, Home Department (Special) No. 3092 Date: 8-10-1942. File 1110 (31) II 1942.

17. Home Department (Special) No.3201 Date: 10-11-1942. File 1110 (31) II 1942.

18. Transcript of the broadcast on 14 October 1942, 8.53 p.m., Police Wireless Monitoring Report; Transcript of the broadcast on 25 October 1942, 8.45 p.m., Police Wireless Monitoring Report; Transcript of the broadcast on 26 October 1942, 8.45 p.m., Police Wireless Monitoring Report.

19. Personal communication of the author with Ushaben.

20. Transcript of the broadcast on 18 September 1942: It was pointed out in this broadcast that after a particularly bad day of firing in Nagpur, Mr Sullivan, one of the undersecretaries to the government of the Central Provinces, remarked that he felt exhilarated after a good day's *shikar* (hunt). Moreover, the Viceroy issued his

annual circular in the middle of August to the major princes inviting offers for his cold weather shooting. The Congress Radio reacted sharply to it: 'Why does His Excellency risk the discomforts of a swamp on a jungle when his subordinates find bigger, better, more exciting game so close at hand—the Indian people? The Christians were thrown to the lions to make sport for the Roman emperors. Today in India taking a pot-shot at the native is a fine sport which satisfies the blood lust of these white Nabobs of the East.'

21. Transcript of the broadcast on 19 September 1942: In Madras Alladi Krishnaswamy Ayyar, the Accountant General of Madras, wanted to withdraw Rs 20 lakh from his account of Rs 86 lakh in the Reserve Bank. Sensing the impending collapse of British currency in India, he desired to secure his fortune through much safer investment in land. But the government prohibited him from withdrawing more than Rs 20,000 at a time. This incident caused great uneasiness in the richer class in Madras.

22. Transcript of the broadcast on 18 September 1942.

23. Transcript of the broadcast on 20 September 1942: When the police sub-inspector was aiming to shoot little girls, Shirish Mehta, a young boy, rushed to the scene and asked the policeman to shoot him instead of the innocent girls; and he was shot. Four more boys under ten years were shot dead and 15 were wounded. No medical aid was allowed to reach them. In Chinchni, young boys and girls were whipped until they were unconscious. In Dombivli, a sub-inspector tried to intimidate small boys by caning and whipping them indiscriminately. In Nandurbar, a pleader, dressed in khadi and going in a tonga (a horse-drawn two-wheeled vehicle), was arrested and taken to a police station; he was whipped all along the road. Persons holding responsible positions

had started resigning. For example, 80 police patels in
Karad resigned.

24. Transcript of the broadcast on 22 September 1942: Every
few days the workers took out peaceful processions. On
10 September, Uma Shankar Pandya, a promising and
young mechanical engineer of the Works, was leading the
procession. He and others in the procession were asked
by the police to disperse. When they did not listen, he was
shot dead. Other places in the province were also restless.
In Poona, 1,000 students of the Ferguson College held a
meeting in the college compound, denouncing Churchill's
last speech. In Vaduj in Satara district, people took
procession to the court and the police post. Subsequently
four persons were killed and several were injured by the
police firing. In Dharwar, an appeal had been issued to
the government and the University of Bombay under the
signatures of Sir S.T. Kambli, ex-minister of Education,
Rao Bahadur B.L. Patil and other prominent persons to
close all educational institutions in view of the prevailing
political atmosphere.

25. Transcript of the broadcast on 27 September 1942.

26. Transcript of the broadcast on 26 September 1942.

27. Transcript of the broadcast on 26 September 1942: It was
reported that a ship was sunk by the enemy action between
250 and 300 miles from Bombay. By this time 14 ships had
been sunk in the Arabian Sea.

28. Transcript of the broadcast on 22 September 1942.

29. Transcript of the broadcast on 20 September 1942.

30. Transcript of the broadcast on 22 September 1942.

31. Transcript of the broadcast on 18 September 1942.

32. Transcript of the broadcast on 24 September 1942.

33. Transcript of the broadcast on 19 September 1942: Certain
sections of the Grand Trunk Road were also damaged or
blocked and telephone and telegram wires cut at various
places. In addition, the GTC corps of the Benares University

and the trainees of the Aeronautics department, in a mood of defiance, protested against the British rule.

34. Transcript of the broadcast on 19 September 1942.

35. Transcript of the broadcast on 24 September 1942.

36. Transcript of the broadcast on 27 September 1942.

37. Transcript of the broadcast on 22 September 1942.

38. Transcript of the broadcast on 22 September 1942.

39. Transcript of the broadcast on 25 September 1942. Collective fines of Rs 2,000 and Rs 5,000 were imposed on Waraseoni (Balaghat) and Katra Bazar (Saugar) respectively.

40. Transcript of the broadcast on 22 September 1942.

41. Transcript of the broadcast on 18 September 1942.

42. Transcript of the broadcast on 24 September 1942.

43. Transcript of the broadcast on 24 September 1942: In Assam, 100 Rajput soldiers with their rifles were found missing from their barracks. Subsequently, 15 were captured. However, since the incident, Indian soldiers in Assam were not allowed to keep their rifles at night.

44. Transcript of the broadcast on 20 September 1942.

45. Transcript of the broadcast on 20 September 1942: On 18 August the government attempted to negotiate the purchase of 50,000 maunds of rice for war purposes and called a meeting. But the Congress volunteers came to the meeting and persuaded the merchants to withdraw. The Sub Divisional Officer (SDO) was induced to put on a Gandhi cap and lead the procession with the national flag. On the 20th, the court was picketed, and on the 21st, the Congress flag flew over the court building. The magistrate and SDO arrived there on the 22nd with armed police but an amicable settlement was made with the Congress workers. These officers were allowed to enter the court building on the condition that the national flag flew over it. Troubles started when the government officials tried again to purchase rice in secret from one or two merchants. After

5,000 bags had been carried to the station, the Congress volunteers intervened and started picketing. Military patrols arrived on the 25th. At this juncture, the merchants refused to sell to the government. On the 28th a public meeting was held, a special train arrived at midnight and took away five workers who were under arrest. Next day Bolepur had a complete strike and a public meeting was held. Three to four thousand Santhals of Birbhum came to the meeting and burnt a part of the station, the records and other property. The railway superintendent of police telephoned for the military patrol from the next station. He himself started to fire upon the assembled Santhals. The military patrol also shot people indiscriminately. Two were killed and several were seriously injured. On 4 and 5 September, extensive arrests were made of the Congress workers and students of Shanti Niketan. Bolepur station was cut off from the rest of Bengal due to extensive damage on the railway tracks.

46. Transcript of the broadcast on 19 September 1942: At Faridpur, Nadia, when the police came to arrest Dr Sureshchandra Banerjee, MLA and former president of the Trade Union Congress, 4,000–5,000 villagers gathered and declared that Dr Banerjee could not be removed unless they all were killed. The officers were unable to arrest Dr Sureshchandra Banerjee. In Midnapur Mahesadal, similar resistance was offered at the arrest of nine workers on 2 September. In this case the SDO withdrew the warrants. At Contai in Ramnagar, the police attempted to arrest the speaker at a meeting but could not succeed due to people's opposition. In Malda, 40 armed police had to return unsuccessful when they tried to arrest Subodh Chandra Misra, a popular worker. In Delhi, 125 clerks in the AGCR (Accountant General Central Revenues) office submitted their resignations.

47. Transcript of the broadcast on 27 September 1942.

48. Transcript of the broadcast on 26 September 1942.
49. Transcript of the broadcast on 25 September 1942.
50. Transcript of the broadcast on 24 September 1942: Four ships had been sunk near the Diamond Harbour. On one occasion leaflets containing Subhash Chandra Bose's message were also dropped near the Diamond Harbour area.
51. Transcript of the broadcast on 19 September 1942.
52. Transcript of the broadcast on 22 September 1942: In Rangiya, the station was burnt, all properties damaged and rails removed. In Bhaluka (between Malda and Katihar), telephone and telegraph wires were cut. In Kampur, the station was burnt and all property damaged. On the East Indian Railway, a ballast train was derailed between Rampurhat and Mollarpur.
53. Transcript of the broadcast on 26 September 1942.
54. Transcript of the broadcast on 24 September 1942.
55. Transcript of the broadcast on 25 September 1942.
56. Transcript of the broadcast on 22 September 1942.
57. Transcript of the broadcast on 22 September 1942.
58. Transcript of the broadcast on 24 September 1942.
59. Transcript of the broadcast on 12 October 1942, 9.20 p.m., Police Wireless Monitoring Report.
60. Transcript of the broadcast on 25 October 1942, 8.30 a.m., Police Wireless Monitoring Report. The procession was led by the owner representing the Viceroy. Those donkeys were arrested by the police and kept in custody and placed before the City Magistrate for trial. The man was convicted and the donkeys were released.
61. Transcript of the broadcast on 29 October 1942, 8.45 p.m., Police Wireless Monitoring Report: These men went from house to house and shot down the people. Twenty-five Congressmen were murdered and their homes were burnt. The Collector took strong exception to the situation.

62. Transcript of the broadcast on 20 October 1942, 9.10 p.m., Police Wireless Monitoring Report.

63. Transcript of the broadcast on 12 October 1942, 9.20 p.m., Police Wireless Monitoring Report.

64. Transcript of the broadcast on 22 October 1942, 8.45 p.m., Police Wireless Monitoring Report: In the Central Provinces a girl of about thirteen years died two days after her arrest. In Bihar soldiers killed six women. A landlord from Bengal, who was himself a Hon. Magistrate, had a tale of harassment by the military and policemen in his village.

65. Transcript of the broadcast on 29 October 1942, 8.45 p.m., Police Wireless Monitoring Report.

66. Transcript of the broadcast on 28 October 1942, 8.45 p.m., Police Wireless Monitoring Report: This report was prepared by Vimala Deshpande, Vimla Abhyankar, Dwarkabai Devaskar, Ramabai Tambe and Dr (Mrs) Valazkar. They visited Chimur on 19 and 20 September. Soldiers had taken possession of all the houses, had looted them and had outraged women. Women were frightened, panic-stricken and afraid to talk. They talked about the men who had been jailed and about the looting/damage of their property, but found it very difficult to reveal the instances of molestation. However, they managed to tell Dr Valazkar about molestations that occurred in Chambharpura and Telipura, etc. Six cases were related of ruthless rape even of pregnant women. Since the military entered on 14 August, only children and women were left behind, as all men had been taken away. Many women hid themselves. They were in groups of 25 and 30. For two whole days the women and children had nothing to eat, not even water to drink. Houses were taken over by the soldiers. The Congress Radio urged that 'India must prevent the rape of their women. Mukami in Bihar, Chimur in Central Provinces and Devakovat in Madras have

shaken the soul of India. Hindu and Muslim women have been raped by thousands.' The Congress Radio declared, 'We shudder to think of Indians who are still serving this administration and who have dealings with it, who expect something from it.'

67.   Transcript of the broadcast on 20 October 1942, 8.45 p.m., Police Wireless Monitoring Report. Further, the broadcast on 26 October 1942, 8.45 p.m., mentioned that the Congress Radio gave information about a telegram sent to the newspapers in India on 23 October by the Associated Press. Initially, the Press Censor had passed this telegram, but later it was withheld. This showed the anxiety of the government. The telegram conveyed that Ahmedabad, the city of Gandhiji, had gone ahead in carrying out the Congress programme and civil disobedience. Since 9 August, after the arrest of the Congress leaders, the textile mills of Ahmedabad remained closed. The municipal staff was also on strike. Educational institutions also followed the orders of the Congress and were closed. One third of the mill workers left the city after 9 August as they had great respect for Gandhiji who established the Mill Mazdoor Union in Ahmedabad. On 7 October women in Surat took out a procession from Gandhi Chowk and 14 girls who took part in the procession were arrested. They were treated badly by the police. However, later, all the girls, except one, were released. Transcript of the broadcast on 26 October 1942, 8.45 p.m., Police Wireless Monitoring Report.

68.   Transcript of the broadcast on 20 October 1942, 8.45 p.m., Police Wireless Monitoring Report.

69.   Transcript of the broadcast on 24 October 1942, 8.45 p.m., Police Wireless Monitoring Report.

70.   Transcript of the broadcast on 20 October 1942, 8.45 p.m., Police Wireless Monitoring Report: A police sub-inspector Ramnad Singh was arrested for taking part

in an agitation. When the police was escorting him and Haricharan Bansi (who had escaped from Hajipur jail), the police were attacked by 50 villagers armed with different kinds of weapons. The police opened fire and Rajnarin Singh, who was leading the mob, was killed. However, the brave villagers did not allow his body to fall into the hands of the police.

71. Transcript of the broadcast on 27 October, night, 1942. Thakur Ram Nandan Singh in Sitamarhi jail, who was unwilling to be released this way, sent a message to the people to desist. The people left after hoisting the National Tricolour on the jail building. It was significant that at none of these four jails the Indian staff and police attempted to resist the people or fire at them. Some railway lines were also broken up. Some trains were suspended including Darbhanga–Champaran lines, Muzaffarpur–Mokamah lines, Patna–Mogalsarai and Patna–Asansol lines for some time. Hundreds of stations including Mokama, Barauni and Bhagalpur were burnt and looted.

72. Transcript of the broadcast on 24 October 1942, 8.45 p.m., Police Wireless Monitoring Report.

73. Transcript of the broadcast on 20 October 1942, Police Wireless Monitoring Report. 144 policemen were suspended and detained in their barracks and 36 put under arrest on 18 October as they refused to submit to a medical examination preliminary to sending them abroad. Moreover, there was a loud explosion in the Government Finishing Factory in the Allahabad fort and two first-class railway bogeys were burnt at Allahabad station. Emphasizing that the Indian police would not hold arms against their own people, the Congress Radio was pleased to announce on 12 October 1942 that the Muslim officers had followed the same course in Allahabad. Transcript of the broadcast on 12 October 1942, 9.20 p.m., Police Wireless Monitoring Report.

74. Transcript of the broadcast on 12 October 1942, 9.20 p.m., Police Wireless Monitoring Report.

75. Transcript of the broadcast on 13 October 1942, 8.45 p.m., Police Wireless Monitoring Report.

76. Transcript of the broadcast on 23 October 1942, 8.45 p.m., Police Wireless Monitoring Report.

77. Transcript of the broadcast on 23 October 1942, 8.45 p.m., Police Wireless Monitoring Report: Many policemen had resigned there and some were prosecuted by the government and sentenced to two years' rigorous imprisonment. The Ahmedabad textile workers decided to continue their strike till swaraj was won.

78. Transcript of the broadcast on 30 October 1942, 8.45 p.m., Police Wireless Monitoring Report: Six political prisoners went on hunger strike as a protest against the quality of food in Porbunder in Gujarat. Since the commencement of the movement, the Indian Collector at Motihari, Bihar, was deprived of his power; instead, two Europeans were given full authority to deal with the local situation. Many were killed. In Govindganj, students started a successful village campaign against the Chowkidari tax. In Kolhapur, Sahu's place on 13th Road which was occupied by government officers was gutted by fire on 28 September. All important documents and records were destroyed. A stock of two years was burnt in the fire in the Times Godown in Bombay. There was only 15 days' stock for newsprint in the press. Further stock of three months had just arrived from Calcutta.

79. Transcript of the broadcast on 12 October 1942, 9.20 p.m., Police Wireless Monitoring Report.

80. Transcript of the broadcast on 30 October 1942, 8.45 p.m., Police Wireless Monitoring Report: On 11 September, when the college reopened after the holidays, the National Flag was flying on the building and also on the High School. The posters/notices calling upon the students to go an on indefinite strike were plastered all over the city.

81. Transcript of the broadcast on 29 October 1942, 8.45 p.m., Police Wireless Monitoring Report: In Travancore jail the political prisoners were kept with other prisoners in the cells having no sanitary arrangements. There were 100 prisoners in Cochin. Students in Trivandrum conducted a successful strike on Gandhi Jayanti. More than 40 of them were arrested and badly treated.

82. Transcript of the broadcast on 24 October 1942, 8.45 p.m., Police Wireless Monitoring Report.

83. Transcript of the broadcast on 24 October 1942, 8.45 p.m., Police Wireless Monitoring Report: It prompted the Congress Radio to say: 'Even God is against the British government and is with the Indian nation.'

84. Transcript of the broadcast on 26 October 1942, 8.45 p.m., Police Wireless Monitoring Report.

85. Transcript of the broadcast on 22 October 1942.

86. Transcript of the broadcast on 30 October 1942.

87. Transcript of the broadcast on 21 October, night, 1942.

88. Transcript of the broadcast on 21 October, night, 1942.

89. Transcript of the broadcast on 18 October 1942, 7.30 a.m., Police Wireless Monitoring Report: On the day of Vijaya Dashmi the broadcast bulletin remembered the victory of justice over injustice thousands of years ago in the context of the ongoing war between good and evil.

90. Transcript of the broadcast on 20 October 1942, 9.10 p.m., Police Wireless Monitoring Report: On 5 October, 280 Red Shirts were seriously wounded: the total number of injured was 400. The city of Peshawar observed a complete hartal on 6 October as a protest against the arrest of the city Congress Committee workers and others. There were reports from Mardan that government offices and courts were picketed. The police opened fire several times and some workers were killed. The people of Peshawar and other parts of the province broke and cut off telephone and telegraph poles and raided police stations. The Congress

Radio also disseminated the shocking news that students and boys arrested on suspicion were taken to a nearby canal and drowned.

91. Transcript of the broadcast on 22 October, 8.45 p.m., Police Wireless Monitoring Report: Attention was also drawn to the ongoing agitation in the firing at Mardan and several other places. In Peshawar about 300 persons were injured. Students had pulled down telephone and telegraph posts.

92. Transcript of the broadcast on 28 October 1942, 8.45 p.m., Police Wireless Monitoring Report: 800 Khudai Khidmatgars were arrested and very badly treated by the police. On 21 October an unknown person entered the Khudai Khidmatgars' camp and poisoned their tea. One died and 100 were seriously ill. A post office was burnt in Nowshera. An effigy of Churchill was set on fire instead of that of Ravana in Karachi on 20 October.

93. Transcript of the broadcast on 29 October 1942, 8.45 p.m., Police Wireless Monitoring Report.

94. Transcript of the broadcast on 18 October, 7.30 a.m., Police Wireless Monitoring Report.

95. Transcript of the broadcast on 5 November 1942 morning.

96. Transcript of the broadcast on 1 November 1942, 8.30 a.m., Police Wireless Monitoring Report.

97. Transcript of the broadcast on 2 November 1942, 8.45 p.m., Police Wireless Monitoring Report.

98. Transcript of the broadcast on 1 November 1942, 8.45 p.m., Police Wireless Monitoring Report.

99. Transcript of the broadcast on 8 November 1942.

100. Transcript of the broadcast on 6 November 1942: In Zalod (Gujarat), telegraph wires were cut at three places. In Kathiawar, telegraph wires had been cut and were removed at Vinchhiva in Jasdan state and at Wadhwan. In Surat, 45 businessmen were arrested for observing hartal.

101. Transcript of the broadcast on 8 November 1942.

102. Transcript of the broadcast on 9 November 1942: On 4 November, 15 Desh Sevikas who were on hunger strike at gate of Mafatlal Mill for the last few days gave up their fast as the proprietors had agreed to close the mills and accept the terms of the Congress.

103. Transcript of the broadcast on 7 November 1942: On 28 October, a cooperative society godown in Belgaum was burnt. Telephone and telegraph wires had been cut in Shahpur and Hosatti. A report about the brutal assault on student under-trials in Mysore was received. On 27 October, about 30 students-under-trial prisoners were taken to court for trial. They were not given the usual midday meal. On their return in the evening they asked for food. The jail superintendent, after lengthy discussions, said that he would arrange for it. At midnight all of a sudden, about 150 reserve police, badly drunk and armed with lathis, were let loose on them. The under-trial prisoners were badly beaten. 17 were seriously injured. No medical aid was given: Shankarappa died on the morning of 30 October. The government doctor declared that the death was due to broncho-pneumonia, even though several of his ribs were broken. His parents were permitted to take the body only when they agreed to take him under police escort and have his last rites performed in the presence of his murderers. One more student died thereafter. In Mysore also there were some instances of the destruction of electric and telephone wires and posts.

104. Transcript of the broadcast on 8 November 1942.

105. Transcript of the broadcast on 10 November 1942: SDO of Hassan was pressing for his transfer. The DC of Shimoga also asked for transfer. Many village patils were anxious to resign as they did not want to associate with the repressive steps of the government. The Congress Radio advised the government servants: 'A traitor to one's own people will never find peace. The people's freedom movement will dog them wherever they

go. If they want peace let them decide once and for all to leave the enemy's camp and be with the people.'

106. Transcript of the broadcast on 10 November 1942: The use of brutal and repressive methods by the police angered the people further. Contractors gave up their contracts and demanded a refund of their deposits from the government. On the one hand, the contractors refused to cooperate, and on the other, the people picketed or assembled in another area and held their bazaar where the contractor had no right of collection. At some places, the police tried to force the people to go to the usual site of the bazaar but were not successful. Some persons were arrested, but the villagers did not allow the police van with the prisoners to proceed. The arrested persons had to be released. At some places the military was sent to frighten the people from holding the usual bazaar. But the villagers refused to hold any bazaar as long as the military remained there.

107. Transcript of the broadcast on 5 November 1942.

108. Transcript of the broadcast on 6 November 1942.

109. Transcript of the broadcast on 5 November 1942.

110. Transcript of the broadcast on 2 November 1942, 8.45 p.m., Police Wireless Monitoring Report.

111. Transcript of the broadcast on the morning of 5 November 1942: One of the victims of this ill-treatment was Nandita Devi, the granddaughter of Rabindranath Tagore. The government intended to control the dissemination of information about the movement.

112. Transcript of the broadcast on 2 November 1942, 8.45 p.m., Police Wireless Monitoring Report.

113. Transcript of the broadcast on 5 November 1942.

114. Transcript of the broadcast on 9 November 1942.

115. Transcript of the broadcast on 2 November 1942, 8.45 p.m., Police Wireless Monitoring Report.

116. Transcript of the broadcast on the morning of 5 November 1942: Moreover, two derailments took place

at Bishesharganj (between Allahabad and Pratapgarh) on 22 and 23 October, and on 25 October the railway line was breached on the Delhi–Karnal sections. The Dariba post office in Chandni Chowk, Delhi, was also completely gutted by fire on 21 October.

117. Transcript of the broadcast on 8 November 1942: During the previous fortnight about 400 were arrested: more than half of them were women. Women volunteers were harassed by the Karachi police and were abused in filthy language. They were released very often at midnight at far-off lonely places. Sentences with heavy fines were being imposed on all. Whipping for political offences had become common in Karachi and other districts. Even children between the ages of 8 and 13 were arrested and kept huddled together with criminal juveniles at the remand house. Three prominent businessmen were arrested since this ministry took charge. In Karachi, a fire broke out in the Small Causes Court and some records were burnt. In Shikarpur, a fire broke out in the Civil Court and some furniture was burnt. A post office in Sukkur was set on fire and its contents burnt and the office of the Barrage Mukhtiarkar was also set on fire.

118. Transcript of the broadcast on the night of 8 November 1942: On 21 October, in a village in Rajapur, the peasants were called for the recovery of old arrears: the official was accompanied by the police. But the peasants had become conscious of the new situation created by the struggle. The Congress bulletins were regularly reaching the villages. The Congress volunteers addressed this gathering first by beat of drum and then read out the message of the Congress. They carried the National Flag and also read out a leaflet warning the government servants against becoming tools of the terror regime. The official could not dare to arrest anyone on the spot. The whole village and the neighbouring villages also learnt to renounce the fear of bureaucracy. In another village the police collected some local goondas and

arrested a Congress volunteer unawares. But the defiance and courage of the people in a small village they were passing by forced the police to release this volunteer who was then led through the village in a triumphant procession which terminated in a meeting.

119. Transcript of the broadcast on the night of 9 November 1942: Professor Bhansali, an inmate of the Sevagram Ashram and a close associate of Mahatma Gandhi, had met M.S. Aney, a member of the Viceroy's Executive Council, at his official residence on the morning of 1 November to bring to his notice the excesses committed by the police and the military during the disturbances in the Central Provinces. Atrocities perpetrated against the villagers and women in particular pained Professor Bhansali. He opined that Aney had a good reputation and he should have courage to demand an independent investigation into the facts. By his inaction, he had become a silent partner in the sin against his own daughters and sisters. Professor Bhansali put two facts to Aney. Firstly, such horrifying events were a challenge, not purely political in significance, but a challenge to the very core of our humanness. The second question that he posed to Aney was more personal. He pointed out that Amery, the Secretary of State, had been proclaiming to the Parliament and the world that the present policy of repression had full support of all the Indian members of the Viceroy's Council. The world would be justified in thinking that Aney was a party not only to the ordinances but also to the lawless laws of the goondaraj: he became a party to the perpetration of atrocities to his own sisters and daughters. Aney was not willing to undertake a personal investigation into the Chimur atrocities. Moreover, he blamed Mahatma Gandhi and the Congress for launching the struggle in spite of all the warnings. Professor Bhansali said that if Aney could not even secure an independent inquiry, he should resign.

Thereafter, Professor Bhansali mentioned his decision to fast without food or water, until his demand for an independent inquiry into the Chimur atrocities was met. Professor Bhansali's demands to Aney were: soldiers and police should not be allowed to commit excesses hereafter; atrocities being committed in jails should be stopped and those that had occurred in the past should be investigated; and excesses committed by the police and the military must be investigated. Prof. Bhansali started his fast without food and water; he also imposed upon himself the vow of silence. By 8 p.m. several press representatives were around the professor. Around 9 p.m. the police took Bhansali and his companion Balwantsingh and they were sent to the jail next morning. Before being taken into custody he gave the following message in writing: 'No nation can achieve freedom which suffers outrages on the women and receives them lying down. We must be up and fight against a government intoxicated with the lust of power. God gives the utmost to those who fight for their honour.' The broadcast bulletin praised Professor Bhansali's courage and spirit. (He ended his fast on 14 January 1943.)

120. Transcript of the broadcast on the morning of 9 November and the night of 10 November 1942.

121. Transcript of the broadcast on the morning of 12 November 1942.

CHAPTER 6

Note: Copies of the transcripts of the broadcasts for most of the days during the Congress Radio's functioning are found in Usha Mehta Congress Radio Papers, Mani Bhavan Gandhi Sangrahalaya, Mumbai. All the transcripts of the broadcasts referred to in this chapter are from Usha Mehta Congress Radio Papers, Mani Bhavan Gandhi Sangrahalaya, Mumbai. The copies of the transcripts of the broadcasts from 9 October to 2 November prepared by Police Wireless Monitoring Report (for 'Illegal Congress Radio' Station) are available in these papers and also in File 1110 (31) 1 1942.

1.   Transcript of the broadcast on 9 November morning and 10 November night. It was announced that, 'To our listeners, to the Indian people, we admit our inadequacies. But do not forget that we are a secret centre. Certain technical difficulties we can never overcome. And yet we will continue to bring you the voice of truth and freedom; it may sometimes falter or break, but we give you our pledge, it will never die out.'

2.   Personal communication of the author with Ushaben.

3.   Transcript of the broadcast on 21 October 1942, 8.30 a.m., Police Wireless Monitoring Report: The broadcast referred to the French and Russian revolutions and proclaimed that India could not accept the traditional revolutionary way for some reasons. Firstly, the people here had been disarmed for very long time and not prepared for an armed insurrection. Secondly, the British state evolved a method whereby concentrated armed might of tanks, artillery and aeroplanes was centred in the hands of the British soldiers and Indian army, infantrymen and subordinate ranks. It further stated that, 'Thirdly, our long tradition of peace and our continued disarmament and the great teachings of Mahatma Gandhi have combined to produce a grand new weapon of war against injustice and tyranny. Our weapon claims to show a new way to the world so our revolution cannot be based on a traditional pattern or known example. It is its own model and path-finder.'

4.   Transcript of the broadcast on 29 October 1942, 8.30 a.m., Police Wireless Monitoring Report.

5.   Transcript of the broadcast on 18 September 1942.

6.   Analysing the ideologies and work of the underground activities, Hutchins makes relevant observations. In

his opinion, the ultimate goals of all the underground revolutionaries were vague. The main differences within the movement were on questions of method. With the waning of the spontaneous mass activity, the need for active stimulation and direction was clear. As the thinking of the individuals began to clarify, groups began to emerge which represented a commitment to turning the movement in one direction or another. Alternative plans were formulated, but no one group or plan ever became dominant. The movement remained too fugitive and scattered for any one group to feel that they could afford to dissociate themselves from colleagues espousing different methods. No one was prepared to betray an old associate over a difference of opinion about the method to pursue the common goal. Further, Hutchins locates groups with three main points of view. One group, represented most notably by Jayaprakash Narayan, wanted to see the movement substantially reorganized into a disciplined guerrilla effort in which violence would be systematically employed. A 'Centrist' group, consisting primarily of the Congress socialists who had, during the fall, taken a major responsibility in coordinating activities, were prepared to carry on in a roughly similar way in future, providing encouragement to resistance efforts spontaneously undertaken by volunteers in different parts of the country. The third group, the Gandhians such as Sucheta Kriplani and Sadiq Ali who had been closely associated with the Congress organization before 9 August, were beginning to feel that secret activities should be either given up altogether or at least made more 'Gandhian' by focusing on constructive activities. Francis G. Hutchins, *Spontaneous Revolution: The Quit India Movement* (Delhi: Manohar Book Service, 1971), pp. 302–3.

The perspectives of all the three groups were based on (their) interpretations of Gandhi's teachings. All underground workers—not simply the Gandhians—were strongly influenced by Gandhi. Beyond intellectual debt, all were bound to Gandhi by the intense ties of personal respect and affection which made them anxious for Gandhi's approval, and distraught to think of India deprived of his presence. Hutchins, *Spontaneous Revolution*, p. 311. Also, Gandhi was not inclined to exert pressure on the underground workers to surrender themselves if they wanted to continue their activities. Hutchins, *Spontaneous Revolution*, p. 309.

7. Transcript of the broadcast on 21 October 1942, 8.30 a.m., Police Wireless Monitoring Report.

8. Transcript of the broadcast on 27 September 1942: Days were mentioned as: 2 October - Prayer Day; 3 October - Martyrs' Day (a tribute to all those who sacrificed their lives for the country's freedom); 4 October - Flag Day; 5 October - Charkha Day; 6 October - Harmony Day among various communities; 7 October - World Peace Day and 8 October - Celebration Day (Indians belonging to any party want the independence of India through non-violence).

9. Transcript of the broadcast on 13 October 1942, 8.45 p.m., Police Wireless Monitoring Report.

10. *Harijan*, 24-5-1942; CWMG 76 (1 April 1941—17 December 1942), The Publications Division, Ministry of Information and Broadcasting, Government of India, New Delhi, 1979, p. 119.

11. He was getting impatient and had expressed his feeling in May 1942 while talking to the members of the Rashtriya Yuvak Sangha (of the C.P. at Sevagram). He was asked, 'There will be, in the course of the resistance, in spite of all our will to prevent them, clashes and resultant anarchy. May not that anarchy be worse than the present anarchy which you have called ordered anarchy?' Saying that it was 'a very proper question', Gandhi replied, 'That is the consideration that has weighed with me all these 22 years. I waited and waited until the country should develop the

nonviolent strength necessary to throw off the foreign yoke. But my attitude has now undergone a change. I feel that I cannot afford to wait. If I continue to wait, I might have to wait till doomsday. For the preparation that I have prayed for and worked for may never come, and in the meantime I may be enveloped and overwhelmed by the flames that threaten all of us. That is why I have decided that even at certain risks which are obviously involved I must ask the people to resist the slavery . . . The people have not my ahimsa, but mine should help them.' Sevagram, 28-5-42, *Harijan*, Vol. IX, No. 21, 7 June 1942, p. 184.

12.   Transcript of the broadcast on 31 October 1942, 8.30 a.m., Police Wireless Monitoring Report.

13.   Personal communication of the author with Ushaben.
       In 1934 some young intellectuals who had participated in Gandhiji's Satyagraha movement met at Patna under the leadership of Acharya Narendra Dev and formed the Congress Socialist Party. The party had leaders of integrity and intelligence like Acharya Narendra Dev, Yusuf Meherally, Jayaprakash Narayan, Achyut Patwardhan, Ram Manohar Lohia, S.M. Joshi, Purshottam Trikamdas, Kamala Devi, Ashok Mehta and M.l. Dantwalla. The Congress Socialist Party gained great popular support when its leading members played an important role in the 1942 Quit India movement. They had close affinity with Gandhi at a personal level despite their ideological differences.

14.   *Harijan*, 20-4-1940, CWMG Vol. 71 (1 December 1939–15 April 1940), The Publications Division, Ministry of Information and Broadcasting, Government of India, New Delhi, 1978, p. 424.

15.   Speech at the special convention of the Socialist Party, Betul, 14–18 June 1953. Jayaprakash Narayan, *Politics in India: Towards Total Revolution 2*. With an introduction by Brahmanand (Bombay: Popular Prakashan, 1978), p. 211.

16. Transcript of the broadcast on the night of 10 November 1942.

17. Transcript of the broadcast on 12 October 1942, 8.45 p.m., Police Wireless Monitoring Report.

18. Transcript of the broadcast on 2 November night 1942. A speech on 'Double Standard' exposed the hollowness of the British policy towards India. If it was good for the people of Europe to rebel against the Nazi domination and if this was a great force that was to be Hitler's undoing, must not the same logic apply in Asia as it did in Europe? So long as Europe and America did not recognize the existence of racialism in their war policies, they could not hope to defeat the Axis. The decisive factor of this war was the role of the people of India and the Middle East as well as the people of China and Russia.

19. Transcript of the broadcast on 8 November 1942. Referring to this in a talk on 'A Worthless Promise', it was said that no government could last which made enemies of the entire people. The government servants and particularly the police were asked by the Congress Radio not to be lulled by the worthless promises given by the British government. 50,000 men and women boldly faced death, whole villages were looted and burnt and women were raped. A pointed question was asked: 'Can these wrongs be forgotten?' and the passionate answer was 'Never, Never, Never. India will not allow such acts of treachery to go unpunished.'

20. Transcript of the broadcast on 1 November 1942, 8.45 p.m., Police Wireless Monitoring Report. Moreover, in its broadcast on 4 November 1942 about the exploitation of India by the British and worthlessness of the paper currency, the Congress Radio drew attention to the grim situation in the country. There was acute shortage in India of articles of everyday use, like kerosene, rice, jowar, wheat, sugar and petrol. Moreover, the prices of essential things were rising. This was the inevitable out-growth

of the war economy. The British currency and banking system in India was a close parallel to the Nazi methods of financial manipulations. Sterling was becoming weak and England was buying from India her war material and paying for it by means of paper transactions and book entries. That was another form of loot. Under the circumstances the Congress Radio advised the people to buy silver, goods, houses, jewellery, land, etc. and not to hold the paper currency that was scrap of paper. They were further advised to go to villages, store grain and not to sell the grain and the cattle. Transcript of the broadcast on the night of 4 November 1942.

21. Transcript of the broadcast on 20 October 1942, 8.30 a.m., Police Wireless Monitoring Report.

22. Transcript of the broadcast on 31 October, night, 1942: The Congress Radio appealed to the people that 'Our leaders may be in prison at the moment. But their voice, which is the voice of free India, is far from silenced. . . . Our only strength lies in a daily growing resistance to the usurper regime in every village and in every street of every Indian town.'

23. Transcript of the broadcast on 20 October 1942, 8.45 p.m., Police Wireless Monitoring Report.

24. Transcript of the broadcast on the night of 27 October 1942.

25. Transcript of the broadcast on 12 October 1942, 9.20 p.m., Police Wireless Monitoring Report. In another talk on 29 October 1942, the Congress Radio advised the people that in case of the invasion: 'Break away all connections with the British government. Bring intoxication of freedom in your eyes and a fever of independence in your brains. Move your feet towards freedom and keep the tricolour flag in your hands.' The broadcast expressed its faith in the strength of the

people. Transcript of the broadcast on 29 October 1942, 8.30 a.m., Police Wireless Monitoring Report.

26. Transcript of the broadcast on 20 October 1942, 8.30 a.m., Police Wireless Monitoring Report. On 30 October 1942 the Congress Radio broadcasted Khan Abdul Gafar Khan's instructions to Congressmen who came to him from different provinces after the arrest of the Congress leaders in every province. According to him, 'It is the paramount duty of all residents in every province to hold meetings and processions and broadcast the Congress programme to the masses by means of literature. Later, every province at one appointed time and on one day should make a declaration of independence. Every effort should be made to paralyse the present machinery of the government. After the declaration of independence, necessary instructions should be issued in each province according to the situation. The programme should be followed in its various phases.' Transcript of the broadcast on 30 October 1942, 8.45 p.m., Police Wireless Monitoring Report.

27. Transcript of the broadcast on 8 November 1942: Passionate words conveyed the message of Diwali: 'A renewed determination to fight the usurper, a sincere effort not to defile the sacred memory of thousands of our countrymen who have offered their best for our freedom, an unflinching fidelity to the cause of Indian freedom expressed through daily acts of defiance of this goonda regime—let these be your Diwali offerings to Mahatma Gandhi and his numberless soldiers of freedom all over India.'

28. Transcript of the broadcast on 29 October 1942, 8.30 a.m., Police Wireless Monitoring Report. The enumerated 10 duties were:
1. Do not transact any business either with the Britishers or their government because whatever money you give

them or take from them is dipped in the blood of your
countrymen.

2. From every house and window exhibit a tricoloured
flag.

3. Do not see movies or allow others to see because by
doing this some money goes to the tyrant government.

4. Consider it a sin to enter the courts.

5. Do not purchase foreign goods.

6. Withdraw your money from government banks.

7. Boycott the servants of a repressive government.

8. Do not transact any business for which you are required
to go to court.

9. Leave the cities and go to villages.

10. Let the grain and other things remain with the peasant.
At the end of the bulletin, the speech of Maulana Abul
Kalam Azad was played.

29. Transcript of the broadcast on 13 October 1942, 8.45 p.m.,
Police Wireless Monitoring Report.

30. Transcript of the broadcast on 19 October 1942,
9.07 p.m., Police Wireless Monitoring Report. Listeners
were engaged in a question–answer session. To a question
asking the reason behind the appeal of the Congress Radio
to leave cities, the listeners were told that the British
government was carrying away food crops, sugar and the
like outside the country, resulting in food shortage in the
cities. One would at least find food in the villages in case
the peasant did not sell his crop. Answers were provided
to other questions also. Advising the people regarding
deposits in post offices, the Congress Radio stated that
large sums, kept by the people in the post offices, were
being used to keep India in bondage and to buttress the
collapsing credit of the usurper government. So it was
the duty of all to withdraw their balances and to encash
the certificates forthwith. The Congress Radio had its
own views regarding the income tax and going to cinema.

It drew the attention to the fact that modern life is like a spider's web and there are thousands of threads going into one another. By going to the cinema, people not only paid revenue to the usurper government but also supported the newspapers by giving them a large advertisement income. Hence, this needed to be avoided. The Congress Radio asked all the people, including the rich, to cease paying tax to the usurper government and maintained that 'our real strength lies in the action by the masses and the people'. To a question regarding the use of paper money and inflation, the Congress Radio explained that the volume of paper currency circulation had increased by about 75 per cent since the outbreak of the war while production and trade had gone up only about 35 per cent. The currency extension had been mainly responsible for the speedy rise in prices. Increase in paper notes had led to shortage of food for the people and inflation.

31. Transcript of the broadcast on 20 September 1942.

32. Transcript of the broadcast on 26 October 1942, 8.30 a.m., Police Wireless Monitoring Report.

33. Transcript of the broadcast 7 and 8 November 1942.

34. Transcript of the broadcast on 19 October 1942, 9.07 p.m., Police Wireless Monitoring Report. In another broadcast on 28 October it was announced that, 'Prevent any act of rape non-violently, failing which, kill or get killed. Women of India, there is no shame in such rapes. There is suffering. There is agony. There is pride in the struggle to be free.' Hope was expressed in the efficacy of the 'new weapon which Mahatma Gandhi has given.' Transcript of the broadcast on 28 October 1942, 8.45 p.m., Police Wireless Monitoring Report.

35. Transcript of the broadcast on 27 October 1942, 8.30 a.m., Police Wireless Monitoring Report.

36. *Congress Responsibility for the Disturbances, 1942–43* (published with authority), The Manager of Publications,

Delhi, 1943, p. 41. There is also another important report. Justice Wickenden was required to go through the voluminous material (reports of the CID agents, police reports, interceptions of correspondence, published statements of Gandhi and other leaders, and other rare materials) placed at his disposal and find out whether it was possible to fix the responsibility for the disturbances on the Congress and to advise the government whether it would be desirable to bring the Congress leaders to trial in a court of law. Wickenden held Gandhi and the Congress responsible not only for the launching of the movement but also for the consequent violent character it assumed. However, interestingly he opined that most of the evidence was utterly inadmissible in a court of law and the conviction not a certainty if the Congress leaders were brought to trial. P.N. Chopra, ed., *Quit India Movement: British Secret Report* (Faridabad: Thomson Press, 1976), p. 14–15. According to Wickenden Gandhi, though retaining his personal belief in nonviolence, was forced to discard it when practical considerations arose. The urgency and gravity of the situation left neither time nor place for nonviolence as he had always conceived it. Chopra, ed., *Quit India Movement*, p. 208.

37.   No. 1769 dated 23 October 1942, To, The Secretary to the Government of India, Department of Information and Broadcasting, New Delhi. From, Additional Secretary to the Government of Bombay, Home Department. File 1110 (31) II 1942.

38.   No. 6563 dated 5-12-1942, From Home Department, Government of India, New Delhi to J.M. Sladen, Home Secretary to the Government of Bombay, Bombay. File 1110 (31) 1942–1943.

39.   Report by the Commissioner of Police, Bombay, on the Congress Radio Case, No. 1419 dated 26-1-1943 from Commissioner of Police, Bombay, to the Additional

Secretary to the Government of Bombay, Home Department (Special), Bombay. File 1110 (31) 1942–43.

40. D.O. No. 981, 3 February 1943, from Home Department (Special), Bombay, to the Additional Secretary to the Government of India, Home Department. File 1110 (31) 1942–43.

41. Khwaja Ahmad Abbas, *I Am Not an Island: An Experiment in Autobiography* (New Delhi: Vikas Publishing House), pp. 252–54.

42. Archive/Audio/Interview: K.A. Abbas-Part 2, Centre of South Asian Studies, University of Cambridge, Cambridge, https://www.s-asian.cam.ac.uk/archive/audio/item/interview-k-a-abbas-part-2/.

43. Transcript of the broadcast on the morning of 9 November and the night of 10 November 1942. Interestingly it was said in this broadcast that 'It is over a week since we received news from Bombay that a powerful transmission set used for Congress broadcasts had been seized by the usurper administration. The Bombay administration had apparently doled out conflicting reports. This set, we are told, is only one of many . . . But we have been also told that this set was seized, while in operation and along with the announcers. It is not our intention to unravel this mystery. It shall remain a mystery until India is free. And to our people we say, do not bother about us, do not talk about us, let us carry on our work. Should anyone of you get to know or guess the persons doing this work or places where this work is done, God damn you if you talk about it to the best of your friends. Had it not been for the high and strong walls of popular sympathy that protect us, we would have died long ago. We have been careless. We have done things far too openly. But India is our land, let the British usurpers sneak about, if we do things at all, it will be with a bang and not a whimper. It is not for nothing, that Congress Radio Calling is the best

secret centre the world has so far seen. The reason does not lie in our competence; we know we are not competent enough, though slightly less incompetent than the British. The reason does not lie in our money resources; we are far too poor. Congress Radio calling is the best secret centre of the world because it is the voice not of a minority, not mere majority, but of an entire people, the voice of the Indian people.' The transmission set referred to here seems to be the one seized by Inspector Kokje when he arrested Manukumar Madhavji and Madhavji Sunderji just as they were carrying a complete transmitter unit in a taxi.

AFTERWORD

1. No. 2064/A/320/W/2871 dated 20-2-1943; To, The Additional Secretary to the Government of Bombay, Home Department (Special), Bombay, From, The Commissioner of Police, Bombay, Subject: The Congress Radio, File 1110 (31) 1942–43.

2. Subject: Congress mass movement, Incidents on 10-3-1943,No. 2766/A-320 from the Office of the Commissioner of Police, Special Branch I, CID, Bombay, 11 March 1943. To, The Secretary to the Government of Bombay, Home Department (Special), Bombay. File 1110 (6)A(1) VI 1943.

3. P.N. Chopra, ed., *Quit India Movement: British Secret Report* (Faridabad: Thomson Press, 1976), p. 338.

4. 26 January 1944, 'Calendar of the Quit India Movement in the Bombay Presidency' ed. by Sanjiv P. Desai, Department of Archives, Government of Maharashtra, Bombay, 1985, p. 368.

5. Lohia's statement, Intelligence Bureau, Home, New Delhi, to Special Branch, Bombay, 21 Oct. 1944, CP File No. 1581/B/I, cited in K. K. Chaudhari, *Quit India Revolution: The Ethos of its Central Direction*, (Mumbai: Popular Prakashan, 1996), p. 245.

6. Transcript of the broadcast on 9 November and 10 November night 1942, Usha Mehta Congress Radio Papers, Mani Bhavan Gandhi Sangrahalaya, Mumbai.
7. Rajabhau Kulkarni, *Punyatil Bhumigat Akashvanicha Aanakhi Ek Prayog* (in Marathi), *Sadhana*, Pune, 15 August 1992, year 45, issue 1, p. 39.
8. *Bombay Chronicle*, 7 April 1946.
9. Chopra, ed., *Quit India Movement*, p. 116. It is to be noted that the Quit India movement was widespread, especially in the United Provinces, Bombay, Bihar, Bengal, Orissa and Andhra, and independent/parallel governments were formed in places like Satara, Ballia, Midnapore and Balasore.
10. Chopra, ed., *Quit India Movement*, p. 212.
11. Chopra, ed., *Quit India Movement*, p. 112.
12. *K. K. Chaudhari, Quit India Revolution: The Ethos of its Central Direction*, p. 141.
13. Information from Ram Sewak Pande's statement after his arrest on 1 June 1943, 'Ram Sewak Pande, in his statement after his arrest on 1 June 1943', in Chopra, *Quit India Movement*, p.136.
14. T.K. Tope, *Bombay and Congress Movement* (Bombay: Maharashtra State Board for Literature and Culture, 1986), p. 125.
15. Francis G. Hutchins, *Spontaneous Revolution: The Quit India Movement* (Delhi: Manohar Book Service, 1971), p. 291.
16. Chandrakant Mehta, *Hind Chhodo* (in Gujarati) (New Delhi: National Book Trust, 1997), pp. 36–37.
17. Statement of Ram Sevak Mataprasad Pandey, in Chopra, ed., *Quit India Movement*, p. 332.
18. *Congress Responsibility for the Disturbances 1942–43* (Published with the authority), Manager of Publications, Delhi, 1943, p. 27. For references to underground publications see Chopra, ed., *Quit India Movement*, pp.100–103; for some extracts and examples see Appendix

C, pp. 317–27. Also: Y.B. Mathur, *Quit India Movement* (Delhi: Pragati Publications, 1979), pp. 30–37, 45–46, 54–57, 67–71, 86–88, 90, 97.

19. Hutchins, *Spontaneous Revolution*, p. 303.
20. *Bombay Chronicle*, 30 August 1942.
21. Chaudhari, *Quit India Revolution*, pp. 138–39.
22. Chaudhari, *Quit India Revolution*, p. 121.
23. *Ninth August*, No. 1, 9 August 1943, p. 16, File 1110 (6) A(1) VIII 1943.
24. *Ninth August*, No. 2, 23 August 1943, File 1110(6)A(1) VIII 1943. Jayaprakash Narayan had written in the issue that 'As we complete a year of our National Revolution, the thought that is uppermost in my mind is that if we fail it will only be because we lack FAITH in ourselves.' (p. 4) In Aruna Asaf Ali's fiery words, 'For us 9 August 1942 will ever be a memorable day. By their unprovoked assault the British in India on that day brought about a revolution that is unique in all history.' (p. 8) Ram Manohar Lohia thundered, 'We must be hard and carry on the fight never thinking of surrendering.' (p. 9).
25. *Ninth August*, No. 11, 9 January 1944, pp. 1–4, File 1110 (6)A(1) VIII 1943 .
26. *Inquilab*, Nos 6–7, 25 November 1943, p.6, File 1110 (6) A(1) VIII 1943.
27. 350, Lohia's letter to Prof. H.J. Laski, in Mastram Kapoor, ed., *Collected Works of Dr. Rammanohar Lohia*: 9 (New Delhi: Anamika Publishers & Distributors, 2011), p. 173.

Bibliography

Abbas, Khwaja Ahmad. 1943. 'Let India Fight for Freedom'. *Sound Magazine*, Bombay.

———. 1977. *I Am Not an Island: An Experiment in Autobiography*. New Delhi: Vikas Publishing House.

———. Archive/Audio/Interview: K.A. Abbas-Part 2. Centre of South Asian Studies, University of Cambridge, Cambridge. Retrieved from: https://www.s-asian.cam. ac.uk/archive/audio/collection/k-a-abbas/

Ali, Sadiq. 16–31 December 1985. 'Gandhi and Nehru Threatened to Resign from the Congress!' *Bhavan's Journal*, Congress Centenary issue, 32 (10).

August 9, 25th anniversary, All India Congress Committee, New Delhi, 1967. (This copy is published on the 25th anniversary in 1967.)

Awasthy, G.C. 1965. *Broadcasting in India*. Bombay: Allied Publishers.

Bapat, Vasant, and G.P. Pradhan. eds. 15 August 1992. *Sadhana* (Marathi), August Kranti Suvarna Mahotsav Visheshank Vol. 45, no. 1.

Bhavan's Journal, Vol. 39, no. 1, Quit India Golden Jubilee Number, 15 August 1992.

Bhuyan, Arun Chandra. 1975. *The Quit India Movement: The Second World War and Indian Nationalism*. New Delhi: Manas Publications.

Chakrabarty, Bidyut. 1997. *Local Politics and Indian Nationalism: Midnapur 1919–1944* New Delhi: Manohar.

Chandra, Bipin. 2009. *History of Modern India*. Hyderabad: Orient Blackswan.

Chandra, Bipin, Mridula Mukherjee, Aditya Mukherjee, K.N. Panikkar and Sucheta Mahajan. 1988. *India's Struggle for Independence 1857–1947*. New Delhi: Penguin Books.

Chaudhari, K.K. 1996. *Quit India Revolution: The Ethos of Its Central Direction*. Mumbai: Popular Prakashan.

Chopra, P.N., ed., 1976. *Quit India Movement: British Secret Report*. Faridabad: Thomson Press.

———. ed. 1989. *Historic Judgement on Quit India Movement: Justice Wickenden's Report*. Delhi: Konark Publishers.

Clymer, Kenton J. 1997. *Quest For Freedom: The United States and India's Independence*. New Delhi: Prentice-Hall.

Congress Responsibility for the Disturbances 1942-43, (published with the authority), Manager of Publications, Delhi, 1943.

Desai, A.R. 1966. *Social Background of Indian Nationalism*. Bombay: Popular Prakashan.

Desai, Sanjiv P. ed. 1985. *Calendar of the Quit India Movement in the Bombay Presidency*. Bombay: Department of Archives, Government of Maharashtra.

Dwivedy, Surendranath. 1993. *Untold Story of August Revolution*. Delhi: Ajanta Publications.

Gordon, Johnson. 1973. *Provincial Politics and Indian Nationalism: Bombay and the Indian National Congress 1880–1915*. Cambridge: Cambridge University Press.

Government of India. 1978. *The Collected Works of Mahatma Gandhi* Vol. 71: (1 December 1939–15 April 1940). New Delhi: Publications Division, Ministry of Information and Broadcasting, Government of India.

———. 1979. *The Collected Works of Mahatma Gandhi* Vol. 76: 1 April 1942–17 December 1942. New Delhi: Publications Division, Ministry of Information and Broadcasting, Government of India.

Greenough, Paul R. 1999. 'Political Mobilization and the Underground Literature of the Quit India Movement, 1942–44'. *Social Scientist* 27 (7/8), pp. 11–47.

Gupta, Partha Sarathi. 'Radio and the Raj'. In Sabyasachi Bhattacharya. ed. 2002. *Power, Politics and the People: Studies in British Imperialism and Indian Nationalism*. London: Anthem Press.

Hutchins, Francis G. 1971. *Spontaneous Revolution: The Quit India Movement*. Delhi: Manohar Book Service.

———. 2017. *Gandhi's Battlefield Choice: The Mahatma, the Bhagvad Gita and World War II*. New Delhi: Manohar Publishers & Distributors.

India Ravaged (Being an account of atrocities committed, under the British Aegis, over the whole subcontinent of India in the latter part of 1942), January 1943.

Hindustan Times, New Delhi. 'India Unreconciled: A Documented History of Indian Political Events from the Crisis of August 1942 to February 1944'. First edition 1943, Second edition 1944.

Janata Vol. XXIII, Nos. 37–38, 12 October 1968.

Joshi, P.M. 1972. *Student Revolts in India: Story of Pre-Independence Youth Movement.* Bombay: P.M. Joshi.

Kapoor, Mastram. ed., 2011. *Collected Works of Dr. Rammanohar Lohia – 9: Collected Papers (1939–1963).* New Delhi: Anamika Publishers & Distributors.

Krishnan, Bhaskaran. 1999. *Quit India Movement: A People's Revolt in Maharashtra.* Mumbai: Himalaya Publishing House.

Lal, Ramji. 1986. *Political India 1935–42, Anatomy of Indian Politics.* Delhi: Ajanta Publications.

Low, D.A. ed. 2004. *Congress and the Raj: Facets of the Indian Struggle 1917–1947.* New Delhi: Oxford University Press.

Maity, Pradyot Kumar. 2002. *Quit India Movement in Bengal and the Tamralipta Jatiya Sarkar.* Kolkata: Purvadri Prakasani.

Mansergh, Nicholas, ed., and E.W.R. Lumby, asst. ed. 1971. *Constitutional Relations between Britain and India: The Transfer of Power, 1942–7* Vol. II, 30 April–21 September 1942. London: Her Majesty's Stationery Office.

———. 1971. *Constitutional Relations between Britain and India: The Transfer of Power, 1942–7* Vol. III, 21 September 1942–12 June 1943. London: Her Majesty's Stationery Office.

Masselos, Jim. 2007. *The City in Action: Bombay Struggles for Power.* New Delhi: Oxford University Press.

Mathur, Y.B. 1979. *Quit India Movement.* Delhi: Pragati Publications.

Mehta, Chandrakant. 1997. *Hind Chodo* (Gujarati). New Delhi: National Book Trust.

Mehta, Usha. Interview. Centre of South Asian Studies, University of Cambridge, Cambridge. Retrieved from: https://www.s-asian.cam.ac.uk/archive/audio/item/ interview-dr-usha-mehta/.

Mitra, Bejan, and Phani Chakraborty, ed.s, *Rebel India*, Orient Book Company, Calcutta, 1946.

Nadkarni Brahmanand, ed., Girija Keer, asst. ed., *Anuradha* (Marathi) Vol. 13, no. 6, Kranti Visheshank August 1969.

Nayar, Sushila. 1997. *Mahatma Gandhi Vol. VIII: Final Flight for Freedom*. Ahmedabad: Navjivan Publishing House.

Pande, B.N. General Editor, 1985. *A Centenary History of the Indian National Congress Vol. III: 1935–1947*. Edited by M.N. Das. New Delhi: AICC and Vikas Publishing House.

Patankar, Arun (editor-in-chief), R.G. Maydeo (managing editor) and Veena Gawade (editor). *Lokrajya*, August 1992, Quit India Movement Golden Jubilee Celebrations, Vol. 49, no. 4, Bombay.

Pati, Biswamoy. 1998. *Turbulent Times India 1940–44*. Mumbai: Popular Prakashan.

Pradhan, G.P. 1990. *India's Freedom Struggle: An Epic of Sacrifice and Suffering*. Bombay: Popular Prakashan.

Pyarelal. 1956. *Mahatma Gandhi: The Last Phase Vol. I*. Ahmedabad: Navjivan Publishing House.

Sahai, Govind. 1947. '*42 Rebellion: An Authentic Review of the Great Upheaval of 1942*. Delhi: Rajkamal Publications.

Shroff, Zenobia E. 2005. 'Professor Kamal Wood: The Voice of Nationalism'. In Nawaz B. Mody, ed.,

Enduring Legacy: Parsis of the Twentieth Century Vol. II. Mumbai: Nawaz B. Mody.

Sengupta, Syamlendu, and Gautam Chatterjee. 1988. *Secret Congress Broadcasts and Storming Railway Tracks during Quit India Movement*. New Delhi: Navrang.

Sitaramayya, Pattabhi. 1947. *History of the Indian National Congress Vol. II: 1935–1947*. Bombay: Padma Publications.

Shinde, A.B. 1990. *The Parallel Government of Satara: A Phase of the Quit India Movement*. New Delhi: Allied Publishers.

SOUND – Quit India Number Vol. VI, NO. 8, AUG 1947

Thakkar, Neel. 2013. 'The Congress Radio Calling: Underground Broadcasts during the Quit India Movement'. *Stanford Storytelling Project*. Stories from Branden Grant Winners.

Tope, T.K. 1986. *Bombay and Congress Movement*. Bombay: Maharashtra State Board for Literature and Culture.

Virmani, Arundhati. 2008. *A National Flag for India: Rituals, Nationalism and the Politics of Sentiment*. Ranikhet: Permanent Black.

Zaidi, A.M. 1973. *The Way Out to Freedom: An Inquiry into the Quit India Movement Conducted by Participants*. New Delhi: Orientalia (India).
————. ed. 1986. *Defying a Distant King: A Study of the Quit India Movement*. New Delhi: Publication Department, Indian Institute of Applied Political Research.

Primary Sources

Usha Mehta Congress Radio Papers, Mani Bhavan Gandhi
   Sangrahalaya, Mumbai.
Home Department (Special) Files-1020(5)C1 1940-41;
   1110(1) 1942; 1110(31)I 1942;1110 (31)II 1942;
   1110(31) 1942-1943; 1110(6)A(1)1 1942; 1110(6)
   A(2)1942;1110(6)A(1)VI 1943;1110(6)A(1)VIII 1943;
   Maharashtra State Archives (MSA).

Index

A

Abbas, Khwaja Ahmad, 13
  autobiography, 154
  in Communist Party office,
    156
Agitation
  during November 1942,
    132–137
  during October 1942,
    127–132
Ali, Sadiq, 13
Allahabad, situation in,
  130
All India Congress Committee
  (AICC), 2, 13
  agitations and protests in,
    14
  Complete Independence'
    resolution, 2
  Congress Radio started
    after, 48

Hindustan Hamara' song,
  86
meeting
  people outside, 4
  on 7-8th August 1942,
    179
session in August 1942,
  10–14
Sucheta Kriplani in, 34
Wardha session, 4
All India Radio (AIR), 23
Amritlal Nathuchand Trust,
  43
Anglo-Saxon Britishers, 127
Announcer, perspective of,
  154–57
Appeal to College Students, in
  1942, 37
Assam Bengal Railway, 126
9 August 1942, arrests on,
  44–45

353